Game Design
SECRETS

Game Design
SECRETS

DO WHAT YOU NEVER THOUGHT POSSIBLE TO MARKET
AND MONETIZE YOUR IOS, FACEBOOK, AND WEB GAMES

Wagner James Au

WILEY

John Wiley & Sons, Inc.

ACQUISITIONS EDITOR: Mary James

PROJECT EDITOR: Jennifer Lynn

TECHNICAL EDITOR: Billy Pidgeon

PRODUCTION EDITOR: Daniel Scribner

COPY EDITOR: Kezia Endsley

EDITORIAL MANAGER: Mary Beth Wakefield

FREELANCER EDITORIAL MANAGER: Rosemarie Graham

ASSOCIATE DIRECTOR OF MARKETING: David Mayhew

MARKETING MANAGER: Ashley Zurcher

BUSINESS MANAGER: Amy Knies

PRODUCTION MANAGER: Tim Tate

VICE PRESIDENT AND EXECUTIVE GROUP PUBLISHER: Richard Swadley

VICE PRESIDENT AND EXECUTIVE PUBLISHER: Neil Edde

ASSOCIATE PUBLISHER: Jim Minatel

PROJECT COORDINATOR, COVER: Katie Crocker

COMPOSITOR: Kate Kaminski, Happenstance Type-O-Rama

PROOFREADER: Louise Watson, Word One

INDEXER: John Sleeva

COVER DESIGNER: Ryan Sneed

COVER IMAGE: © Chad Baker / Lifesize / Getty Images

Game Design Secrets

Published by
John Wiley & Sons, Inc.
10475 Crosspoint Boulevard
Indianapolis, IN 46256
www.wiley.com

Copyright © 2012 by John Wiley & Sons, Inc., Indianapolis, Indiana

Published simultaneously in Canada

ISBN: 978-1-118-33774-5
ISBN: 978-1-118-46391-8 (ebk)
ISBN: 978-1-118-41646-4 (ebk)
ISBN: 978-1-118-43420-8 (ebk)

Manufactured in the United States of America

10 9 8 7 6 5 4 3 2 1

For general information on our other products and services please contact our Customer Care Department within the United States at (877) 762-2974, outside the United States at (317) 572-3993 or fax (317) 572-4002.

Wiley publishes in a variety of print and electronic formats and by print-on-demand. Some material included with standard print versions of this book may not be included in e-books or in print-on-demand. If this book refers to media such as a CD or DVD that is not included in the version you purchased, you may download this material at http://booksupport.wiley.com. For more information about Wiley products, visit www.wiley.com.

Library of Congress Control Number: 2012944690

Here's to all the game developers who've inspired and entertained me all these years—including, yes, all those whose iOS, web, and Facebook games often distracted me from finishing this book about iOS, web, and Facebook games.

Ardent thanks to the lovely and beloved Rachel, whose face and thoughts were always at my periphery through this book's long march, making all the milestones along the way worthwhile.

About the Author

Wagner James Au is a writer, consultant, and sometime game designer/writer. He wrote *The Making of Second Life* (HarperCollins) in 2008 based on his experiences as Linden Lab's virtual "embedded journalist" in the groundbreaking 3-D virtual world. As a game developer, he was lead writer and a mission designer for City of Eternals, a Facebook-based MMO from ohai (subsequently acquired by Electronic Arts), a writer at Outspark, an MMO publisher, and a writer on Majestic, EA's innovative alternate reality game. He's written on gaming and tech culture for Internet Evolution, Inside Social Games, GigaOM, Kotaku, Salon, and *Wired*, was an industry analyst for Social Times Pro and GigaOM Pro, and has been interviewed on these topics in *The New York Times* and by the BBC and ABC. He's a frequent speaker at and conference advisor for South by Southwest.

Read his gaming, tech, and virtual culture blog, New World Notes, at nwn.blogs.com. Follow him on Twitter @SLHamlet, or drop him an e-mail at wjamesau@gmail.com.

About the Technical Editor

Billy Pidgeon is a senior analyst at M2 Research, a boutique market research firm covering the games industry since March 2010. With 24 years in the electronic entertainment industry, including extensive experience in research, management, and product development specializing in the PC, console, and mobile games market, Billy is an industry expert appearing regularly in print, on radio, and on television and at events as keynote speaker, moderator, and panelist.

Since becoming a market research analyst with Jupiter Media Metrix in 1999, Billy has authored dozens of market research reports, bulletins, and articles covering a wide range of game hardware, software, services, and technology. His topics include tracking and contextualizing gamer behavior, intention, and purchasing patterns, in-game advertising and microtransactions, covering sales, use and development of online and offline games, single and multiplayer games, and games designed for enthusiast and mass-market players. Billy is an advisor to manufacturers, publishers, developers, carriers, and retailers on market forecasting, business, and marketing strategy.

Billy began his career in video games in 1988 as a producer for Hi Tech Expressions, a small computer and console software publisher (notable titles include Big Bird's Hide and Speak and The Chessmaster) and was hired as an executive producer from 1992 to 1996 for Acclaim Entertainment (Mortal Kombat, The Simpsons, and many others).

Acknowledgments

A huge mahalo to all the game developers, analysts, and assorted experts I spoke to for this book—thanks for bringing your particular wisdom to the proceedings. Extra thanks to Billy Pidgeon, analyst with M2 Research (www.m2research.com) for doing double duty as both an interview subject and this book's technical editor. Thanks just as profusely to all the folks supporting this book at Wiley, especially Ms. Mary James, the editor who first gave me the call. Also, much gratitude to Jennifer Lynn of Page One Editing and copy editor Kezia Endsley, for helping make this book coherent and whole. Cheers always to David Fugate of Launch Books (www.launchbooks.com), my agent of six years, for his unflagging support where it matters most.

Contents at a Glance

Contents

Read This First

Once upon a time (2007 to be exact), a British programmer named Paul Preece designed a fun little web game in his spare time. After a month of work he put it online and promoted it by posting a link to the game on a few sites. Then the funniest thing happened: A lot of people started to play it. Tens, then hundreds of thousands. Then millions. Then tens of millions. It was called Desktop Tower Defense, and you've probably played it at least once, but likely many times more. People kept playing. Five years later, Preece estimates now, 100–150 million people have played his fun little web game.

But here's what Preece says about it now: "I actually consider Desktop Tower Defense to be a failure. Yes, it was popular, but it wasn't successful." Because the problem, he says with hindsight, was this: "I had no thought in my head of making money. I just made a game I wanted to play." Had he designed it a bit differently and converted just 2 percent of the people who played the game into paying customers, it would have been a blockbuster success in every sense of the word. Things ultimately worked out well for Preece (as you'll read down the way), but he still expresses regret at this early, missed opportunity. "Success," as Preece puts it now, "is really measured in your ability to keep making games, and to keep making games, you have to earn money from them."

So the goal of this book, dear game designer, is to help make you a lot of money. If you love games like I do, that might seem like a strange thing to say. Because after all, shouldn't you be making games for the love of games? Yes, absolutely. But to keep on making games and to keep on having the freedom to make them the way you want… well, you need to make a fair amount of money, too. That is what this book is for.

Who This Book Is For

Since you're reading this book, you've likely got a lot of great game ideas, and maybe got even more inspiration from books like Raph Koster's *A Theory of Fun for Game Design* or Jesse Schell's *The Art of Game Design*. If you've come this far, you probably also have a lot of game development skills, say in programming or level editing. This book is meant to be an addition to volumes like those, because it's primarily about the business of game design for the largest game platforms on the market—both for new, indie game designers and relatively established designers. For that reason, it's also intended for managers, executives, and investors who help guide and finance designers and want a reference to help them help their games succeed as a business.

And believe me, it is a business. I've talked with dozens of established game developers and execs in the last few years, and one refrain kept coming up: We wish game designers would design monetization into their games from the very beginning and not just add it on as a last-minute afterthought, which almost never works.

I heard that complaint so often, as a matter of fact, that I decided to write this book.

What You'll Learn in This Book

This book covers the business of game design, walking you through gaming's three largest markets: Facebook, iOS, and the web. By only writing about these three, I'm not criticizing other popular platforms and online game distribution channels, such as Google's Android platform and its associated online markets, such as Google Play and the Amazon App Store. Independent game developers can also make games for Microsoft's Xbox Live Arcade (XBLA) or Valve's Steam. But as of Spring 2012, there are only some 65 million Xbox 360 owners who can access XBLA and only some 40 million active Steam accounts. Even combined, both of these are a fraction of the user base for iOS, let alone Facebook or the web. There are sometimes good reasons for making games for a smaller market. But generally speaking, if you are an indie designer or a designer working with a small budget, you want to get your games to where they have the best chance at finding the largest possible audience.

How This Book Is Structured

The first part of this book provides you with a market overview for each of the largest markets—again, Facebook, iOS, and the web—as well as a guide to finding the right platform for your indie game. Then, the next three parts of the book walk you through the basics of each platform, explain how money is made on each (and just how much), and how the best developers create games designed to gain a large and/or passionate audience willing and eager to pay for them. This includes in-depth interviews with some of the very best developers on those platforms, including Preece, Randy Smith, and the team behind Kingdom of Loathing. Finally, the book wraps up with a discussion of funding and some final thoughts. Be sure to check out the appendix, "Resources," which provides myriad resources for designing games for Facebook, iOS, and the web.

What You Need to Use This Book

This book assumes basic knowledge of games on Facebook, iOS, and the broader web, both from a consumer's perspective and from a developer's vantage point. If you're already developing games on any or all of these platforms, even better; if you're planning to make the leap soon, that's just as good. As mentioned already, this book doesn't cover many of the technical aspects of game design, but it will help guide your decisions when it comes to finding an audience and encouraging them to pay you for the pleasure of playing.

Many games are featured in this book, so it's also a good idea to get some hands-on gameplay with them before you read about how they were designed. In addition to major classics like Desktop Tower Defense and Angry Birds, here's a selected list to start with:

On Facebook: Backyard Monsters, Battle Pirates, Draw Something, Legacy of a Thousand Suns, and Tetris Battle.

On iOS: Dimensions, The Heist, Spider: The Secret of Bryce Manor, Waking Mars, and ZOMBIES RUN!

On the web: kingdomofloathing.com, games on JayisGames.com, Kongregate.com, and Nitrome.com; War Metal Tyrant on synapse-games.com.

Features and Icons Used in This Book

The following features and icons are used in this book to help draw your attention to some of the most important and useful information in the book, some of the most valuable tips, insights, and advice that can help you unlock the secrets of game design.

▶ Watch for margin notes like this one that highlight some key piece of information or discuss a poorly documented or hard-to-find technique or approach.

SIDEBARS

Sidebars like this one feature additional information about topics related to the nearby text.

TIP The Tip icon indicates a helpful trick or technique.

NOTE The Note icon points out or expands on items of importance or interest.

CROSSREF The Cross-Reference icon points to chapters where additional information can be found.

WARNING The Warning icon warns you about possible negative side effects or precautions you should take before making a change.

Part I
OVERVIEW

CHAPTER 1

Market Overview: iOS, Facebook, and the Web

IN THIS CHAPTER

▶ Understanding why to target these platforms

▶ Surveying the iOS game market

▶ Surveying the Facebook game market

▶ Surveying the web game market

This chapter gives you an overview of the three game platforms featured in this book—iOs, Facebook, and the web—and describes who plays on them, how many there are, and how much larger they're expected to grow.

UNDERSTANDING WHY TO CHOOSE THESE PLATFORMS OVER OTHERS

The combined audience size of these three game platforms—iOS, Facebook, and the web—is massive. Drawing from the estimates in this chapter, the audience size is between 600 and 800 million total. Besides that, there are at least three reasons for small and indie game designers to create for them in particular: market acceptance of low-budget games, direct connection to social media, and portability to other platforms. These reasons are discussed in more detail in the following sections.

Market Acceptance of Low-Budget Games

Due to their presence on multiple-use platforms (the iPhone is also a phone, Facebook is also for social networking, and so on), the market has proven to be far more accepting of games on Facebook, the web, and iOS. This is true even when the games are produced for low budgets and come with no-frills graphics, short playtimes, and extremely simple interactivity. Tap Pet Hotel (see Figure 1-1) is just one example of a best-selling, no-frills game.

FIGURE 1-1: App Store screenshots of Tap Pet Hotel, a top-grossing 2011 iOS game with no-frills 2D graphics.

Most of the best-selling iOS games, for instance, are not made with high-end graphics and other features that are typically costly to deploy.

Reviewing the 20 top-grossing iOS games of 2011, only one, Infinity Blade, boasted high-resolution 3D graphics. We see a similar pattern on Facebook, where games with simple, non-3D cartoon-graphics, like CityVille, Texas HoldEm Poker, and Draw Something (the graphics are provided by the actual players) dominate, and on the web, where the biggest online games, like RuneScape and Club Penguin, are also graphically low-frills.

▶ The mega-blockbuster Angry Birds was reportedly developed by a core team of four.

Direct, Frictionless Connection to Social Media

All three platforms can be seamlessly integrated with social media and e-mail, making it extremely easy for fans to promote their favorite games to friends: Click a Tweet that links to a new Facebook game, and start playing it within a few seconds. Or, post a link to an iOS game on your Facebook wall, and anyone who clicks it will be taken directly to its purchasing page in Apple's App Store. Yes, the three major game consoles have at least some integration with Facebook and other web- or phone-based social media, but this is mainly for promotional purposes and there are several barriers and serious lag time between, for example, recommending a favorite PS3 game on your Facebook wall and your friends being able to buy/download and play it. (By contrast, Facebook and, increasingly, the web and iOS games, *encourage* players to share game content and gameplay with each other—an important viral marketing and growth mechanism for these games.)

Portability to Other Platforms

As you'll see in later chapters, these three platforms are compatible with a number of development platforms, which makes porting between them relatively easy. For instance, web games made in HTML5 or Unity are compatible with iOS, and Facebook games can and have been ported to other social networks. (Yes, they do exist, and are often surprisingly large.)

With all that established, here's a bird's-eye view of each platform in terms of users and market size.

SURVEYING THE IOS MARKET

Now let's look deeper at the state of games on the platform that Steve Jobs made (see Figure 1-2).

FIGURE 1-2: iOS App Store page for games

Overall Install Base

The total install base of iOS devices currently exceeds 200 million, and, according to ReadWriteWeb, 90 percent of iOS owners are running iOS version 4.x or higher. Within this market, the iPad has an install base of approximately 60 million.

Player Demographics

According to top smartphone app analyst Flurry.com, as of February 2012, a reasonable estimate of the iOS gaming market is 110 million, with a roughly 50/50 gender ratio. "Between 0.5 and 6 percent of players—depending on game genres—use in-app purchases," Flurry analyst Patrick Minotti told me.

NOTE See Flurry's blog, blog.flurry.com, and the posts "Mobile Freemium Games: Women Thrifty, Men Binge" and "Mobile Freemium Games: Gen Y Plays But Gen X Pays" for more details on iOS gamer demographics.

"In terms of geographical location," says Minotti, "I would say it's about 50 percent North America, 30 percent European Union, and 20 percent Asia."

iOS games are primarily monetized through in-app purchases, with hardcore titles gaining most of their revenue. Fortunately for indie developers, the overwhelming share of games on the iOS market are made by them and not by established companies coming from another platform. This does not mean indie developers have it easy on iOS, however. In a survey, 63 percent said they've made less than $10K from their iOS games *in their entire lifetime*.

CROSSREF Read more about all this in Chapter 11, "Quick Survey of the iOS Game Market."

Projected Growth

Flurry projects the iOS game market to grow to more than $1.25 billion in 2013.

SURVEYING THE FACEBOOK GAME MARKET

Now let's turn to Facebook and get a quick read on who's playing games on Mark Zuckerberg's social network (usually when they're in the office, supposedly getting work done.) See Figure 1-3.

FIGURE 1-3: Facebook's Apps and Games page

Overall User Base

As of mid-2012, shortly after its May IPO, Facebook has about 900 million monthly active users and 500 million daily active users. Since the company reports that 20 percent of this user base is in the United States and Canada, it's safe to estimate that more than 160 million Americans—that is, more than half the entire U.S. population—are on Facebook.

Player Demographics

As for Facebook users who play Facebook games, the social network reports that 70 percent of active users also use Facebook games and applications. So assuming 30–60 percent of them play games, it's reasonable to estimate there are about 255 to 510 million users who play one or more Facebook games a month. This user base is so large, it's also safe to say that it encompasses all the major demographics who use Facebook, from late teens up to people in their 60s.

> **NOTE** One example of Facebook gaming's wide demographics: According to AppData.com, Playdom's hidden object game Hidden Chronicles has about 20 percent of fans who are in their mid-20s to mid-30s, and about as many who are over 55.

Monetization rates for Facebook games tend to be between 2 and 9 percent of each game's player base. (In other words, players who purchase and use Facebook Credits in a given game.)

Projected Growth

Facebook's penetration rate in developed countries is really high, and therefore, growth in the developed world is slowing. However, Justin Smith, a leading social media analyst at Inside Network, tells me that the social network is now strongly growing in Brazil and India. At current growth rates, it's reasonable to forecast that Facebook will have more than a billion users by 2013.

▶ And 30–60 percent of these users will be playing Facebook games.

Facebook also has strong traction in other emerging markets in southern Asia, although Facebook may lose share in Asian markets if local social networks, such as China's Sina Weibo and Japan's mixi, maintain their popularity.

SURVEYING THE WEB GAME MARKET

Finally, here's the big picture of web games, sometimes overlooked by game developers and the tech industry but still quite large.

Overall Install Base

Web games are primarily developed in Flash, a platform that has a market penetration of more than 99 percent of all personal computers. Other web-based platforms, such as HTML5, WebGL, and Unity will probably gain more prominence in the next few years (these are discussed in Chapter 10), but in the short to medium term, "web game" and Flash are almost synonymous.

> **CROSSREF** For more about web-based platforms, see Chapter 10, "Future Trends and Opportunities for Web Gaming."

Player Demographics

David Cole, head analyst with DFC Intelligence (`www.dfcint.com`), one of the game industry's leading research firms, gave me this overview of the web-based gaming market in March 2012:

"Growth got hard hit by Facebook games on one hand and large client-based games on the other. The number of monthly active users is still high—about 200 million—but only about 10 million users are paying—that is, 5 percent.

"In terms of audience, you have primarily a teenage/young adult audience that skews more male. Very different than Facebook games, which skew older and more female. There is also a much larger percentage from Europe and emerging markets: Latin America, Russia, Turkey, and so on. North America is only about 20 percent."

On this point, Mochi Media's Colin Cupp concurred: "A lot of the players on the Mochi Media network are based in Brazil." (Mochi is a leading web game advertising platform. See Figure 1.4) He added this explanation: "Consoles are typically too expensive for most of the gamers there, so they play online games. This has also resulted in a large (and thriving) game developer base in the region."

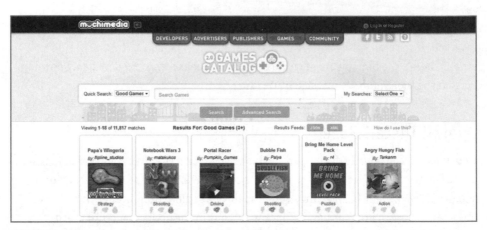

FIGURE 1-4: Web games on Mochi Media

Projected Growth

Cole's firm, DFC Intelligence, forecasts total revenue for browser-based games will be $916 million in 2012, growing to $1.20 billion in 2014 and $1.46 billion in 2016.

SUMMARY

Here are the key points we covered in this chapter:

- ▶ Facebook, the web, and iOS have three major advantages besides being the most popular game platforms: market acceptance of low-budget games, frictionless connection to social media, and portability to other platforms.

- ▶ Facebook has more than 900 million monthly users, about 30–60 percent who play games on the social network. This includes both genders and all the major age demographics.

- ▶ About 200 million people play web-based games, with an audience that skews teen/young adult and male. Only 20 percent are based in North America, with most of the audience in Europe and in emerging markets like Latin America, Russia, and Turkey.

- ▶ iOS has a total install base of more than 200 million, including 60 million iPads and 110 million monthly game players. About 0.5–6 percent of them (depending on genre) make in-app payments for games.

▶ Although only a small percentage of the browser market spends money on games, remember that developers can still earn indirect revenue from all their players through web ads and sponsorships.

iOS versus Facebook versus the Web: What's the Right Platform?

IN THIS CHAPTER

▶ Reviewing what works and what doesn't on iOS

▶ Reviewing what works and what doesn't on Facebook

▶ Reviewing what works and what doesn't in web games

As you saw in the last chapter, the three platforms that are the focus of this book have a massive user base. But they're all far more cluttered with losers than winners, and there are opportunity costs to investing your game-development resources in one over the others. Apple's submission process for apps can be time-consuming and arduous, for example, not to mention that Apple and Facebook take a 30 percent commission on revenue, placing a substantial barrier on profit. The broader web, although offering more options and markets for publishing games, lacks the concentrated and direct monetization options that iOS and Facebook boast. (In other words, App Store users already have their credit cards registered in the system, while many Facebook gamers already have a bank of virtual currency, both of which make them more likely to spend on your game.) At the same time, some game

12

CHAPTER 2   iOS versus Facebook versus the Web: What's the Right Platform?

genres generally work better on one platform than others, and all else being equal, offer a better opportunity for success. This chapter briefly sketches out the game genres and features that tend to perform well on each platform—and the kinds that usually don't.

REVIEWING WHAT WORKS AND WHAT DOESN'T ON IOS

A simple review of top App Store sales and downloads, regularly published by Apple and tracked daily by sites like AppData.com, will give you a pretty good picture of the game genres doing best on this platform. However, pay less attention to titles in the Top Paid Apps chart, and more to those on the Top Grossing Apps chart, because this chart will give you a better indication of the iOS games that bring in the most money.

As we'll discuss in more detail in Chapter 11, "Quick Survey of the iOS Game Market," hardcore games, particularly MMOs and RPGs, make the most money, with the biggest spenders from the U.S., Japan, and Korea. As I write this chapter in June of 2012, for example, nine of the top grossing iOS game apps fit in the hardcore gamer category:

- ▶ DragonVale
- ▶ Kingdoms of Camelot: Battle for the North
- ▶ Rage of Bahamut
- ▶ Minecraft—Pocket Edition
- ▶ Plague Inc.
- ▶ Castle Age HD
- ▶ Dragon Story
- ▶ Global War
- ▶ Kingdom Age

Six are casual/puzzle/social gaming:

- ▶ Bejeweled Blitz
- ▶ Tap Paradise Cove

- ▶ Smurfs' Village
- ▶ The Sims FreePlay
- ▶ Draw Something

And the remaining five are casino:

- ▶ Slotomania
- ▶ Zynga Poker
- ▶ Card Ace: Casino
- ▶ Slots Journey
- ▶ Texas Poker

This is more or less a typical spread.

WHAT WORKS BEST ON IOS

Although hardcore titles are generally most likely to gross the most money on iOS, the games that are most successful on the platform have less to do with genre and more to do with their gameplay.

Games That Leverage iOS's Touch Interface

Although this may seem like an obvious point, the high number of games that are mere ports of handheld console games (see the section cleverly titled "Gaming Console Ports" later in this chapter) makes it worth stating here: Most top-selling iOS games emphasize use of the iOS unique touch/slide screen interface in gameplay. It is evident, of course, in blockbusters like Angry Birds, but almost all of 2011's top-grossing games also made central use of the touch/slide feature, including Tap Zoo (see Figure 2-1) and Tap Pet Hotel, which even emphasize the iOS interface in the actual game title.

Related to this, it's worth noting that the iPad, with its much larger screen, works even better than its smaller cousin for touch-based gameplay. It's for this reason that missing object games, in which players have to locate and point out items located within a large game environment, do particularly well on the iPad.

14

CHAPTER 2   iOS versus Facebook versus the Web: What's the Right Platform?

FIGURE 2-1: Tap Zoo, 2011's top-grossing iOS game

Short, Discrete Gameplay Sessions

Here's the thing about the iOS: For the most part, it's still mainly a mobile phone. Which means an iOS game is often (or usually) played in contexts where a mobile device comes in handy most: in remote locations away from the living room or office, during idle times. (Say, waiting for a bus, traveling on a plane and, yes, sitting in a bathroom.) For that reason, the iOS is better suited to games with short, discrete gameplay sessions that the player can easily quit and return to at any given time. To take an iconic case, a complete Angry Birds level can be played in less than a minute, but typically takes several minutes. This is a good time frame to aim for.

2D or 2.5D Games

▶ While many 2.5D games may appear to be 3D, using an isometric perspective, camera control over the game scene is severely limited. Hence the term 2.5D.

Another common feature in top-selling iOS games is 2D or 2.5D graphics, where gameplay is depicted on a flat, single-plane surface, or in a 3D space limited to a single perspective. This is probably due in part to the comparable difficulty of playing a 3D game on the flat surface of an iOS (see the section "Full 3D Games") and iOS touchscreen interface (see "Games That Leverage iOS's Touch Interface"), which works much better with 2D/2.5 gameplay, because touch literally connects the player to the screen.

WHAT DOESN'T WORK ON IOS

Now that you know what works best on iOS, take a look at what doesn't work so well.

Full 3D Games

The App Store's top-grossing list for 2011 is scant on games with full 3D graphics, which display a first-person perspective or display the game space with a camera that rotates along the full X/Y/Z axis. Indeed, the only 3D game to make the top-grossing chart in 2011 was the fighting/RPG game Infinity Blade (see Figure 2-2).

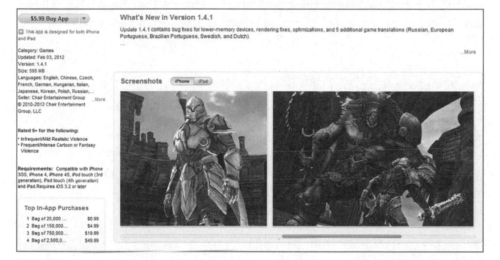

FIGURE 2-2: Infinity Blade, one of the few 3D games that performs extremely well on iOS

There are probably a number of reasons for the lack of top-selling 3D games on iOS, chief among them the gameplay context. Unlike a couch or desk, where 3D games are traditionally played, an iOS game is often played in open, public, and semi-public areas, where it's difficult for a player to devote the high degree of focus and time that 3D games typically demand. Further, maneuvering in a 3D space is difficult to do without the keyboard/joystick controls that PCs and consoles have but the iOS lacks. And if you've ever tried playing a 3D game on iOS, you're probably familiar with the calluses they tend to give your fingertips!

16

CHAPTER 2   iOS versus Facebook versus the Web: What's the Right Platform?

Gaming Console Ports

Games that are based on or ported from bestselling console and PC games are also scant on the App Store's top-grossing and top-paid lists. Although titles like Grand Theft Auto : Chinatown Wars and Street Fighter IV for the iOS draw respectable sales, they are consistently beat by indie games made on smaller budgets without any pre-existing brand recognition. Part of the problem is that most of these adaptations and ports use full 3D graphics (see "Full 3D Games"). Further, game ports often do not make use of the iOS touchscreen interface. And because they typically require higher production values and budgets, publishers feel pressured to sell their iOS ports at relatively high cost (the Grand Theft Auto and Street Fighter games currently sell for $4.99 and $9.99), which makes them less appealing to the larger iOS gaming market. (They can play countless games of near or equal quality at little cost, or even free.)

▶ The top PC/ console game publishers are thus at a double disadvantage on iOS—which is good news for the indie iOS developer.

REVIEWING WHAT WORKS AND WHAT DOESN'T IN FACEBOOK GAMES

I'll survey the most and least successful genres on the Facebook platform in more detail in the next chapter, but here's a broad and brief overview of key features that are best suited to games in Mark Zuckerberg's playland.

WHAT WORKS BEST ON FACEBOOK

Socially Networked Gameplay

As you'll read more about further on, all the popular Facebook games make heavy use of the social network's social features in myriad ways, such as game updates that can be posted to the player's profile wall and in-game leaderboards that track a player's success in relation to other Facebook friends playing the game. Doing this leverages the core aspect of Facebook that has made the social network so popular—the ability to rapidly share experiences with friends.

Short Game Sessions

▶ That translates to an average of about 14 minutes on Facebook per day.

According to the Nielsen ratings service, U.S. Facebook users log in to the site an average of seven hours a month.

For the Facebook game developer, that translates into very short individual gameplay sessions—from three to five minutes. Of course, the ideal is to draw players into longer and more engaged gaming sessions, but designers need to *anticipate* the short session, "lunch break" activity pattern that most Facebook users follow.

Point-and-Click Gameplay

Despite Facebook's continued predominance as a social network used on PC desktops and laptops, almost all its successful games make primary or exclusive use of point-and-click mouse-based interaction, with minimal use of the keyboard. This is in line with the user interface of Facebook itself, which emphasizes mouse-based interaction as much as possible, and the preferences of most Facebook gamers, who are casual, light gamers accustomed to simple gameplay interaction.

Tetris Battle, the only top Facebook game with keyboard-driven play, is an exception that proves this rule (see Figure 2-3).

▶ Tetris Battle became popular, its lead designer told me, only after they added a loading page and tutorial that carefully explained its keyboard-based gameplay.

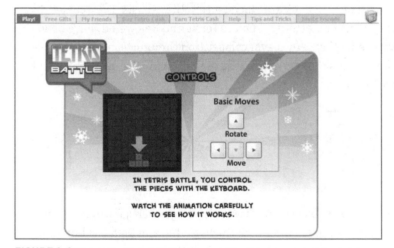

FIGURE 2-3: Tetris Battle's tutorial teaches Facebook gamers how to use the keyboard for play.

WHAT DOESN'T WORK ON FACEBOOK

After four years of Facebook games, it's also possible to make some pretty fair generalizations of what doesn't work on the platform, as described in the following sections.

18

CHAPTER 2   iOS versus Facebook versus the Web: What's the Right Platform?

3D Graphics

Although Flash and other web platforms can now display robust 3D graphics, and some 3D games are popular on the larger web, no Facebook game with 3D graphics has achieved any significant popularity. This is due in part to the longer load times associated with graphics-heavy games and Facebook's preference for short session gameplay. It's probably just as much due to the mismatch of the attention required for a 3D game versus the lightly engaged, text-driven experience of the social network. As proof of this, consider Gaikai, the successful cloud-deployment service. In April 2012, it began offering high-quality 3D console games for free on Facebook, but as of June, it had gained fewer than 9,000 fans.

▶ That is, monthly users in the six figures.

Poorly Networked Games

Just as all the top Facebook games heavily leverage the platform's social sharing features, most successful games emphasize gaming interaction between players. Very few, if any, games on Facebook are played on a solitary basis. Even games that were primarily solo on other platforms, such as Tetris and Bejeweled, have been re-designed to emphasize player-to-player competition through leaderboards, live matches, and other features that emphasize the fun of playing the game with (and against) others on Facebook.

REVIEWING WHAT WORKS AND WHAT DOESN'T IN WEB GAMES

For this section, I spoke with experts from two of the larger web game publishers— Colin Cupp, Product Marketing Manager with Mochi Media, and Greg McClanahan, Director of Games and Achievements with Kongregate. Although their insights are most directly related to their respective companies' platforms, both publishers are large enough that they also apply to web games in general. That both of them mostly publish indie/low-budget games also points to the fact that the web is particularly well suited to grassroots, DIY developers.

> **CROSSREF** You can find more information on Mochi Media and Kongregate in Chapter 7.

WHAT WORKS BEST IN WEB GAMES

First, starting with what works best on the web...

Demographic-Specific Genres

Colin Cupp of Mochi Media says, "Genres tend to map to specific audience types. For example, match-3 puzzles, such as Jade Monkey, tend to be really popular among women; the dress-up genre is popular with younger girls; and shooter/action genres, such as SAS: Zombie Assault 3, Raze 2, and so on, are very popular among teenage males." See Figure 2-4.

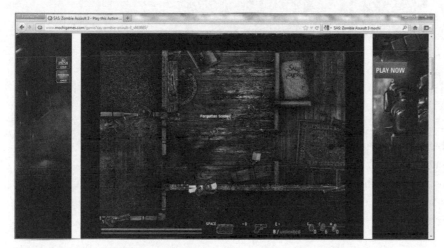

FIGURE 2-4: SAS: Zombie Assault 3

"With that being said," says Cupp, "changing themes of games can often change the audience. An example of this is Bio Gems—a fighting or combat element is added to a match-3 puzzle, making it more attractive to teenage males compared to the typical match-3 game." (See "Hybrid Genre or 'Twist' Games" for more information.)

Tower Defense, Launcher, and (on Kongregate) High-Budget Games

Greg McClanahan of Kongregate says, "Tower defense and launcher games are especially popular right now." See Figure 2-5.

"If you sort Kongregate by rating, you'll see these two types dominating by a degree disproportionate to how many of them we have on the site."

▶ For Kongregate's top-rated games, go to www .kongregate.com/ games?sort=rating.

20

CHAPTER 2   iOS versus Facebook versus the Web: What's the Right Platform?

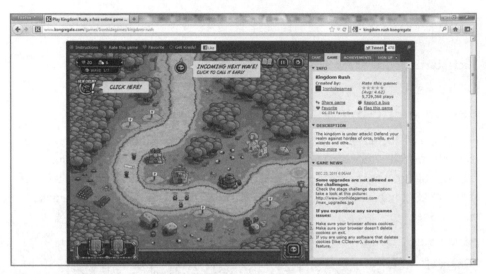

FIGURE 2-5: Kingdom Rush, an extremely popular tower defense game on Kongregate

"I'm not entirely sure why this is," says McClanahan. "It could be that the genres lend themselves well to games that are quick to get into and immediately fun. They're also game experiences that are far less common on other platforms. Additionally, large, deep, high-production-value, polished games seem to do disproportionately well on Kongregate relative to the rest of the web—the Mardek series is a great example of this. When I'm doing Flash sponsorships, it often seems like short and simple games spread to other sites a lot better, even if their ratings on Kongregate aren't great."

Hybrid Genre or "Twist" Games

Again, Greg McClanahan of Kongregate: "Another genre popular in the Flash world is games that don't fit into a predefined genre very easily. Oftentimes developers can score big points with players by showing them something unique and fun. For example, most games by [Kongregate developer] Nerdook are difficult to characterize by genre.

▶ http://www
.kongregate.com/
accounts/nerdook

"Elephant Quest [see Figure 2-6] is a blend between platformer, RPG, and shooter. Platformer games by themselves usually aren't very popular, but platform games with some kind of unique twist are popular, such as Company of Myself, One and One Story, Enough Plumbers, Chronotron, Adventure Story, and Spewer. Other games, like Dolphin Olympics, Pandemic, and Music Catch, are difficult to place into a genre.

FIGURE 2-6: Elephant Quest: hybrid platformer, RPG, and shooter

> **NOTE** To play the games mentioned here, visit www.kongregate.com.

"Because most of our players already have console games, it's difficult to create a popular Flash game by simply picking a genre and creating a well-made (yet uninspired) game of that type—most games need to have some kind of special hook, or some fun little mechanic at the core."

WHAT DOESN'T WORK IN WEB GAMES

Now let's turn to web games that don't work as well.

Poorly Designed/Executed Games

Mochi Media's Cupp says, "I don't actually believe there is a genre that works *least well*; rather, there are games that don't perform well—or at least not as well as expected. There are myriad reasons for this, including not understanding the audience—therefore no real connection with the player, poor game design, not enough polish, too many bugs, et cetera."

22

CHAPTER 2 iOS versus Facebook versus the Web: What's the Right Platform?

Sports and (Most) Puzzle Games

Kongregate's McClanahan, says "[A]ny genre can be made to work well, but there's definitely a lack of successful sports games—aside from racing. I'm not entirely sure why, but if I had to guess I'd say that the complexity and depth required in the sports genre—both from the players understanding the rules/interface and the developer programming all the rules and the AI—is at odds with the nature of the Flash industry, where games that are simple, immediately fun, and have broad appeal are the most successful. There are also a lot of failed puzzle games released every day, but this is probably just due to how easy they are for new developers to program. There's no shortage of great puzzle games among the cream of the crop."

SUMMARY

Here are the key points we covered in this chapter:

▶ On iOS, 2D or 2.5D games that leverage the touch interface tend to do better than full 3D games and ports of game console titles.

▶ On Facebook, games that make use of the social network's friend-sharing features, and are designed for quick gameplay sessions and point-and-click control, do better than 3D games and those with a solo gameplay focus.

▶ On the web, genres targeted at specific demographics (match-3 puzzles for women, dress-up games for younger girls, shooter/action games for young males, and so on) tend to do well. In addition, tower defense, launcher games, and hybrid games that combine genre elements or add a twist to popular gameplay features also perform well. By contrast, sports and most puzzles games are usually less successful (the latter due to overabundance).

Part II

FACEBOOK

CHAPTER 3

Facebook Games: The Users, the Money, and the Major Players

IN THIS CHAPTER

▶ Understanding who plays Facebook games and who pays for them
▶ Understanding the anatomy of a successful Facebook game
▶ Making money in Facebook games
▶ Pitching publishers: who buys/publishes indie games

In the first few years after Facebook launched in 2004, Mark Zuckerberg and company gave short shrift to the games launched on their platform. But fast-growing successes like Zombies and Scrabulous in 2007 quickly convinced the social network and Silicon Valley investors that a new market for games was emerging. Although most of the early games had limited interaction and little resemblance to games as they were usually understood, Facebook games gradually began to replicate the early computer games. Early hits like Vampire Wars and Mob Wars (2008) resembled text-based roleplaying games (RPGs) from the 80s and 90s, while FarmVille and CityVille (2009 and 2010) seemed like the original Sim games from that era. By 2011 and 2012, the most popular Facebook games included arcade games (Tetris Battle, Diamond Dash), strategy games (CastleVille and Empires & Allies), and RPGs (The Sims Social).

▶ When Facebook officially announced its entry on the stock market, the company reported that a solid chunk of its total revenue—15 percent!—was generated by leading social game developer Zynga.

This chapter takes a look at the marketplace for Facebook games and the leading developers that currently serve it. You'll then review the game genres that are doing well on the platform and those that are floundering. From there, you'll learn about the guidelines for spotting a successful Facebook game, and learn how developers make money from them. Finally, the chapter closes with a survey of some top Facebook publishers who accept indie submissions—or at the very least, have great advice for developers just starting out.

UNDERSTANDING WHO PLAYS FACEBOOK GAMES AND WHO PAYS FOR THEM

Many designers from the traditional game industry assume that Facebook games are only popular with casual female gamers, sometimes called "Facebook moms." This stereotype, although somewhat true in the social network's early years, has become less accurate in recent times. Whereas a 2010 PopCap-sponsored study suggested that 55 percent of U.S. Facebook gamers were women with an average age of 48, a 2011 study sponsored by Kabam showed a significant presence of gamers as we generally understand them. Of the people who play strategy games on Facebook, 82 percent reported they were also frequent console gamers, and 77 percent played PC games like WoW and Starcraft. So clearly there's a large market for a variety of games. Generally speaking, about 5 percent of this player base will directly spend money on a game—see the interview with Inside Virtual Goods's Justin Smith in the next chapter.

▶ This is in a market of about 25 million monthly active users, or MAU.

IDENTIFYING FACEBOOK'S BIG THREE IN GAMES AND THREE OF ITS RISING STARS

For a better understanding of how diverse the market for Facebook games is, here's a look at three of the industry's top developer/publishers, along with three successful mid-tier developers.

Zynga

The undisputed market leader of Facebook gaming now counts about 247 million monthly active users of its titles, which include the SimCity-like game CityVille and the strategy game CastleVille. Although many of its top titles were developed in-house, a number of its hits were first developed by smaller studios the company acquired. (Or, as it's sometimes called in Silicon Valley, "acq-hired.") In 2011 alone, Zynga bought several mobile developers—including Wonderland Software, DNA Games, Astro Ape Studios, and Five Mobile—strongly suggesting the company plans to design and develop more cross-platform games like its hits Words With Friends and Texas Hold 'Em. This direction was confirmed in March with the purchase of OMGPOP, developer of the come-from-nowhere cross-platform hit Draw Something, for $180 million.

▶ Mobile game designers, take note.

The flip side of acquisition: Zynga is also known for designing games that very strongly resemble the hits of competitors, and in 2012, two smaller developers, NimbleBit, creator of Tiny Tower, and Buffalo Studios, creator of BINGO Blitz, accused Zynga of copying their games. Zynga defends itself by claiming they are merely improving on games, but for many indie designers, their takeaway is this: Make a popular game, get bought by Zynga.

▶ Or watch as Zynga copies you and uses its huge cross-promotional engine to make its game way bigger than you ever dreamed.

Electronic Arts (EA) Playfish and PopCap

The game industry giant literally bought its way into Facebook gaming with the 2009 purchase of Playfish (maker of Pet Society and other early social game hits) and the 2011 acquisition of PopCap (casual multi-platform game developer of Plants versus Zombies, Bejeweled, and for Facebook, Bejeweled Blitz (see Figure 3-1). The company's current hit is The Sims Social, a collaboration between Playfish developers and developers from EA studio Maxis, creator of the original classic franchise.

FIGURE 3-1: EA PopCap's Bejeweled Blitz

Wooga

This Berlin-based developer and publisher has created a number of games in several genres, including the casual arcade games Diamond Dash and Bubble Island and Monster World, a farming sim with a fantasy twist.

In addition to the big three developers there are three rising stars, notable for their growing size and/or the successful niches they've carved for themselves. These are covered next.

6waves

▶ This includes hits like Ravenskye City.

This developer was originally two separate companies that merged in 2011. 6waves began as an Asian-based publisher of numerous social games, many of them independently developed. It joined with Lolapps, a San Francisco-based quiz, gift, and game app development studio to develop and release an extremely large portfolio of games. (The merged company now counts more than 400 games and entertainment apps on Facebook.)

KIXEYE and Kabam

▶ Kabam and KIXEYE have a combined audience size of about 6.5 million MAU.

KIXEYE and Kabam are Facebook's current leaders in real-time and asynchronous strategy games intended for a hardcore gamer audience that enjoys classic PC games like Starcraft, Command & Conquer, and their many successors. KIXEYE was first launched as Casual Collective, a web game startup led by Paul Preece and Dave Scott, the designers of the 2007 Flash blockbuster Desktop Tower Defense. The startup floundered with several Facebook games before hitting its stride with the real-time strategy game Backyard Monsters in 2010. As the game picked up momentum, the company decided that it would rebrand itself as serving the growing market for hardcore gamers in search of Facebook games to play when they couldn't get to their consoles. (For this reason, it's often called the "mid-core" market.)

▶ Indie developers should be aware of this conflict when approaching one or the other for development gigs or publishing partnerships.

In a similar way, Kabam's RPG-strategy games like Dragons of Atlantis and Kingdoms of Camelot are designed for extremely complex gameplay, and consequently attract a smaller but passionate group of players. Both companies are believed to be earning good revenue, proving there's a market for mid-sized Facebook games.

Speaking of which, the companies also have some competitive tension. For example, in 2011, KIXEYE accused Kabam of copying Backyard Monsters (see Figure 3-2) as Edgeworld.

FIGURE 3-2: KIXEYE's Backyard Monsters

Tetris Online, Inc.

Creator of Tetris® Battle (see Figure 3-3), one of Facebook's top-ten popular games, this Honolulu-based company is the exclusive online licensee of The Tetris Company, LLC and all rights to the world-famous Tetris® game in North America and Europe. Although Tetris Online has been involved with a number of Facebook games that are variations of the original videogame, the company gained runaway success with Tetris Battle, which added several competitive multiplayer features to the design. The company has also published Facebook games not associated with the Tetris brand, and is open to submissions from indie designers.

▶ Yes, one of the top Facebook game developers is based in Hawaii. Keep that in mind if you're hoping to work with Tetris Online.

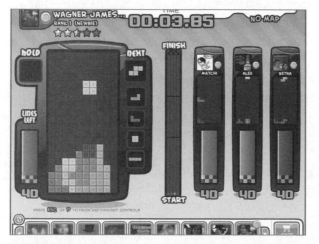

FIGURE 3-3: Tetris Online's Tetris Battle

In the next sections, you'll take a look at the genres that are generally doing well in today's market, those that are on track to grow, and those that aren't doing too well.

GETTING TO KNOW THE PLAYING FIELD: THE GENRES LIKELY TO GO BIG, DO WELL, OR STAY SMALL

Facebook's game market has been highly volatile in the last couple of years, with games and genres that attracted 10s of millions in 2011 now floundering. Here's a quick overview of the genres doing well in 2012—and those not doing as well.

Strategy Games

In addition to Zynga's Empires & Allies (which currently boasts a huge audience, thanks to the company's cross-promotional kung fu), a number of strategy games on Facebook enjoy a passionate following: Battle Pirates and War Commander from KIXEYE (see Chapter 5), Kabam's Edgeworld and Dragons of Atlantis, and Social Point's Social Empires. Although most of these games have players in the hundreds of thousands (relatively small for Facebook), they attract players in the "core gamer" demographic of young males, who tend to spend more money on their games than other gamers.

Roleplaying Games

Although it has a niche on Facebook, the traditional (fantasy/sci-fi) RPG game has a smaller but passionate user base. Even though Dungeons & Dragons–style games have a limited audience on Facebook, a number of games that use RPG mechanics in a non-fantasy setting are performing well. This includes a current top game, EA Playfish's The Sims Social, based on the PC game franchise client of the same name, and Zombie Lane, a comedic survival-horror RPG, except, you know, funny.

Casual Arcade Games

By the end of 2012, games with fast, casual action will probably come to dominate the top of Facebook's charts. As of this writing (summer of 2012), five of them are in the top 20: Diamond Dash, Bubble Witch Saga, Tetris Battle, Bubble Island, and Angry

▶ In 2012, expect several casual arcade games, probably led by Tetris Battle, to take the top slots among Facebook games overall, alongside Draw Something.

Birds Friends. Besides Tetris Battle and Angry Birds, the top three in this category have a similar gameplay mechanic (fast-paced symbol matching), and their millions of fans will probably be in the market for new titles that have similar gameplay, but with new twists.

City Management Sims

Supplanting farm-based sims (see the "Farming Sims" section later in this section), these descendants of early PC classics like SimCity have done well recently, with the successful launch of Wooga's Magic Land, Disney Playdom's Gnome Town, Zynga's CastleVille, and 6waves Lolapps's Ravenskye City. All of these hits have a fantasy theme, which represents a new trend in city-building games (as opposed to Zynga's CityVille, launched in 2010, which has a realistic, modern day theme). These leaders in the genre now have a monthly audience of over 40 million.

Casino Games

Gambling-themed games will probably become very popular by the end of 2012. Although Facebook doesn't currently allow real money gambling, this will probably change by the time this book goes to print. For one thing, in late 2011, the U.S. Department of Justice changed its policy prohibiting online gambling, saying that it's legal if gambling is allowed in the state hosting a given game's servers. For another, Facebook is seeking to allow online gambling among UK users of the social network, and may follow suit in other nations where this kind of gaming is also allowed. Anticipating this future, market leader Zynga recently released Zynga BINGO (putting it in competition with the hit game BINGO Blitz), the casino gaming company International Game Technology bought the developer of DoubleDown Casino for half a billion dollars, and U.S. casino giant Caesars Entertainment Corporation bought Playtika, creator of Slotomania. (Expect to read more gambling game acquisition news after reading this book!)

Although gambling games are not necessarily the most popular of genres among many gamers, development costs are relatively low because the rules of popular card and casino games are in the public domain. It's also likely that popular Facebook/iOS/web gambling games will be licensed for use in real casinos.

Among the genres of games that probably have a bleak future on Facebook are the following.

▶ Casino games: big opportunity for upcoming or low-budget designers.

First-Person Shooters and Other Full 3D Genres

Although there have been a number of attempts to find an audience for FPS games on Facebook, none have done reliably well. One high-profile, heavily promoted entry, 3G Studio's Brave Arms, reached a high of 30,000 MAU in 2010, but rapidly lost these users. The likely reason? Shooters appeal almost exclusively to young males, who make up only a small portion of the Facebook user base, and who are more likely to prefer graphically rich shooters on their game console or Steam, as opposed to lower-quality Flash-based 3D. For that matter, first-person shooters, being full 3D, require a greater investment of attention and time—not ideal on a platform more typically used for short lunch breaks or while multi-tasking in other web tabs. This is probably why few, if any, full 3D games of any variety have found much of an audience on the social network.

Overwhelmingly, Facebook game graphics are 2D or overhead perspective 2.5D. All that said, there's probably some market for first-person shooters on Facebook—just with a very low budget, with low-end graphics, to lower the load time and barrier to entry. Perhaps such games could be intended for younger Facebook users who might not be able to afford a next-gen console or high-end gaming PC.

▶ Interestingly, farm sims other than FarmVille are most popular with Chinese and Turkish/Middle Eastern Facebook users.

Farming Sims

When asked to name a Facebook game, many developers reflexively mention FarmVille, even though that Zynga game's reign as top title on the platform ended years ago. And while it does maintain about 30 million MAU, the other games in the farming sim genre have fewer than 1 million MAU.

▶ For indie/low-budget developers who can't afford to license a well-known property or compete against those who can, the unreliable success rate of Facebook franchise games is another bonus to developing on the platform.

Licensed/Franchise Properties

There's one type of game that usually does well on other platforms, but has a highly unreliable track record on Facebook: games based on pre-existing games, movies, TV shows, and other intellectual property. There are a few exceptions—for example, the top 20 games based on popularity now include Sims Social, Tetris Battle (official spinoff of the arcade classic), and Angry Birds, based on Rovio's cross-platform hit. However, there are far more cases where an association with a well-known brand has done little to improve the game's performance. As the developers of Tetris Battle told me recently, having the name "Tetris" in their game definitely boosted its install rate, but they had to design the game to succeed on its own to convince new players to stay.

Of course, the hard reality is that most Facebook games perform poorly, no matter what the genre. Also, it's often difficult to spot the true winners at first. So let's look at some general guidelines to tell one from the other.

UNDERSTANDING THE ANATOMY OF A SUCCESSFUL FACEBOOK GAME

My strong general advice to beginning Facebook game designers is to learn from the games on Facebook that have reached a provable success point. However, many developers associate total MAUs with success, when there are actually a number of other factors that go into a successful and profitable Facebook game.

To find these game design winners, I recommend using AppData.com, a website service founded by my sometime boss Justin Smith (see sidebar interview), which extracts Facebook game MAU and DAU (daily active user) activity into handy charts (see Figure 3-4). When reviewing the data, look for three factors, covered in the next three sections.

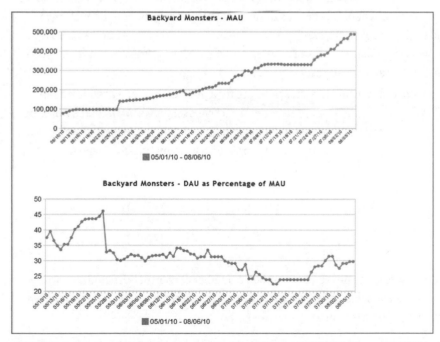

FIGURE 3-4: Successful Facebook game growth: MAU and DAU/MAU (Copyright 2012 Inside Network Inc., a division of WebMediaBrands. All rights reserved. Reprinted with permission from AppData.com.)

Growth or Strong Activity after Three Months

Thanks to cross-promotion and heavy advertising, new Facebook games, especially those from top developers, usually get a big growth spike at launch. But often, that's not because people are really enjoying the game. The real test is how the game performs after the first three months, when cross-promotion and marketing generally has run its course. Then, you need to look at another metric.

Strong DAU/MAU Rates after Three Months

"DAU/MAU" refers to the ratio of a game's daily active users to monthly active users, and it's probably the most crucial indicator of a game that's doing well. As an industry rule of thumb, a DAU/MAU rate of 20 percent or higher means the game is getting good retention and consistent monetization.

▶ DAU/MAU rates aren't very meaningful until about three months after a game launches, when the "try once" players have dropped off.

Strong DAU in Relation to Development Team

Not all or even most Facebook games have to attract millions of players to be profitable (as you'll see in the next chapter.) A good rule of thumb is to look at the number of daily players a Facebook game has in relationship to the number of developers involved with its production and maintenance. If the likely revenue earned from those players significantly exceeds the likely salary of the development team, you're probably looking at a fiscally stable game.

For instance, a typical monetization rate for a puzzle-themed Facebook game is one to two cents in average revenue per daily active user (ARPDAU). That's not a lot, unless the development team is one or two people, which is sometimes the case. Then you're talking about a decent side income or even a healthy full-time wage.

▶ So if a puzzle game has just 10,000 daily players, assume it's earning around $100–200 a day, or $3000 to $6000 a month.

FINDING OUT WHERE THE MONEY'S MADE IN FACEBOOK GAMES

Revenue comes to game developers through a number of channels, including virtual currency and goods sales, in-app offers, advertising, and marketing and promotion. Each of these is discussed next.

Facebook Credits

Facebook's official currency used to be Facebook Credits (see Figure 3-5). The social network made this the mandatory payment method for all Facebook apps in 2011, then reversed course in June 2012, announcing that developers could now sell their own branded virtual currency, while converting users' existing Facebook Credits reserves to their local cash equivalent.

▶ Users can purchase virtual currency in Facebook with credit cards, PayPal, and mobile phones, among other options.

Earn Facebook Credits

Earn Credits for free
Complete an offer below. It's easy and secure. · Terms Apply

Most Popular | Local Deals | Surveys | Categories ▼ | Help

UP TO 50% OFF· FTD	**FTD Flowers & Gifts - $19.99** Up to 50% off Valentine's Day gifts	190 Credits
VALENTINE'S DAY FLOWERS UP TO 50% Off	**ProFlowers & Gifts - $19.99** Only 8 days until Valentine's Day!	180 Credits
f	**Special Facebook Credits Offer** Buy 10 Facebook Credits (just $1!)	40 Credits
DISCOVER	**Discover More Card** Get approved for a credit card	950 Credits
NETFLIX	**Netflix** Instantly watch movies from Netflix	220 Credits
AUTOQUOTES USA Fast, Free Auto Insurance Quotes	**Auto Quotes USA** Get an auto insurance quote	120 Credits

Done

FIGURE 3-5: Facebook Credits offers wall

In-App Offers

As the name suggests, an "in-app offer" is an advertising offer that is displayed within the game (see Figure 3-6). Instead of making direct purchases of virtual currency for use in Facebook, gamers can earn it by signing up for offers made by third-party companies. You can, for example, sign up for a Netflix account and get 10 Facebook Credits to use in CityVille. The game developer takes a cut for each completed offer, making this a good way to monetize most of the players who resist paying straight cash for Facebook Credits.

▶ This year, Facebook allowed these in-app offers to be made in exchange for a game's virtual currency instead of credits, which will likely make them even more attractive to gamers.

FIGURE 3-6: Facebook advertising offer

Advertising

Facebook allows game developers to supply advertising channels to their games (such as links to websites and embedded video ads), which is another indirect revenue stream. It's a relatively small stream at the moment, although it's likely we'll see it grow, especially as Facebook grows in developing nations.

Marketing and Promotion

Many Facebook games are not intended to earn money, but rather are promotional vehicles for other media properties, such as movies or television shows. In that case, the designer's task is not necessarily to increase long-term engagement in the game, but to boost awareness of the sponsoring property.

PITCHING PUBLISHERS: WHO BUYS/PUBLISHES INDIE GAMES AND WHY

Many of Facebook's top game makers often form publishing partnerships with low-budget indie game developers, cross-promoting their titles to their large existing player base. Sometimes, the publisher prefers to buy the smaller developer outright and bring the developing team into the fold. Here's a sample of top developers and what they're looking for.

6waves

Josh Burns, Associate Director, Products at 6waves, estimates the company has published over 75 Facebook games from developers from all over the world.

"We generally do not look to acquire specific Facebook games, but there is always the possibility," he told me. "Unlike many publishers, we aren't looking for a certain type of game, as our goal is to create a network of games that will have multiple titles that will appeal to any one user, which means that we aren't expecting every single game to appeal to all users and be a mass market hit. Many games will only appeal to a certain demographic or affinity group, and we understand that. What we are looking for is a high-quality title that will appeal and engage some segment of users, but will also monetize successfully through virtual goods under the free-to-play model. There aren't any specific types of game design or gameplay features that we want to see, rather [we want to see] that the developer has created a compelling experience for users via the game's design and features."

▶ To arrange a pitch meeting with 6waves, contact the business development team via e-mail at bd@6waves.com.

EA Playfish

Although the Electronic Arts social game company doesn't currently have a live third-party game among its offerings, it offers "publishing services to independent developers to enable them to maximize the full potential of their social games on the Facebook platform," Playfish Public Relations Manager Akiko Abe told me. "Playfish looks to extend its publishing framework to independent social game developers who want to create quality, innovative social game experiences on Facebook."

▶ Check out www.playfish.com/publishing for more info on Playfish's publishing services.

EA PopCap

PopCap develops all its social games in-house. However, Giordano Contestabile, Senior Franchise Director for Bejeweled, offered a number of tips for Facebook designers. He recommends they get familiar with Bejeweled Blitz: "[I]t's one of the few social games that doesn't impose a barrier on players, forcing them to pay or spam their friends to keep playing. Getting the balance right—creating a game that allows for unlimited play, but still finds ways to encourage players to monetize through fun rather than through coercion—is really difficult and probably the most important lesson to be taken from Bejeweled Blitz."

Contestabile also warned against two common mistakes made by beginning Facebook developers: not structuring a studio to iterate and expand on the game after launch, and not treating monetization as part of the game's design:

"Soon after releasing your product to the audience, you'll have to engage on several fronts: There will be a fair amount of bug fixing and general *firefighting*, you will gain insight from metrics and customer feedback that you'll want to act on, and you'll realize that your most engaged (and valuable) players are consuming content at a prodigious rate and risk getting bored and dropping out of the game. This last element is the most important, as new content will have to be developed, tested, and released on a constant basis, which will often require a team as large as (or larger than) the one that developed the game. A good social game needs to be fully balanced in design and economy, and it's crucial for design and monetization teams to be deeply integrated and cooperate from the start," says Contestabile.

> **NOTE** "[Do not] treat design and monetization as two separate entities, and try to tack one on top of the other in the final stage of development."
>
> —Giordano Contestabile, EA PopCap

"If you create an original, fun social game and achieve some degree of success, be it wide mainstream adoption or a small, dedicated user base, publishers will come knocking on your door, as the social gaming market is extremely competitive and talent is very much in demand."

Wooga

The Berlin-based company produces all its games in-house, but Wooga's Head of Communications & Partnerships, Sina Kamala Kaufmann, offered several tips to designers just starting out in Facebook, such as those in smaller indie studios:

- ► **Find a niche genre and target group:** Noting that Wooga's mass audience games have a 3 percent monetization rate and increased competition from major developers, Kaufmann argued that it has probably become quite difficult for a small/indie game to acquire millions of players. Instead, she suggested, "Focus on a niche; focus on something special and unique...and still think out of the box and see the functionality of the Facebook platform. Don't think in the framework of, 'That's a game and that's not a game.'" As an example of the former, she noted that the strategy games produced by Kabam attract smaller user numbers, but because they cater to a very passionate audience of core gamers, they probably have high rates of engagement and paying users. As an example of the latter, she suggested brain-training games, games to organize your life in a fun way, match-making apps, and other entertainment apps that do not necessarily offer a full game experience, but are still engaging.

▶ **Design wall messages that drive growth:** "Be aware that [on Facebook]," Kaufmann told me, "people play with their friends, not with random people." A specific application of this advice is the wall update—those messages that most Facebook games enable players to automatically send to their Facebook wall, where friends can see them. If designers make these fun and challenging (as opposed to spammy), they'll help drive user growth. (By Kaufmann's estimate, 10–15 percent of a game's new users will come to the app from newsfeed posts.)

▶ **Balance A/B testing with love:** Wooga emphasizes the use of A/B testing new game features on select groups of players to see how they improve engagement, growth, and monetization rates. At the same time, Kaufmann added, "The other part is that you combine your game design background with what you love."

For further inspiration, Kaufmann recommended designers check out two Wooga games—Monster World, for its deep user engagement and the way it evolved over time (see the game's Facebook page to track new updates and announcements the company posted to the wall), and Diamond Dash, for its high polish.

▶ Ultimately, Wooga attributes the success of its games to the creation of game characters that both designers and players love.

King.com

"We don't buy indie games at the moment," Lars Jörnow, VP Mobile at King.com told me, but he recommended FlashGameLicense.com as "the most effective way of getting sponsored as an indie developer."

SUMMARY

Here are the key points we covered in this chapter:

- ▶ The audience for Facebook games is large and diverse, and includes successful hits in traditional "gamer" genres like real-time strategy and roleplaying games.

- ▶ In 2012–2013, puzzle/arcade games will probably be most popular, while casino games also have a lot of potential for indie developers.

- ▶ When analyzing Facebook games, don't assume a large number of monthly users means a game is successful. Look for growth and/or strong activity after three months, and a solid user base of daily users that can support the studio's development team.

- ▶ Besides virtual currency sales, designers can make money from their games through advertising and in-app offers.

- ▶ A number of top Facebook game publishers, including 6waves and EA Playfish, consider submissions from indie developers.

CHAPTER 4

Facebook Game Design: Basic Principles for Growth and Revenue

IN THIS CHAPTER

▸ Gaining and retaining players

▸ Earning and growing revenue to make your game more profitable

▸ Talking with Justin Smith of Inside Virtual Goods and AppData about how much you should expect to make from a well-designed Facebook game

Because I wrote this book in part for developers from the traditional side of the game industry, this chapter begins with some words from Nabeel Hyatt, a former game developer turned venture capitalist. Many game veterans come to Facebook assuming the worst about its style of gaming and the people who play Facebook games. Hyatt's advice to them: Don't go into it too cynically, and don't be exploitative. "You're going to get your best viral and design mechanics from things that users are excited to do," says Hyatt.

CROSSREF You can read more about Nabeel Hyatt in Chapter 15.

Consider how Brian Reynolds, designer of Civilization II, Rise of Nations, and other hardcore strategy game classics, first became interested in Facebook games. Playing the early hit Mafia Wars, he once told me for a GigaOM article, he noticed that it fostered play among a broad range of acquaintances. This observation was crystallized in the moment when his much older aunt, also a Mafia Wars player, posted on his Facebook wall: "Hi Brian—Thanks for the energy packs, I love you!" Seen that way, the Facebook game creates a context for socialization, in much the same way that classic parlor games enable play between friends and family members regardless of age or gender. (Reynolds went on to become a lead designer at Zynga.)

So instead of trying to re-create the worst lab rat–style "Skinner box" type Facebook games (which are generally losing popularity, in any case), the goal of good Facebook design, says Hyatt, is that your players have a fun experience, encourage them to tell their friends about it, and give you money. "And ideally, they're smiling through all these things." Chapter 5, "Facebook Design Lessons from KIXEYE and 5th Planet Games," goes in-depth with some designers who've mastered the fun experience part, whereas this chapter focuses on the other two factors—revenue and virality.

TIP Instead of assuming that Facebook games are successful because they are addiction-forming Skinner boxes that force players into a loop of behavior they don't enjoy, talk to people who enjoy playing such games to understand how they play them and why.

GAINING AND KEEPING USERS

With so many games and assorted distractions on Facebook, and a total user base that's so large, it's not enough for a designer to create a fun and challenging game. Just as key is finding the ideal slice of Facebook users who are most likely to enjoy your game, and then designing the game to increase the chance that they'll not only try the game once, but will keep coming back to it every day, over an extended period of time. This can be done through a careful mix of targeted marketing, overall design, user-to-user sharing, and the introduction of features that encourage regular play. These game-creation basics are discussed in more detail in the following sections.

Know Your Market—and Drive Installs with Facebook Marketing

It's a common mistake to assume that most Facebook games gain their popularity through update spam and "forced virality," in which players must send installation requests to friends in order to advance in the game. For most Facebook games, advertising on the platform is a main driver of installs (see Figure 4-1), and it's a core tool to find your audience—especially when you're not Zynga or Wooga, and don't have a large pre-existing audience to cross-promote your games to.

▶ The trick is to identify the ideal audience for your game and precisely target them with Facebook ads.

FIGURE 4-1: Facebook advertising platform

Using Facebook's advertising platform, developers can select the cohort of users they want to market their game to, based on age, gender, geographic region, and so on. Just as important as these demographic factors are the interests that users add to their Facebook profiles.

Consider what 5th Planet did to find an audience for Legacy of a Thousand Suns and Dawn of the Dragons (DoD), text-heavy adventure RPGs that are a far cry from the usual Facebook games. The company marketed the game to Facebook users who played Castle Age and World of Warcraft—as identified by users who added those games to their profile's Likes section. "If you know who wants to play your game," as 5th Planet's Robert Winkler puts it, "Facebook gives you so many tools to find them." In other words, decide who your likely target market is, then go after them via Facebook ads.

5th Planet made their aim even more precise than that: With DoD, the company targeted their ads at males 18-35 who had played Castle Age and who also had friends who played DoD during office hours. The last two variables are important: Since DoD has a strong social component, 5th Planet wanted to market the game to people who were likely to play it with friends (for example, fellow office workers.) This impact worked really well—so well, in fact, that the company was able to decrease the cost per install while increasing their return on investment. In the end, cost per installation for DoD and Legacy was remarkably inexpensive—just 10 to 15 cents per player.

▶ The amount of advertising spent to get a user to try the game.

However, targeted Facebook ads are only the beginning. You will also need to experiment with lots of variations of the ad (different artwork and copy), try out hundreds of keywords, and tweak the age and gender segments you're trying to reach to achieve an optimal install rate.

Design for Long-Term Aspiration

Hyatt has a simple rule for what the design of a Facebook game should immediately convey to players: a long-term aspiration they can achieve in the game by playing over a long period of time. If a developer can successfully communicate this, a player is more likely to transition from being a non-committal player to becoming a dedicated, regular one.

Consider FarmVille, which many traditional game developers see as being boring and mechanical; however, when they make this observation, they are focusing only on the moment-to-moment process of playing FarmVille. What keeps players engaged in FarmVille is not the moment-to-moment process, but the aspiration of what their farm can ultimately be (see Figure 4-2)—as Hyatt puts it, "wanting this beautiful, big, well-working farm."

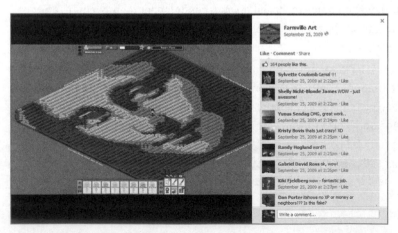

FIGURE 4-2: Customized FarmVille farm

It's this vision in their heads that keeps players returning to the game on a regular basis. This kind of aspiration is applicable to many varieties of games with a building mechanic. For example, in the hardcore strategy game Backyard Monsters by KIXEYE, it's immediately made clear to the players that their long-term aspiration is to create the most badass and impregnable base fortress possible.

> **CROSSREF** You can find out more on Backyard Monsters in Chapter 5.

To take another example, consider Draw Something. The long-term aspiration of that game might not seem obvious, since individual play sessions are brief and disconnected. The long-term aspiration of Draw Something is to become more creative and entertaining, and to be acknowledged by friends and loved ones for that.

Similar to how Flickr's user community fosters the desire to improve the quality of photos they share with each other, Draw Something encourages players to become better or funnier doodlers, so that their drawings will be shared and Liked by others more. (No wonder the game is so huge.)

Encourage Viral Growth by Encouraging Valuable Sharing

Most Facebook games include a feature that allows players to share game content with Facebook friends through an update posted to their wall. In theory, these updates should encourage viral growth—as a player's friends see these updates, they should become interested enough to install the game. However, not all varieties of sharing are equal.

Hyatt puts the distinction in the form of a question: "Is the way you're architecting the game generating two things: a high intent to share—why people would want to share in the first place—and is the thing they're sharing highly shareable, [something] that they'd want to share widely?"

In Hyatt's view, special game decorations or customizations that express a player's personality have a mid-range sharing value (for example, a customized FarmVille farm), whereas fully user-generated content (as in Draw Something) is on the high end of shareability.

Another kind of highly shareable update is humor. Leading Zynga game designer Brian Reynolds once noted that the most popular and viral updates for his game FrontierVille featured a cartoon of a character busily shearing a sheep. This update became highly viral, not because people were particularly interested in wool, but because inadvertently, the cartoon looked like the dude was, well, getting romantic

▶ A player's high scores or other in-game accomplishments are the worst things to share because they're totally irrelevant to non-players—and probably not that interesting even to fellow players.

with the sheep. Once the developers realized that, they pushed for more updates with comical double entendres (lots of LOL-orific references to players who "get wood" or "need a few good screws").

Daily Game Features Help Drive Daily Usage

As noted in Chapter 3, daily usage is generally considered to be among the most important factors of a successful Facebook game and correlates to strong revenue: Someone who plays every day is more likely than not to pay. What's more, daily usage also contributes to the health of the game's ecosystem—players competing with each other and sharing their game content with other Facebook users, both of which in turn encourage even more daily usage.

Designers can encourage players to log in every day by introducing fun features that unlock once every 24-hour cycle. For instance, in Tetris Battle (as in many other Facebook games), a day's first game session begins with a "Daily Bonus Spin" (see Figure 4-3), which offers players a chance to win game bonuses and then invites them to come back tomorrow for another chance at a spin.

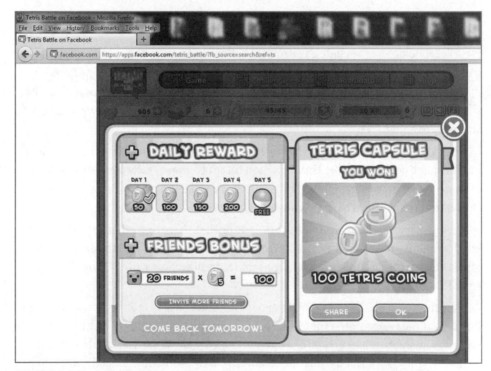

FIGURE 4-3: Tetris Battle's Daily Bonus Spin

Features like Daily Spins explicitly encourage consistent usage, but other features are also incorporated into Facebook games to nudge players to log in often. For instance, leader boards enable players to compete with each other, and leveling systems give players updates on their in-game progress. Above all, regular content updates are an essential component of retention, encouraging players to keep coming back to see the new changes, and in doing so, encouraging them to monetize.

EARNING AND GROWING REVENUE

Besides advertising, sponsorships/tie-ins, and other indirect revenue channels, most Facebook developers make the lion's share of their money by getting players to purchase virtual goods via their in-game currency. Although most players won't pay anything for your game, this section covers some of the tricks veteran designers use to make it more likely that they will.

Make Sure the Game's Monetization is Deeply Integrated into the Game's Design

Ask any game designer the secret to a successful game and they'll say something like "Good game design and fun gameplay" (which would require a whole other book to explain). But ask any Facebook game designer that same question, and the answer will be just a touch different, something like: "Good game design and fun gameplay with monetization deeply integrated into the design and gameplay." Because all Facebook games are free to play, and there are so many, it's not enough to create a good, fun game. Monetization options have to be designed from the start, alongside all the other features that make up the game.

Without being overly obtrusive, artificial, or spammy, the goal is to always make the player aware of how they can pay for the game, and how that payment can make the game more fun. A perfect example of this is found in Backyard Monsters (see Figure 4-4), which is a resource-management strategy game. Players have to harvest enough raw materials to build their base and army. (It's part of the core game loop.)

When players "bank" collected resources, they are sure to notice (because it's embossed in gold) the ability to "Speed Up" the collection process. Clicking this option gives the players the ability to accelerate resource collection with Shiny (the game's official currency, which can be bought with real money cash/credit payments).

► This is really not that different from the monetization mechanic that financed the video game industry for decades, during the arcade era—also known as "Insert Coin to Continue."

Buying this Speed-Up is optional, and the players can have about as much fun playing the game without doing so (as long as they are willing to wait for their harvesters.) But when players are having the most fun and are impatient to keep the fun going, they're most likely to click the Speed-Up option.

"Buy" option speeds up game progress with cash purchase

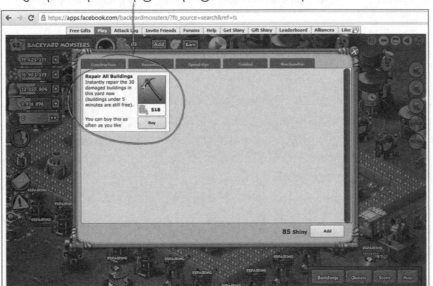

FIGURE 4-4: Speed-Up monetization option in Backyard Monsters

Design the Purchase of Virtual Goods to Be Part of the First-Time Player Experience

In addition to integrating monetization in the design, it should also be integrated very early into the first-time user experience. In other words, from the very start, the players should experience and enjoy the process of purchasing virtual goods for the game. This accomplishes at least two goals—it familiarizes the players with the in-game economy and the buying of items within it as part of the gameplay, and it potentially creates the desire for more purchases down the road.

Emphasize Multiple Virtual Currency Acquisition and Payment Methods

Although most Facebook game developers earn revenue through sales of their virtual currency, there should be a number of ways to pay for it in real life, including PayPal, credit card, cell phone, pre-paid cards sold at retail stores, and advertising engagement offers. See Figure 4-5.

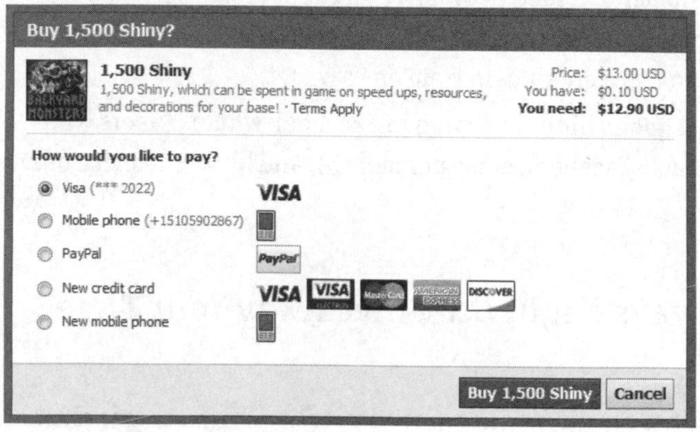

FIGURE 4-5: Multiple option payment wall

It's important to present as many of these payment options as possible in the payment window, so that customers have many options to choose from. Make it as easy as possible for players to give you their money.

Offer Short-Term Virtual Goods Discounts, but Don't Go Nuts

Many developers boost their monetization rates by giving short-term discounts on their virtual goods, generally on Friday and the weekend, when players have more leisure time to play and pay. But you need to provide discounts in moderation, even if they give you a nice short-term revenue boost.

If discounts are too frequent, many players will take advantage of the discount, but then not monetize at all, as they wait for the next discount offer to pop up.

▶ It will usually take some trial and error to optimize discounts with strong overall earnings.

Even Though Virtual Goods Aren't Real, Don't Under-Price Them

A leading Facebook/web game developer once gave me some advice that sounded counter-intuitive at first: "Make sure that you're pricing things appropriately high... it's easy to price items too low." He learned this lesson the hard way, by setting his game's goods at low price points, only to learn that doing this didn't lead to a significant increase in paying customers. In fact, a low price might hurt sales, because it conveys a message that the virtual goods aren't valuable in relation to the game, and aren't even worth the time to fish a credit card from one's wallet.

It's safer to price virtual goods high, in search of Facebook whales (users who spend more than $20 on a single Facebook game per month), and lower the price only if sales are slow.

Promotional Giveaways Might Only Give Away Your Time and Money

Although short-term discounts are a common monetization strategy, some insiders are not fans of promotional giveaways, where players are actually given free in-game currency. In theory, this could "prime the pump," but in practice, top developers have told me these promotions only create "free Credits slushing around in the system, which did not add value" (as one of them put it). The likely problem is that a currency giveaway diminishes the value of the in-game goods they're meant to purchase and the experience of the players who get them.

What to Sell: Functional Items Good, Decorative Items Not So Good

Facebook game developers tell me regularly that the best kind of virtual goods to sell players are functional enhancements that improve their gameplay—power-ups, boosters, upgrades, extra lives—however they're expressed within the framework of the game. These can be permanent enhancements—for example, magic equipment that stays with the players for the game's duration. Another kind of best-selling

> ▶ Traditional gamers have proven they are more than willing to pay $180 in yearly fees just to play a single online game (for example, World of Warcraft), and Facebook game whales will pay nearly as much or more.

> ▶ If the enhancements are permanent, they should probably be relatively high-priced.

functional item is short-term, single-use power-ups, which are often called "consumables" (see Figure 4-6).

Consumables are typically cheaper than permanent items, and consequently, tend to sell in greater volume. They enable players to sample game content more quickly, and often act as a gateway to greater monetization. For that reason, it's a good idea to link these one-time power-ups to bulk sales or better upgrades. For example, "Buy a single power-up for one gold coin...or five power-ups for three coins!"

By contrast, decorative items generally sell less well than functional items. But this isn't to say you shouldn't sell decorative items (for example, stylish clothing for a player's avatar). These decorative items tend to sell relatively well when other players can see them, because players can use them to show off their personalities.

FIGURE 4-6: Consumable power-ups in 5th Planet's Legacy of a Thousand Suns

Decorative items can also have an indirect functionality. For example, EA Playfish's The Sims Social cleverly merges the functional with the decorative by selling virtual goods that are mostly meant to furnish the player's home (see Figure 4-7).

Although these items allow players to customize their space, they also have functional benefits that improve gameplay—an enhanced bed increases energy when used, for example. In addition, buying enhanced items increases the stated, public value of the player's home, which acts as a game metric and leaderboard. (Sims Social players who compete with each other and themselves have a higher home value.)

Decorative game item that also enhances player's character stats

FIGURE 4-7: Functional/decorative items in The Sims Social

Release Regular New Content to Increase Monetization

This point bears repeating: Regular and consistent content updates to your game are important, not only because they help retain existing users, but also because they help turn more of those players into paying customers. New content is also an opportunity to promote monetization. For instance, you can announce a new mission for your RPG, and advise players to buy some power-ups to accomplish it. What's more, new content increases the esteem of buying items associated with it.

When 5th Planet releases a new collection of virtual goods, Winkler tells me, "Some people will buy the whole set in the first half hour, because they know they'll be using it for the next few months." (Not to mention they'll have bragging rights.)

▶ Many players want to be the first among their fellow players to own the latest and coolest game goods.

Don't Hide Your Best Viral and Monetization Features

Finally, one more bit of advice from social game veteran Hyatt on what not to do. "A common mistake that people make when they're trying to invent new virality and revenue is to bury that feature," he says. "If you have a great feature, the most important question is to measure what percentage of players engage with it. Don't lock it up—instead, perhaps show it off before they even play the game, such as in the marketing and load screen art."

Sometimes these key game features emerge from user behavior. While recently preparing a report on gambling-themed Facebook games, I was struck by how many of the players spent more time idly chatting with each other than they did playing the actual game, talking about their families, the weather, and so on. So I was surprised that none of these games highlighted this "social hangout" feature in their advertising or first-time player orientation. Play up the most unique and innovative features of your game, and play up the features that your players love most!

CHATTING WITH JUSTIN SMITH OF INSIDE VIRTUAL GOODS AND APPDATA ABOUT GAME REVENUE

AppData.com is without a doubt the leading site for tracking Facebook game user activity. (And I'm confident that's the case, even though I have to disclose having recently written for it and the parent site, Inside Social Games.) Co-founded in 2008 by Justin Smith, who also co-authors a quarterly *Inside Virtual Goods* report, AppData was conceived at a time when many Facebook games were beginning to gain rapid growth, although it still wasn't clear which apps were truly popular. Drawing on publicly accessible data, AppData's aim is to be a tool for analyzing the Facebook gaming ecosystem.

With that background, it's no surprise that Smith has a lot of secrets to share with developers—on the kind of money they can expect to make from well-made Facebook games, the design elements that help boost revenue, and future changes to the social network that developers should be aware of.

Typical Facebook Game Monetization Rates

Most Facebook games attract a very small number of paying customers—1–3 percent is typical, with rates approaching 5–9 percent considered extremely good. Among these paying players, 10 percent are generally defined as whales, as described earlier. For most Facebook games, it's these players who'll contribute the bulk of a developer's revenue. (As you'll see with web and iOS games, this is typical of most free-to-play games, regardless of platform.)

Facebook Genres That Monetize Well: Poker and Caretaking-Related Games

According to Smith, poker games earn more money than other genres, and speaking more broadly, games with a caretaking mechanic also do well.

▶ *These include simulation games, in which the player regularly takes care of property, pets, fish, and so on.*

Note that this does not necessarily mean just farming and pet games; for example, the Facebook game Army Attack is a turn-based strategy title aimed at the mid-core market, but still contains a strong caretaking element (see Figure 4-8). Players must log in on a regular basis to collect base resources and repair any damage from external attack.

Harvesting resources in strategy game

FIGURE 4-8: Caretaking in Army Attack

Typical ARPU Rates of Successful Facebook Games

A well-designed, well-monetized Facebook game will earn 50 cents to 1 dollar in average revenue per user (or ARPU) per monthly player. In other words, such a game with 100,000 monthly active users (or MAU) will gross $50,000–100,000 a month for the developer. If you're earning that ARPU rate, says Smith, "you're in good company and you're doing something right."

Facebook Design Elements That Monetize Well: Appointment and Crew Mechanics

The caretaking feature monetizes well, Smith explained, because it involves an appointment mechanic, nudging players to return to the game on a consistent basis. (And active players are much more likely to become paying players.) Related to that, Smith pointed out a similar feature—a crew mechanic, in which certain game tasks can be accomplished only with the help of other players. Again, having this feature increases more game activity, which increases the likelihood of turning players into paying users.

In addition to the caretaking and crew mechanics, Smith recommends creating an easy on-ramp for novice players to move to paying players.

This lowers monetization's barrier to entry, and makes it likely that players will go on to buy more items (as opposed to asking players to spend several dollars or more of real currency on their first purchase).

All those numbers and strategies aside, the basic appeal of a game's design and execution remains fundamental. "Any game that's fun," as Smith puts it, "has the potential to monetize well."

▶ The first game items a player encounters that are buyable with virtual currency should be extremely cheap, or given out for free, with advertising-driven offers.

For Early Growth, Create an Acquisition Campaign

Although a Facebook game can earn a lot of organic growth from having a good internal design, Smith recommends integrating a good design with a paid marketing strategy that leverages Facebook's capability to target potential players by age, gender, and so on. By doing so, your games can reach their optimal intended audience. (Check Smith's InsideSocialGames.com for a selection of vendors that provide such services.)

Future Trends and Opportunities: More Mobile, More Facebook Gaming outside of Facebook

Smith sees a couple of important changes to Facebook that designers should be aware of:

▶ **More Facebook-related game activity outside of Facebook.** Smith notes that Facebook is adding more features to the open graph, the company's API that connects social network users' interests to activity happening outside Facebook. He believes this may lead to more opportunities to connect web game stats and updates to Facebook, a feature developers can use to drive traffic and retention. (From my perspective, this drive will likely depend on how successful Zynga is in turning their off-Facebook site Zynga.com, which uses Facebook Connect, into a popular destination site.)

▶ **More Facebook-oriented mobile gaming.** Facebook recently rolled out its mobile platform and is encouraging more development on it, including (especially?) games. It's likely that Facebook will also offer monetization options on its mobile platform (placing it in competition with Apple), both features that developers should consider for their upcoming games.

▶ The sudden growth of Draw Something and Words With Friends, which are mainly played on mobile devices and outside of Facebook, is perhaps an early sign of the two trends Smith anticipates.

How to Use AppData as a Developer

For developers who want to use AppData.com, Smith has this advice: Focus on sub-genres that they are most interested in creating games for and track relative movement to see which games in that sub-genre are growing. Also advised: using the Compare Apps feature to generate a broader picture of the market. When looking at particular apps, developers can use the Traffic Trends > Custom feature to track relative performance of genres and games over specified segments of time.

▶ Although it doesn't always tell the complete story of a game's health, a DAU/MAU that's over 20 percent usually indicates a game with a lot of passionate players who are eager to monetize.

For developers who want to follow their own games on Facebook, Smith recommends watching the DAU as percentage of MAU (or DAU/MAU) metric.

He also recommends closely following AppData's "gainers" leaderboard (see Figure 4-9), which tracks games that are gaining users and activity. Games that earn a place on this leaderboard tend to attract investors.

Leaderboards >> Top Gainers This Week

List: [Applications ▾] By: [MAU ▾] [Find]

Filter by: Size Category Platform Language

	Name	MAU	Gain ▾	Gain,%
1.	Bubble Safari	17,100,000	+11,200,000	+ 190%
2.	Socialcam	79,800,000	+6,400,000	+ 9%
3.	Terra	7,800,000	+1,800,000	+ 30%
4.	Lost Bubble	5,700,000	+1,700,000	+ 43%
5.	Viddy	22,600,000	+1,700,000	+ 8%
6.	TripAdvisor™	20,800,000	+1,500,000	+ 8%
7.	Zynga Bingo	10,000,000	+1,000,000	+ 11%
8.	Glassdoor	1,600,000	+820,000	+ 105%
9.	Song Pop	1,200,000	+810,000	+ 208%
10.	Bubble Blitz	4,700,000	+800,000	+ 27%
11.	DoAlbums	2,500,000	+800,000	+ 47%
12.	MyCalendar - Birthdays	34,000,000	+800,000	+ 2%
13.	Instagram	18,900,000	+700,000	+ 4%
14.	Scribd	25,600,000	+700,000	+ 4%
15.	Candy Crush Saga	11,600,000	+600,000	+ 6%
16.	Truth Game	6,900,000	+600,000	+ 11%
17.	MiCalendario - Cumpleaños	14,600,000	+600,000	+ 4%
18.	Spotify	22,100,000	+600,000	+ 3%
19.	Are YOU Interested?	7,500,000	+600,000	+ 10%
20.	Birthday Reminder	830,000	+570,000	+ 219%

FIGURE 4-9: AppData's top gainers leaderboard (June 2012). Copyright 2012 Inside Network Inc., a division of WebMediaBrands. All rights reserved. Reprinted with permission from AppData.com.

NOTE Justin Smith's next *Inside Virtual Goods* report, co-written with Charles Hudson, will be available for order in Fall 2012 at www.insidevirtualgoods.com.

SUMMARY

Here are the key points we covered in this chapter:

► Know your market. Identify the ideal audience of your game, and precisely target it with Facebook ads.

► Design for long-term aspiration. Communicate what players can do with your game 3, 6, and 12 months down the road, and they're more likely to become dedicated, regular players.

► Encourage viral growth by encouraging valuable sharing. Design content to be shared on Facebook walls. Player customizations are good; user-generated content is even better.

► Include daily game features; they drive daily usage. Encourage players to log in every day by introducing fun features that unlock once every 24-hour cycle.

► Deeply integrate monetization into design. It's not enough to create a good, fun game. The monetization features should be designed from the start, alongside all the other features that make up the game.

► Make buying virtual goods part of the first-time play experience. From the very start, players should have (and enjoy) the process of purchasing virtual goods for the game.

► Price your goods (generally) high, not low. Go in search of whales (paying users who spend more than $20 on a single Facebook game per month), and lower your prices only if sales are slow.

► Include virtual goods. Functional enhancements tend to sell well, decorations not (usually) so much.

► Watch your monetization rates. Between 1–3 percent is typical, 5–9 percent is extremely good. Among paying players, 10 percent are generally whales. A well-designed, well-monetized Facebook game will earn 50 cents to 1 dollar in ARPU per monthly player.

CHAPTER 5

Facebook Design Lessons from KIXEYE and 5th Planet Games

Although it's all well and good to talk about general design principles for building engagement and revenue in Facebook games, it's perhaps even more important to see how they've been applied in specific, successful titles. In this chapter, we will analyze the success of two developers who've managed to prove there's a market for hardcore games on the Facebook platform: the strategy games of KIXEYE and the adventure RPGs of 5th Planet Games.

DESIGNING FACEBOOK STRATEGY GAMES THE KIXEYE WAY

▶ GigaOM (www.gigaom.com) delivers the latest technology news.

Before Paul Preece could help launch KIXEYE, he first had to get fired. That happened after his boss, who expected him to put more energy into his day job as a Visual Basic coder, noticed a widely read *GigaOM* article about Desktop Tower Defense, the breakout success Flash game Preece developed after hours. His boss, Preece told me then, "was not a happy chappy." (This put me in an awkward place, because, you see, I was the one who wrote the *GigaOM* article.) But the game was also noticed by someone else: Lightspeed venture capitalist Jeremy Liew, who put $1 million in seed funding together to fund and launch the company with Preece and his development partner, David Scott.

> **CROSSREF** To read more about Desktop Tower Defense, see Chapter 9, "Web Game Developer Profiles: Kingdom of Loathing and Desktop Tower Defense." Read more about Jeremy Liew in Chapter 15, "Is Your Game Ready to Get VC or Crowdsourced Funding?"

This isn't to say the company's success was preordained or easy. In 2009, KIXEYE (then called Casual Collective) was at a low point and came close to bust. This had nothing to do with the quality of their follow-up games, which were as polished and well designed as Desktop Tower Defense. What they lacked was a good monetization and marketing strategy. Thanks in part to the entrance of Will Harbin, who took over as CEO and helped steer the company's product and revenue plan, and who advocated giving the company a more hardcore, game-sounding moniker, KIXEYE, the turnaround came very quickly.

By 2010, KIXEYE was making as much in a day as it had made in all of 2008 and 2009, and it has been profitable ever since. By 2012, it was one of the most successful game developers on Facebook, proving (and pretty much pioneering) the market for games on the social network that appealed less to fans of FarmVille and more to lovers of Warcraft and Command & Conquer. KIXEYE's games include Backyard Monsters, Battle Pirates (see Figure 5-1), and War Commander, all variations of real-time, resource-management strategy games.

▶ This game was KIXEYE's first breakout success.

But how did KIXEYE reach this high point? To learn the KIXEYE way, I visited Preece at the company headquarters, which, unsurprisingly, was located on the top two floors of an elite San Francisco corporate skyscraper. In a wide-ranging conversation, Preece outlined some of the design principles that helped make KIXEYE games so successful. These principles are discussed in the following sections.

FIGURE 5-1: KIXEYE's Battle Pirates

Wrap the Game Mechanics in a Metaphor That People Understand

"The ideal game mechanic is something you don't have to explain," Preece says, which is especially true for a mass-market audience like Facebook. This is likely why the most popular Facebook games simulate everyday actions like farming or building construction.

> **NOTE** Building up a social game is about building up momentum of player activity. This is quite unlike a packaged console game, which requires an up-front investment of $60 or so—then, a player is willing invest the time learning how to play, to get their money's worth.

Because social games are free, it's all about keeping the players in the game and meeting their expectations minute by minute. A game mechanic that makes no intuitive sense, therefore, becomes a roadblock that will cause many players to simply quit.

Make the Tutorial the Game's Sales Pitch and Immediately Satisfy a Player's Expectations

The point of the game tutorial should not just be teaching how to play the game; the tutorial should just as much act as the game's sales pitch, showing off all the key features of the game. For instance, in KIXEYE's War Commander, the tutorial includes a battle in the first 10 seconds, and before the first minute is over, the player has captured a base—both of which are essential aspects of the game's experience. See Figure 5-2.

FIGURE 5-2: War Commander tutorial

You can see this insight in how Backyard Monsters changed during its development cycle. When it first launched in 2010, the monsters and the combat animations were cute, reflecting the designers' desire to give the game a mass appeal. However, KIXEYE realized that the art assets weren't accurately depicting what the game actually was, and changed the artwork and effects to be much more aggressive and violent. After the change, Backyard Monsters began generating better engagement and revenue numbers.

The reason? "Because we were dressing it up as the game it was, which is a combat game," Preece now says. "You don't want to bc buying people on false advertising...the only reason you lose someone in a game is you haven't met their expectations."

When a player's expectations aren't immediately satisfied in a free-to-play game, they have no incentive to stay a minute longer. "You have to exceed their expectations in the first second, in the first minute, in the first five minutes; you have to keep doing that," says Preece.

▶ So if a game's ad depicts a rocket being fired, the players better be able to fire a rocket in the first two minutes, or they'll feel betrayed.

Crappy Prototypes Are Better Than Amazing Design Documents

In the KIXEYE approach, it's better to create a rudimentary prototype of the game than a highly detailed design document. The prototype will prove whether the core experience is fun, and if not, you can iterate until it does. Once the prototype works, you can build layers (art, effects, and so on) on top of this skeleton.

For that reason, KIXEYE prefers that the prototype be a vertical slice of the entire game, so that you can see how changes in one area of gameplay can impact another. Another reason for preferring prototypes over design documents is Preece's belief that every game has about 70 percent similarity to the games that came before it. "Don't believe there's any more firsts," he says. "It's [about] highly evolved design."

Monetization Lesson, Part I: Speed-Ups Good; Decor and Deals, Not So Good

KIXEYE's main monetization method is the purchase of game speed-ups. For example, in Backyard Monsters, players can harvest resources, upgrade units and buildings, and create new monsters for free, but the process can take anywhere from several minutes to several days to complete. KIXEYE cleverly inserts a Finish Now! option, so that players can buy and spend the game's virtual currency, Shiny, to hasten (or immediately complete) this production process (see Figure 5-3).

It was this change to the revenue strategy, by the way, that helped put KIXEYE on the road to profit. "If the game's doing its job," Preece explains, "the player should be eager to gain access to content in the game." Then, spending $20 becomes more worthwhile to some players, rather than weeks of waiting. "They see it almost like an investment."

Related to this, functional customization items also sell well in KIXEYE games, but Preece and other designers make sure that it's possible to earn the same items with enough free play (although true to their strategy, doing that will take more time.)

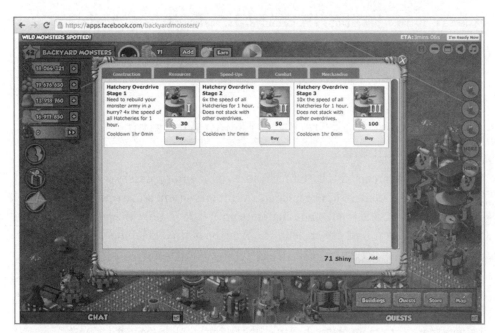

FIGURE 5-3: Speed-up option in Backyard Monsters

Less successful for KIXEYE are decorative customization items, such as those that players can buy to customize their Backyard Monsters base. And while many Facebook developers report success at offering daily discounts for virtual goods, Preece says that KIXEYE's user base does not find that appealing. This is probably because they are motivated to monetize for other reasons—keep reading to find out what they are.

Monetization Lesson, Part II: Emotional Response— Positive or Negative—Monetizes Well

In Backyard Monsters, many players monetize at a key moment: after logging into the game and discovering that their base has been attacked and rampaged by another player. When this happens, they can slowly build up a large enough army to launch a retaliatory strike—or spend money to speed up the creation process and return the attack as soon as possible (see Figure 5-4).

For Preece, the lesson to that player behavior is this: "Emotional response monetizes...I think there's definitely a connection between emotion and monetization." The advertising world has known about this connection for some time—it's not about selling the product, but creating an emotional connection to it. Coca-Cola ads don't sell sugar water, but the feeling you want to have when you're drinking it (fun with

▶ In the case of Backyard Monsters, anger and the desire for revenge.

friends, and so on). The same is true with Apple's ads: "They make you long for their devices... [and] you're not rationally comparing iPhones to any other phone."

FIGURE 5-4: Avenge this! A player's Backyard Monsters base after invasion

How do you know when your game is inspiring emotion? In my experience, one quick way might be to check the game's player forums. If 90 percent of the users are enraged at the developers, it's probably monetizing well. If it's monetizing *extremely* well, half the players will be angry, while the other half are telling the others to shut up.

Speaking of forums, Preece recommends paying close attention to user feedback posted there (because only the most hardcore players will take the time to make comments), but ignoring the outliers—the ones who are screaming the most loudly, but without any clear reason. Instead, listen to the people who have a specific and reasonable grievance about the game that fuels their anger.

Targeted Marketing Leads to Good Monetization

As noted at the start of this chapter, KIXEYE began making money after they figured out how to best market their games. Essentially, this came down to targeting the Facebook users who are most likely to install and play KIXEYE games. Profit comes when the lifetime value (LTV) of a player exceeds the average cost per install (CPI) of each player spent on advertising to acquire them. In the KIXEYE model, LTV is assumed to be

▶ These players are known as "whales."

▶ This marketing strategy will have diminishing returns as you scale upward—since there are only so many users in your target demographic.

around 6–8 months, and averages the revenue earned from players who pay nothing, pay some, or pay quite a lot.

In simple math terms, for example, a game that generates $2.00 in LTV from $1.00 CPI and 10,000 total paid installs makes $10,000 in profit. However, this assumes the right Facebook users have been targeted in your ads. In the case of KIXEYE games, an ideal target is men between 18 and 34 who have "Liked" strategy games like Command & Conquer.

Design a Strong Meta Game

For Preece, there's another key design feature to a successful Facebook game (or for that matter, games on most platforms): A "meta game" that has goals above and beyond the game's specific, explicit objectives. For example, in Battle Pirates, the meta game is effective teamwork—players learning to collaborate in order to find the best ways to minimize their own damage and maximize damage to others.

As an example of this meta game, Preece says some players who inhabit the same sectors of Battle Pirates have come to establish a no-neighbor-attack policy with each other (see Figure 5-5). In other words, players are changing the goals of the game, which is meant to be an all-out PvP-fest. Even FarmVille has a meta game, Preece notes, which is "How do I design the most efficient farm?" Then, he says, "You've gone beyond the mechanics and are looking at it top down." From a business perspective, Preece believes "meta players" are more likely to spend money on the game than more casual players.

Preece offered a sub-rule related to this one—don't punish the meta gamer. As with the no-attack policy that emerged in Battle Pirates, sometimes players create meta game rules that you, the designer, didn't intend. In Preece's view, this is a good thing that is to be encouraged. "You shouldn't remove something that takes skill to acquire," he argues. (You could go even further, I might add, and actively *reward* meta players, by turning their unofficial gameplay behavior into an explicit game mechanic. So, for example, if meta players are forming informal alliances with each other, create an "Ally" feature that confers explicit game bonuses for allying—and explicit penalties for betraying an ally.)

With his web game classic Desktop Tower Defense, Preece was at first bothered by players who'd "juggle" their defense mazes—that is, create a temporary opening in the maze that the invading monsters would rush toward, giving the player extra time to reinforce another section of the maze (see Figure 5-6).

From one point of view, this technique could be seen as an exploit—but from another, it was a clever player strategy. And while Preece originally considered removing the ability to juggle, he ultimately decided it should stay. "If anything," as he says now, "you should double down on that [workaround]…[in KIXEYE games] we try to allow that kind of emergent gameplay to occur."

FIGURE 5-5: A Battle Pirates sector

Juggling "creeps" by creating a temporary opening

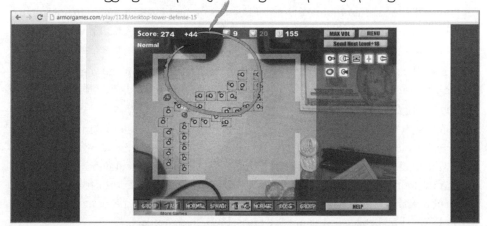

FIGURE 5-6: "Juggling" the invading creeps in Desktop Tower Defense

DESIGNING STORY-RICH FACEBOOK RPGS THE 5TH PLANET WAY

In 2009, Robert Winkler was a full-time student at UC Davis with a wife and three kids, and he'd just been offered a full scholarship to the university. However, he wanted to help launch a game studio, 5th Planet Games, even though he had no background in game development (beyond a love of playing them), and doing this would mean giving up the scholarship. Despite that, his wife gave Winkler the go-ahead, telling him, "This is the one chance to follow your dream." Winkler's co-founder in the nascent company, Steve Pladson, was a programmer, but he didn't know Flash, the platform they intended to develop for, and had to learn it on the job (so to speak) through a book. The first 20 people on their team, for that matter, also had no prior game development experience. The company had no investors and was 100 percent bootstrapped and self-funded.

The original plan, as conceived by the four original founders, was to create a web-based, massively multiplayer online game like Ragnarok or Runescape and hope to get it into a presentable demo they could then shop around, to get a bigger budget. "We knew it wasn't going to happen," Winkler remembers. Instead, he and Pladson argued that they should instead make a Facebook game—even though none of them even had an account on the social network at the time. Rejecting that pivot, two of the founding team members quit.

"[But t]hat's where all the users were," Winkler reasoned, arguing they could create a better game than what was currently offered on Facebook in 2009. "If we grabbed a tiny section [of users], we could make a living doing this."

▶ Dawn of the Dragons was developed for less than $10,000.

5th Planet's first game was Dawn of the Dragons, a text-driven RPG in the vein of early Facebook hits like Mafia Wars (see Figure 5-7). "We put in 40 hours in our normal day job and 60 hours developing the game," as Winkler remembers. It took about four months to go from the game they imagined on whiteboards to a live game on Facebook that was taking paying customers. Their second game, a text- and art-heavy RPG called Legacy of a Thousand Suns, launched soon after.

FIGURE 5-7: 5th Planet's Dawn of the Dragons

Winkler's gamble paid off. He is now co-CEO of 5th Planet Games, based in Roseville, a small town near Sacramento. The company is profitable and counts 32 employees. Although the user base for their games is small—as of this writing, in mid-2012, Dawn of the Dragons has 90,000 MAU and Legacy has 40,000 MAU— for Facebook, their monetization rates are extremely high. ARPU is over $1 per month per user overall, and Legacy of a Thousand Suns is close to $3 per month per user, with some individuals and groups spending up to $5,000 a month, and 15–20 percent of total users monetizing.

"We're playing in a different league," as Winkler puts it. Indeed. As noted in Chapter 3, a well-designed, well-monetized Facebook game will typically earn 50 cents to 1 dollar in ARPU per monthly player, and is extremely lucky to get 5–9 percent of players monetizing. So clearly, 5th Planet Games has found a very successful niche creating games they're passionate about. Legacy of a Thousand Suns, in particular, has beautiful artwork and a deep, highly involving story—both rare in Facebook games.

How did they do it? Winkler shared some secrets to 5th Planet's success. These secrets are discussed in the following sections.

Differentiate the Game with Great Art and Music— Economically

Legacy of a Thousand Suns has some of the most polished art and music of any Facebook game (even compared to the major publishers), a design choice Winkler and team made early on, to differentiate themselves from other social games (see Figure 5-8). "We wanted the game to feel like something special," he explains. "We felt that Facebook lacked a true RPG experience." They found a writer and composer on the developer forum GameDev.net, and paid $1,000 for the music. (This was, Winkler says, "a HUGE part of our budget.") Even though most or many players eventually toggle off the music, Winkler believes it's worthwhile in order to portray Legacy as something unique, from the very first log-in.

For the art, 5th Planet partnered with Concept Art House, a studio that's created visual assets for Blizzard and other major players. Instead of paying the company out of pocket, however, 5th Planet offered a revenue-sharing deal, showing them the earnings of their first game to prove it was a worthwhile partnership.

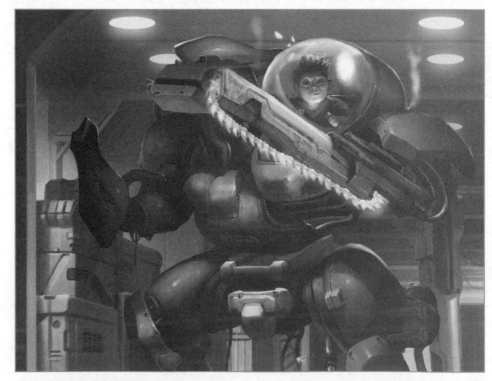

FIGURE 5-8: Art from 5th Planet's Legacy of a Thousand Suns

A Text-Heavy Game Can Work on Facebook—If Your Hard-Core Fans Love It

Another distinguishing feature of Legacy is its heavy use of text, far more than most Facebook games (see Figure 5-9). Winkler believes that most players don't read the storyline prose, and 5th Planet has designed it so users can easily skip it. "We have a wall of text, but it shouldn't take you more than one click to get past," as he puts it.

▶ Just one story zone of Legacy of a Thousand Suns is about 39,000 words, the size of a short novel.

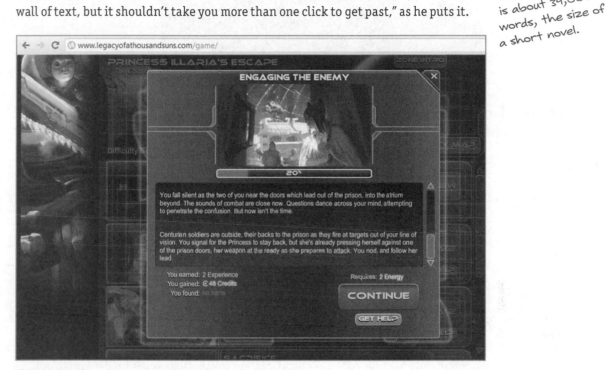

FIGURE 5-9: Sample game text in Legacy of a Thousand Suns

At the same time, Winkler argues that the game's most hard-core users do read most of the text, and relate the gist of the story and background to other players, in forums and other channels. To prove his case, Winkler notes that Legacy players had a strong emotional reaction to a plot twist in the last game zone.

Drive Viral Growth with Group Experiences

Winkler says that adding group raids was the best design decision to Legacy and Dawn. In this play mode, players are challenged to defeat a game boss within a certain time frame (such as 72 hours), with each participating player promised huge amounts of loot if the boss can be killed by then. See Figure 5-10.

FIGURE 5-10: Boss Battle in Legacy of a Thousand Suns

▶ One raid in Dawn of the Dragons involved 23,000 players!

This creates a major incentive for active players to invite their friends and fellow players to join them on the raid, and promote the game to them. (They can post raid announcements as links on Facebook walls or as links on third-party websites, which take anyone who clicks it directly to the raid.) These raids have been enormously popular, encouraging viral growth. They have also become great for user retention, because they often bring back lapsed players. "It's such a fun, engaging time," says Winkler, "people come out of retirement." (This kind of symmetrical play, by the way, isn't typical of most Facebook games, which are asymmetrical.)

Interestingly, because raids require player cooperation, they encourage people to buy items to help their guild beat a boss, instead of just buying upgrades that only benefit themselves. (For both Dawn and Legacy, the majority of monetized items are player energy and stamina refills.) "People want to be part of something bigger than themselves," Winkler explains.

Get a Lawyer Early On

Beyond game design, Winkler emphasizes a point developers may not consider at the start: "One of the smartest decisions we made was hiring a good lawyer early on." In

5th Planet's case, they found someone involved in entertainment law, and the reason for doing that is very simple: "Facebook gaming, social gaming...this is just the Wild West, and there are very few rules, so it's very important to have good legal counsel." This was most valuable when negotiating a publishing agreement—a lawyer can better explain how much revenue such a deal will cost you, what rights it will grant you, and so on.

SUMMARY

Here are the key points we covered in this chapter:

- ► Paul Preece, co-founder and lead designer for the successful Facebook strategy developer KIXEYE, recommends game mechanics that are wrapped in metaphors that people immediately understand. He believes the game's tutorial should act as its sales pitch and immediately satisfy the players' expectations raised by the art, marketing, and branding. He recommends developing a rough prototype rather than a detailed design document. For KIXEYE (and probably other developers of strategy games), speed-up boosters monetize well, but decorative items and weekly discounts do not. Preece believes that linking monetization to a player's emotional response (good or bad) does very well, and Facebook marketing that targets your game's desired demographic is crucial for good monetization. Finally, he recommends designing a strong "meta game," which is a way of playing the game beyond its specific objectives and goals.

- ► Robert Winkler, co-CEO of the successful 5th Planet Games, gained success from the company's RPGs by differentiating them with high-quality art and music, and discovered that there is a market for text-heavy games on Facebook. 5th Planet drives viral growth and retention with regular group experiences in which hundreds or thousands of players can participate in a giant boss battle. For new developers, he recommends hiring a lawyer early on to help you negotiate publishing deals and protect your intellectual property in the social gaming's "Wild West" frontier.

CHAPTER 6

Future Trends and Opportunities for Facebook Games

IN THIS CHAPTER

▶ Developing for cross-platform and mobile connectivity—especially via Facebook Connect

▶ Creating shareable user-generated content

▶ Seeing the end of updates as a viral channel

▶ Forecasting *unlikely* Facebook gaming trends

As a game platform, Facebook changes and evolves so quickly. It's been difficult to keep up with its evolution, even during the four months it took to write this book. When I began writing it in January 2012, for example, Zynga's dominance of the market was utterly unquestioned. Then came March, and within a few weeks, a Pictionary-like game called Draw Something (from a small developer called OMGPOP), launched, grew wildly, and was suddenly the most popular Facebook game overall. (Unsurprisingly, Zynga purchased OMGPOP days after this "most popular" milestone was reached.) Played on iOS and Android using Facebook Connect functionality, its success strongly suggested the strength of at least two future trends (discussed in the section "Cross-Platform and Mobile Connectivity").

FORECASTING FUTURE (LIKELY) FACEBOOK GAMING TRENDS

The success of Draw Something also illustrates how rapidly trends can appear from unexpected places. With that understanding in mind, the following sections sketch the likely trends that Facebook developers should pay close attention to.

> ▶ Unsurprisingly, Zynga purchased OMGPOP days after this "most popular" milestone was reached.

Cross-Platform and Mobile Connectivity—Especially Facebook Connect

In its IPO filing in early 2012, Facebook reported a surprising stat: 50 percent of its traffic now comes from mobile devices. Game designers have not devoted much creative energy to this user behavior, with most Facebook games mainly or exclusively developed to play on the web version of Facebook. This will change very soon, and designers should immediately begin thinking about how their upcoming Facebook games can fully leverage mobile devices, including tablets (see Figure 6-1). Doing this also gives players the freedom to play their favorite games across multiple devices, each of them tailored to their particular platform.

FIGURE 6-1: OMGPOP/Zynga's Draw Something in iTunes' App Store

An early sign of this trend was Spring 2012's breakout success, Draw Something. Although it's primarily played on smartphones and tablets, players of OMGPOP's game are counted as Facebook gamers due to the app's use of Facebook Connect (in both the iOS and Android versions). Although the use of Connect defines it as a Facebook game, the ability of players to share Draw Something content with friends in their social graphs also encourages viral growth.

Unlike most games that have come before it, Draw Something does something different with the cross-platform concept—most of the game experience is staged within the iOS/Android environment, whereas Facebook is mainly used as a connectivity, communication, and sharing method. This is an extremely promising use of the Facebook platform, because it makes sharing frictionless and automatically networked. We will probably see even more of this with the Fall 2012 release of iOS 6, which deeply integrates Facebook sharing and connectivity with iOS, including with Apple's Game Center, the company's social gaming network.

▶ Up until now, cross-platform play between Facebook games and smartphones has been infrequent. Zynga's Texas HoldEm Poker had been a rare popular exception.

Speaking of sharing, this trend dovetails into another likely market move.

Shareable User-Generated Content (UGC)

As previously discussed, the use of Facebook wall updates for games is a common tactic to increase virality. However, it's long ago become too viral, primarily because game updates in themselves are not directly relevant or interesting to other Facebook users (even other players). However, user-generated and customized content is more likely to be relevant to a player's friends. This is one of the other keys to Draw Something's success—shared as Facebook updates, Draw Something doodles are user-created, unique, and reflect the user's personality and talent in an accessible way. This makes them ideal for Facebook's social architecture. What's more, because the drawings are user-generated, it's also an inexhaustible resource for new content.

▶ In the negative, spammy sense.

Nabeel Hyatt, a venture capitalist whose firm, Spark Capital, backed Draw Something, echoes this point, noting that OMGPOP's game also gained a lot of growth through the uploading of doodles on Twitter and Instagram, even before the game had a sharing mechanism. As Hyatt puts it, "People have pride in the drawings they've done."

CROSSREF You can learn more about Nabeel Hyatt in Chapter 15, "Is Your Game Ready to Get VC or Crowdsourced Funding?"

Hyatt then went on to make a crucial distinction about user-generated content that designers should note: "What you want is a set of things that people would want to share"—for instance, drawings of Lady Gaga versus hamburgers. In other words, it's not enough to leverage user-generated content—the UGC should also have broad appeal.

The End of Updates as a Viral Channel—and Rise as a Retention Mechanism

Spark Capital's Nabeel Hyatt sees the waning of Facebook updates and requests as a viral growth channel. Instead, they'll become more important for maintaining user engagement. "When you get a request, that's a reminder to play the game," he says. Hyatt advises developers to think about ways to bring customers back with updates—in other words, sending and receiving those messages should be part of the value and fun of the game. A savvy developer, he suggested, could innovate ways to design a game whereby those channels are used as a way to play the game itself. (Updates which incorporate user-generated content, for example, are a good option.)

FORECASTING *UNLIKELY* FACEBOOK GAMING TRENDS

Now it's time to forecast some negative trends that will likely appear in the next year or two.

3D Games on Facebook: Not Likely, Except in a Limited Way

▶ Indeed,
Facebook the
company is helping
drive development
of 3D graphics in
HTML5.

The growing popularity of Unity (which can now be exported to Flash) and interest in HTML5 has encouraged some speculation that we'll soon see 3D games and rich graphics in Facebook. It's likely we'll see some elements of rich 3D graphics integrated into social games in the near future, but it's also just as likely that it will be a far more limited version of 3D than what most PC and console gamers are accustomed to.

As of this writing, for example, KIXEYE is working on a 3D Facebook game, which will probably launch some months after this book reaches the shelves. However, KIXEYE's Paul Preece warns that 3D games on Facebook should probably not require users to control the camera or do anything more complicated than simple view rotation. Adding more 3D features will lengthen the tutorial session, and it's just not feasible to expect Facebook players to spend 30 minutes learning how to play such a game.

Despite this, Preece believes it's likely that large game developers will attempt to deploy more 3D games in Facebook because they are accustomed to working with such graphics. However, "[T]he size of the playing population, even on consoles, who know how to control an FPS camera is small." This isn't to say there will never be 3D games on Facebook. Preece notes that Zynga trained its users to play strategy games with its Empires & Allies, which familiarized a large audience with the genre (including those made by KIXEYE). Consequently, he believes there may be a market for FPS shooter-type 3D games on Facebook. For now, however, "If I create an FPS game on Facebook, I'm going to be pissing off almost everyone attempting to play it."

With the biggest Facebook games still resolutely 2D, 5th Planet's Robert Winkler is also not convinced that 3D graphics will work in the social network, in great part because they're usually played by people while they're at work, who can't afford the extra time commitment—or worse, unwanted attention from the boss.

As evidence of this trend, consider the early status of Gaikai on Facebook (see Figure 6-2). In April 2012, the company launched an open beta of its cloud deployment technology, which streams AAA, high-quality 3D games directly to Facebook, so they can be played by anyone on the social network, whether or not their computer has 3D graphics hardware. However, as of this writing (Summer 2012), the service was attracting just 9,000 monthly users. This may change in the future, but for now, it's another indication that the market for 3D games on Facebook is small.

FIGURE 6-2: Gaikai Cloud Streaming 3D Games on Facebook Store

Google+ Not a Likely Viable Facebook Competitor (Though a Good Secondary Market)

As of this writing, the status of Google+ as an alternative social network to Facebook is very much in doubt. Although Google claims G+ has more than 100 million active users, the definition of "active" remains unclear, especially in terms that are relevant to game developers. For that reason, although Google is attempting to make its social network more conducive to games (see Figure 6-3), it doesn't seem to have enough users to be a good ecosystem for gaming, especially compared to Facebook. What's more, at the moment, average user sessions on Google+ are much shorter than they are on Facebook. And as 5th Planet's Robert Winkler argues, "For the most part, [Facebook's] going to be where all the users are...people will always fall back to their social network where they share."

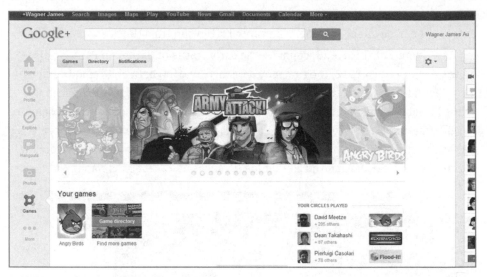

FIGURE 6-3: Google+'s game channel

That said, it's certainly worth exploring Google+ as a secondary market for your Facebook or web games (once they become successful on those platforms), especially as the company is offering competitive revenue sharing deals in an attempt to woo game developers onto the G+ platform. It's also likely that integration with Android phones, YouTube, Chromebooks, and other Google+ products will eventually turn it into a viable platform.

Farm/City/Kingdom-Type Simulation Games Not Likely to Grow

As this book goes to print in mid-2012, Facebook's top simulation games—CityVille, FarmVille, CastleVille, etc.—have been steadily losing users. This does not seem attributable to problems with Zynga, because during the same time period, non-simulation games from Zynga, such as Texas HoldEm Poker and Words With Friends, have enjoyed relatively steady growth. For that matter, other popular simulation games not from Zynga, such as Wooga's Monster World and 6waves's Ravenskye City, are also showing decline. It's likely that interest in the genre has finally reached a saturation point, especially as people gravitate to casual/arcade games which better enable cross-platform, head-to-head play on mobile devices—games like the aforementioned Texas and Words, along with Bubble Safari, Diamond Dash, and so on. In the next year or two, it's quite possible that all the "Ville" games will entirely fall from the top of Facebook's popularity charts. And FarmVille, which many still consider the typical Facebook game, will become a distant memory in this new upcoming era of mobile, cross-platform Facebook gaming.

SUMMARY

Here are the key points we covered in this chapter:

- ▶ The evolution of the Facebook game platform happens very rapidly, with sudden, unexpected changes sometimes occurring in a matter of weeks. Despite the speed of evolution, there are some trends you can probably count on.

- ▶ In the near future, cross-platform games, especially those that use Facebook Connect to enable play and sharing between smartphones/tablets and the web, will likely experience major growth. Also, games with shareable user-generated content will probably become a popular category. Simulation games of the CityVille/FarmVille variety, however, will likely continue to wane.

- ▶ Designers should also think about how to leverage updates on Facebook, not to drive viral growth, but to retain existing users.

- ▶ While 3D graphics may also enjoy growth on Facebook, they will do so in a limited, constrained fashion.

- ▶ The same is true for Google+. At the moment and for the next year or two, Google+ does not seem to be a viable competitor with Facebook as a game platform, but will probably become an important secondary market for social games.

Part III

THE WEB

Deep Dive into Web Gaming: Who Plays, Who Pays

This chapter will introduce you to some of the most important big-picture points about web gaming—the money they make, how to make more, and how to get your games in front of the biggest audience possible.

STARTING OUT: AN OVERVIEW OF THE WEB GAMING MARKET

As discussed in Chapter 1, web games have a markedly different audience than Facebook, skewing toward teen/young adult and male, with a player base that's disproportionately based in developing nations such as Brazil and Turkey, as well as in Eastern Europe. As of 2012, according to DFC Intelligence, the total market for free-to-play browser-based games is 200 million, with 5 percent of that market (10 million) directly paying to play. However, keep in mind that web developers can still earn indirect revenue from all their players, such as through web ads (see "Where the Money's Made" later in this chapter).

Although young guys make up the bulk of web game players, as M2 Research's Billy Pidgeon explains, the web gamers likeliest to monetize are somewhat different:

"Paying web game customers are mostly in the 20- to 45-year-old demographic, and the gender split follows population and web user demographics—slightly more female. Big spenders—aka 'whales'—with higher ARPU [average revenue per user] tend to be mainly in North America, Europe, and parts of Asia, South Korea in particular," Pidgeon says. But this doesn't mean teens aren't paying to play too: "[N]ote that many young players are spending, albeit with their parents' cash and so are not counted as payers."

"ARPUs are lower, with lower-spending whales, in emerging regions, but volume makes a big difference in South and Central America, developing Asian regions, Eastern Europe, India, Africa, and the Middle East. Advertising blends are likely to contribute heavily." Pidgeon adds that mobile games are rapidly outpacing web games in the developing world, something to remember if you're pursuing a market in those regions.

> In a 2011 survey by Mochi Media, the largest browser-based games network, a majority of web game developers reported making most of their money from ads and sponsorships.

> This may partly explain why so many paying web gamers seem to be in their 30s and 40s—at least some of that likely reflects kids "borrowing" their parents' credit cards!

Where the Money's Made in Web Games

The following sections break down the core ways web game developers typically make their money—through advertising, third-party service providers, prepaid cards, mobile usage, and credit cards/PayPal.

ADVERTISING

As with most web content in general, most web games are largely monetized with advertising, from general networks like Google's AdSense to Mochi Media, which has advertising solutions specifically made for web games. As you'll read in the next chapter, there are ways to optimize your website to boost your ad revenue, but there are also methods to hone the ad stream itself. Matthew Annal, Managing Director of web game developer Nitrome Limited, which makes most of its money through web ads, offers some advice here.

VARY YOUR AD NETWORK BY COUNTRY

"For preroll, we have found video networks such as Intergi, Alfy, Spot Exchange, Adapt TV, Brightroll, and so on outperform AdSense and Mochi's solutions," Annal tells me. However, he adds, "they mainly perform well in western territories, so in order to make that work for you, it is best to show different ad solutions based on geo-targeting, so that you can better fill territories that video ad networks do not cover. It is also worth noting that some networks will not work with smaller sites, so it may be necessary to wait until you have grown a bit before you can get on them."

▶ Ads that appear before a game launches.

INCORPORATE A LARGE, RELIABLE AD NETWORK

When you develop a web game, expect to have it distributed on third-party sites you do not directly control; this adds some complexity to the ad network you embed in your game. As Nitrome's Annal explains, "Unlike games on your own site, you cannot change your game on another person's site once it has been placed there. If an ad network stops working for you, you're unable to change the network remotely." For that reason, Annal recommends going with established advertisers like Google, Mochi, or CPM Star.

Nitrome developed an even better solution, by distributing their games in a Flash container that streams the game from the company's servers. That way, they can control the ad network delivery (see Figure 7-1).

FIGURE 7-1: Nitrome advertising on a third-party site

▶ This advice is more likely to apply to developers who gain the millions of players that Nitrome has, rather than to small studios.

"The downside of this is that we have to pay for the bandwidth of the games that are played," Annal acknowledges, "so it is not ideal, but if you can get the right ad partners, as we have, you more than make up for the money you lose."

USE GOOGLE AD MANAGER FOR MULTIPLE AD NETWORKS

Originally, Nitrome would "daisy chain" the ad networks it used for its games. Explains Annal, "You put one ad network first and then whatever they don't fill over a set floor rate, they pass on to the next person in your chain." However, this caused problems, because advertisers always want to be first to display in the game.

Nitrome's solution is to use Google Ad Manager (see Figure 7-2), so "all the networks can be at the top level competing with each other and with Google for the best price, before things that don't get filled drop down the chain. You end up filling more at a higher price than if you use a daisy chain." Still, Annal cautions, even when you're using Ad Manager, finding the optimal advertising solution takes some trial and error.

FIGURE 7-2: Google Ad Manager

> **NOTE** "[I]t is only through using multiple networks and ad solutions that you will find what works best for you, and I don't believe there is a single solution that best suits everyone, so it pays to experiment, but manage your risk," says Nitrome's Matthew Annal.

THIRD-PARTY SERVICE PROVIDERS

Because monetizing web games is such a big business, third-party service providers dominate the way players pay for their games: "Companies like Vindicia, Digital River, PlaySpan, Live Gamer, Xsolla, and ZipZap are making deals with portals, distributors, publishers, and developers of all sizes," M2's Pidgeon explains.

Often, game sites will somewhat mask this relationship: "Large portals, publishers, and distributors can white-label services to obscure third-party participation, or can use 'powered by' co-branding or straight-up third-party branding by payment services." These services primarily support credit card and PayPal, but allow other payment means that are easier based on the player's age, income level, and region.

Pidgeon says, "Distributors want to own the customer account no matter how the customer provides payment, and the top priority is to reduce friction—whatever payment scheme is easiest and most comfortable for the customers, payment services want to be able to accept. Also, payment may be a transfer as a parental allowance, friend gifting, advertiser-based tokening, or player-to-player transactions." Although third-party payment services generally operate by commissions, and will take a cut of your revenue, their ability to offer and handle multiple payment methods is extremely valuable, and worth considering.

PROVIDE A PAYMENT SERVICE LIKE VINDICIA CASHBOX

A customer relationship management and billing platform, Vindicia CashBox (see Figure 7-3) provides payment solutions for gaming companies like Mind Candy, creator of the extremely popular web game Moshi Monsters. Sanjay Sarathy, Senior Vice President with Vindicia, recommends their service to developers who expect to make about $2 million a year or more. "[They] tend to find the greatest value in our service." He says developers and publishers who sign with the company see a 15 percent or higher increase in annual revenue from their baseline earning rate, "assuming they had revenue before launching with us."

How Vindicia CashBox Is Different from Competitors

"First, our focus on helping game developers and publishers maximizes long-term player 'lives,'" says Sarathy. "We track the revenue uplift from our customer retention capabilities and that number, as indicated earlier, is 15 percent+ on an annualized basis. Second is the flexibility and ease with which our clients can change business models to support changing environments. We've had game clients who have shifted from a pure-play subscription model to a free-to-play game that monetized with micro-transactions, and they were able to easily make the changes in CashBox to support this business model shift."

Advice for Web Developers on How to Best Monetize with Vindicia CashBox

Sarathy adds, "Make it easy for players to leave your game, but ensure you have retention offers as they leave. Players will leave with a positive experience and often come back later to play your game.

FIGURE 7-3: Vindicia CashBox

"If a significant percentage of your customer base is outside your home country, be cognizant of supporting your game in different currencies. One of our clients who moved to localized currencies increased their acquisition rates by 5 percent on an annualized basis as a result of expanding from just U.S. dollars to incorporate UK sterling, euros, Australian dollars, and New Zealand dollars."

Part of making money through a service like Vindicia is expecting customers to change their minds during the payment process—or reverse charges afterward.

"If you do get chargebacks," advises Sarathy, "understand the reasons for those chargebacks—it could be a result of internal business processes that, if changed, can improve revenue and reduce costs. Every chargeback is not just lost revenue but also involves fees from your processor, and so on."

Finally, Sarathy advises, "Take the time to understand which marketing tactics lead to your longer-term customer lives and greatest revenue, not just your highest conversion rates."

▶ Players who "convert" to regular players are not necessarily paying players.

"We've seen publishers who realize that the marketing tactic that leads to the highest customer life might only be third or fourth best in terms of conversion rates," says Sarathy.

PREPAID CARDS

Now ubiquitous in department and drug stores, prepaid game cards enjoy a large market share in North America and the EU—up to 50 percent for some kinds of web games, by Pidgeon's estimate.

Offered by companies like Ultimate Game Card (see Figure 7-4), Rixty, and Zeevex, they're an excellent payment option for young players who aren't old enough to qualify for credit. (Plus that means they can nag others to give them as gifts.)

FIGURE 7-4: Ultimate Game Card prepaid card

MOBILE

Although less popular as a payment method in the United States, many gamers prefer to pay via mobile SMS, especially in Western Europe and even more so in the East. "Mobile payments are quickly grabbing market share in Asia (60 percent+)," as M2's Pidgeon notes, "and in the emerging markets as mobile phones are ubiquitous, personal finances are often tied to mobile phone accounts, secondary transfers—gifts, allowances, and so on—are easy, and fraud is more manageable. This is why we're seeing big investments from web-based payment services, banks, and credit card issuers in prepaid and mobile payment solutions."

CREDIT CARDS/PAYPAL

In contrast to mobile, credit cards tend to be a more popular payment option in the United States (and parts of Europe and Asia), but are not generally common on a global scale: "[C]redit cards are the most vulnerable in overall market share worldwide," as Pidgeon puts it, "because not everyone has a credit card, fraud is very high in this category, and security is an issue for consumers." Even in the United States, in a 2009 Rasmussen survey, nearly half of American shoppers reported that they are still wary of using credit cards online.

PayPal, another popular online payment option, gives users a number of options for "filling up" the amount of money they can spend in that service via bank transfer, credit card, and prepaid card. At the end of 2011, PayPal counted 100 million registered users—a large audience, but based on general Internet activity, it's likely that only a fraction of that user base uses the service to regularly pay for online games.

MONETIZATION ADVICE FOR INDIE DEVELOPERS

Although developers with a large player base will probably want to go with a third-party service provider (see the Vindicia CashBox profile earlier in this chapter), that option likely won't be feasible for smaller/indie developers. For them in particular, M2's Billy Pidgeon has the following advice.

Go with Name-Brand Payment Option(s)

Pidgeon recommends that you use a service layer with a name, such as PayPal, Visa, or possibly Digital River, to increase gamers' comfort zone with a recognizable name. The more trust users have with your payment option, the more likely they will be to buy.

Offer Multiple Payment Options and Multiple Revenue Streams

"Friction is always the primary issue with monetization," says Pidgeon. "If gamers want to pay, any barriers to payments such as time, filling out forms, going to secondary sites, and so on are going to be very significant. For this reason, indie developers and micro-publishers should offer any and all payment solutions their customers might want, and they should troubleshoot payment procedures to make sure these are easy and comfortable for all their customers.

> **NOTE** "The payment experience is easily as important as the initial play session, and the same issues are involved. Is it clear and understandable? Is it easy? Is it comfortable? Is it satisfying?" says Billy Pidgeon of M2.

"Besides making payments frictionless and fun, I'd suggest considering multiple revenue stream concepts, such as advertising-based, downloadable add-ons, rare resources, performance and appearance enhancing goods, services allowing for more control over gameplay and personalization, player-to-player payments, and so on."

▶ Independent developers should apply as much creativity to monetization methods and structures as they do to game design for a successful free-to-play game.

Reward Players for Paying

"Gamer payments are a reward to the developer. How does the game reward the paying player? If a player pays, will it improve the experience so that the player will consider paying again? Also, will the paying player still enjoy the game without payments?" asks Pidgeon. Further, he adds, "A game session should be rewarding and should lead to another, and this should be true whether or not a player is paying." Because whether or not they pay, players who keep returning are more likely than not to eventually pay.

PITCHING PUBLISHERS: WHO BUYS/PUBLISHES INDIE GAMES, WHY THEY DO, AND WHAT YOU CAN EXPECT TO EARN

A number of major websites and companies publish indie/third-party web games— among them are Gamehouse, Mochi Games, Flash Game License, Miniclip, Addicting Games, Big Fish Games, and Armor Games. These are surveyed in greater detail in Appendix A, "Resources for Designers." For now, let's have an in-depth conversation with a market leader in web games—Kongregate.

Publisher Profile: Kongregate.com

The following are some key stats about Kongregate:

- ▶ **Web address for developers:** developers.kongregate.com.
- ▶ **Monthly visitors:** 15 million, about 5 million from the United States (according to Kongregate, citing Google Analytics).

▶ **Key demographic stats:** "Our registration data and surveys show us having an average age of about 20 and that we're about 85 percent male," says Kongregate co-founder Emily Greer, who adds that the site has strong overlap with hardcore gamers. "In Comscore we index on console ownership and game purchasing at almost exactly the same rates as IGN and GameSpot."

▶ **Site snapshot:** Along with skewing toward hardcore gamers (who are mostly young and male), Kongregate (see Figure 7-5) is owned by video game and software retail chain GameStop, which also has a large presence online and has a prominent link to the web game portal.

▶ *Gamestop.com gets 4.2 million monthly visitors.*

FIGURE 7-5: Kongregate's homepage

Kongregate's Game Director Greg McClanahan offered these insights for developers interested in submitting their works to the site. You can get in touch with McClanahan directly by e-mailing him at greg@kongregate.com.

What Developers Can Expect to Make on Kongregate

"The success of Flash games is all over the map," says McClanahan. "They can be total duds or earn $100,000 from sponsorships, ad revenue, licensing, and micro-transaction revenue if the game is really successful. Five to ten thousand dollars is a more normal range for what I'd consider a moderately successful Flash game, but again, it's all over the place, and creating a moderately successful Flash game is actually pretty difficult to do."

Kongregate's Unique Features

Live player chat and staff-created achievements for players are two of Kongregate's most unique features. Game achievements (see Figure 7-5 earlier in this section) encourage players to compete with each other and themselves to play the same game repeated times, while live player chat fosters community and socialization among the user base, which in turn leads to more players staying on the site for longer periods of time.

Kongregate's Most Important Monetization Features

Kreds, the site's internal currency, can be used to purchase in-game items and is also where Kongregate earns most of its money. "Games with micro-transactions do really well on Kongregate, and we also share ad revenue," says McClanahan.

Prepaid Kreds cards can be bought at Kongregate's owner GameStop, along with major retailers like Walgreens, CVS, and 7-Eleven. And as we discussed with the Ultimate Game Card earlier in this chapter, having a prepaid card available in retail stores makes it easier for gamers to spend money on your games—especially if they don't have credit cards and Paypal (as younger gamers likely won't).

▶ Read more about Kreds at kongregate.com/kreds.

Mistakes Developers Often Make When Submitting to Kongregate

"The first mistake is forgetting the fun—they might spend months creating a well-crafted, bug-free, fairly polished game that's simply not fun to play. It's usually much better to focus on first making a fun core mechanic, then building a game around that," says McClanahan. "The second big mistake is simply a lack of polish—confusing interfaces, lack of a mute button, unbalanced levels, over- or under-tuned bosses, lack of key remapping, and so on. There's a lot of basic stuff that players come to expect from a game on Kongregate, and developers shouldn't ignore these expectations while striving for a high user rating."

Advice for Developers Submitting to Kongregate

Take risks and be unique: "[In] the free-to-play Flash gaming world, there's a lot of variety in game mechanics. You can spend an hour playing several different games, and those games might have completely unique mechanics not found in bigger games with higher production values," says McClanahan. This is because Flash game developers can afford to take risks—they can create a neat little game within a few days and upload it to Kongregate, and if it's fun, it'll gain exposure and traffic. If it fails, no big deal. A lot of Kongregate players also play console games, and they don't just play games on Kongregate because they're free—they play on Kongregate because the gaming experience is different and unique."

Where to Get More Help from Kongregate

"If you have a game with micro-transactions, submit it to Kongregate and we can take a look, and make revenue optimization suggestions as well as provide general feedback," says McClanahan. "I personally spend a lot of time working with developers on sponsored games. We don't have a ton of time to coach developers on games early in their development cycle, but I'm usually available over IM to give developers feedback and potentially a sponsorship offer."

GETTING YOUR GAME ON JAY IS GAMES, THE WEB GAME KINGMAKER

▶ Jay Is Games happens to be my personal favorite for web game recommendations.

Many sites host web games, but Jay Is Games (`jayisgames.com`) is among the largest and the most influential. At the moment, 1.5 million people visit the site 2.5 million times; a well-made game hosted on the site averages about 250,000 plays, whereas some of the biggest hits will draw 2-3 million. See Figure 7-6.

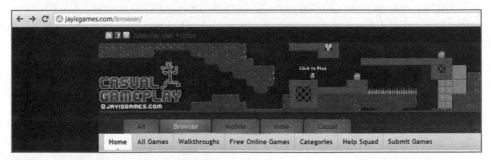

FIGURE 7-6: The Jay Is Games homepage

Through its annual Casual Gameplay Design Competition, games like Gimme Friction Baby and ...But That Was [Yesterday] have become viral hits. So clearly the site is a web game kingmaker. Trouble is, JiG features only a limited number of games that developers submit to the site. How do you increase the odds that yours will become one of them? Editors Jay Bibby, John Bardinelli, and the rest of the team share some insights and advice.

What They're Looking for in Games: Quality, Ease of Use, and Fun

"Lots of factors go into the decision to host a game, including overall quality, ease of use, and of course, how much fun it is. Each time we evaluate a game we get as many of our reviewers to play it as possible. That gives us a wide range of opinions to pull from, since some people will be die-hard fans of the genre and others just occasional dabblers. Once we play the game, we start our discussion, which touches on aspects ranging from level design to puzzles, artwork, sounds, menu screens, and so on. If the general consensus is positive, we'll go ahead with the review.

"Quality is the biggest factor we look at, but some people confuse 'quality' with 'has nice graphics.' We're more concerned with quality as in how the game is written, how the controls feel, and how intuitive it is to play. If your game has an overall high level of polish and smart design, people will notice it. Inspired games can transcend genre preferences, so even if you hate strategy games, for example, you'll recognize a good one when you see it.

"Ease of use is easy to overlook when you're knee deep in designing a game, but it's arguably the most important thing we look at. If you want more people to play your game, don't set up obstacles to keep them from diving right in.

> **NOTE** Unskippable cinematics, lengthy tutorials, or overly complex gameplay early in the game can drive casual players away," say the Jay Is Games editors.

"And yes, we also evaluate games based on how fun they are! A game can have the most stunning visuals ever or the best soundtrack, but if the gameplay isn't as strong or stronger, what's the point?"

How Developers Miss the Mark: Bugs, Glitches, and Lack of Passion for the Game

"You might be surprised how many games have obvious mistakes like typos, glitches, or clumsy interfaces. Bugs are another nasty problem, and we expect games to have these issues ironed out before we take a look at them. Ease of use is also a factor, and games that alienate groups of potential players based on operating system, browser preference, or even common physical disabilities (color blindness, for example) are essentially putting up a barrier to keep players out.

"On a subtler level, we look for effort and passion in a game, and when it's not there, it shows. As a developer, you need to find something you enjoy and work from that. When you're enthusiastic about what you do, it can be felt in every aspect of the game. Similarly, we're not looking for cynicism and soapboxing. Games that exist solely to hammer home an opinion or message and aren't actually fun to play aren't really games at all, so we'll pass on them even if we might personally agree with the developer's thoughts on the matter."

Some Game Sub-Genres Need More Innovation

"We don't really look at any sub-genre as being overdone, more as being underutilized. There are too many people out there who say that shooters are boring and stupid, when what they should really be saying is, 'The type of shooter that gets churned out on a daily basis is boring and stupid.' There is no genre out there that can't be made fresh and engaging if you put effort into it.

"Developers who throw out cookie-cutter games that look and feel like every other game on the market are putting genres in coffins. If we had a nickel for every 'top-down survive the night and upgrade stuff zombie shooter' they've played, we'd...well, we'd have a lot of nickels." That doesn't mean you shouldn't make those games; just pour some creativity into them and show everyone that talent and drive can turn any concept into a winner."

Big Design Opportunity: Hybrids of Different Sub-Genres

▶ Hybrids that combine puzzles with roleplaying elements or adventure-type quests with point-and-click gameplay are good examples of hybrids.

"Developers are figuring out that by marrying different sub-genres, they can play off their strengths and weaknesses to create something really dynamic.

"Another good example of a hybrid is Kingdom Rush, a game that combines real-time strategy with tower defense elements (see Figure 7-7). Even people who don't like tower defense games are eating it up." (In Chapter 3, Greg McClanahan of Kongregate also stressed the appeal of hybrid games.)

"We're also seeing more games with real heart behind them, games that are willing to tackle important issues in a mature, engaging fashion. Developers are learning how to weave their stories and ideas into the gameplay, creating meaningful experiences that capitalize on the interactivity of games to deliver a much stronger emotional message."

To Get Your Game Going Viral: Passion, Practice, Persistence

"Make the game you always wanted to play. Work on it as often as you can, don't get discouraged, and never stop learning new things, whether they be nuances to your programming language, new design concepts, or informative podcasts about badgers for your upcoming game about badgers.

FIGURE 7-7: Hybrid game hit Kingdom Rush

"Be objective about your work and don't let the good things about your game blind you to the criticisms you'll receive. On the same coin, don't let negative comments weigh you down so you can't see the positives. Pay attention to what people tell you about your work and incorporate that feedback. Game design isn't a destination; it's an interactive process just like anything else creative. Start with a core element you find fun, and then iterate—prototype, refine, rinse, repeat—until you find something that works and works extremely well.

"Code something random, even if it's just a simple Tetris clone, and you'll be surprised what you learn. That way, when your big idea inevitably comes up, you'll have the skills and tools to make it happen. Growth is the key, both in your own process and with your games, and if you don't grow in this industry, you won't survive very long."

SUMMARY

Here are the key points we covered in this chapter:

▶ Paying web game customers are primarily between 20 and 45 years old, skewing slightly female. Big spenders tend to be in North America, Europe, and parts of Asia (particularly in South Korea).

▶ Major sources of revenue for web games include advertising, third-party service providers, prepaid cards, and credit cards/PayPal.

▶ When monetizing with advertising, experiment by varying your ad network by country and using Google Ad Manager for multiple ad networks. For distributed games, incorporate a large, reliable ad network or stream the game from your servers.

▶ Small/indie web game developers should go with a name brand payment option(s), reduce payment friction, and offer multiple payment options and multiple revenue streams. They should also reward players for paying, and retain nonpaying customers by making sure it's fun to play the game for free.

▶ Kongregate, a leading web game publisher, has about 15 million monthly visitors. Developers who publish their games on Kongregate and attract a good audience can expect to earn about $5,000–10,000 on average.

▶ When submitting to Kongregate, many developers fail by forgetting the fun aspect of the game, or allowing bugs and other glitches to go unfixed. Instead, when designing games for the Kongregate audience, take risks and be unique.

▶ Jay Is Games is a leading "kingmaker" site for web games—it has about 2.5 million visitors. A well-made game hosted on the site averages about 250,000 plays, whereas some of the biggest hits draw 2–3 million. When looking for games to cover, JiG editors are looking for games of quality, ease of use, and fun.

CHAPTER 8

Web Game Design: Basic Principles for Growth and Revenue

IN THIS CHAPTER

- ► Conceiving and branding your game
- ► Distributing, promoting, and licensing your game
- ► Optimizing your web presence
- ► Earning revenue from your game

As you saw in the previous chapter, web games have a large combined market, but are spread around the wider Internet, making it tough for designers to find their audience. This chapter walks you through some key design decisions that can help get your game in front of the folks most likely to enjoy it, and the steps you should take to keep them there—and hopefully, paying for the pleasure of playing.

CONCEIVING AND BRANDING YOUR GAME

Because web gamers tend to be casual and young males, it's challenging to convince would-be players that your game is for them, and is worth playing—if you can even find them. To help you increase your odds of both, the following sections describe some design approaches that some of the better developers take.

Match Game Theme to Gameplay—or Wrap Gameplay into a New Form

▶ Players judge the games they are about to play from the very first loading screen, deciding second by second whether they should continue or just click away to another page.

KIXEYE game designers Paul Preece and David Scott make a point that's generally applicable to all game platforms, but probably applies most directly to web games—from the very point a player hits a game's site, everything about the game should suggest the kind of gameplay it promises. Unlike iOS, on which a game must first be downloaded from a descriptive App Store page, and unlike Facebook, on which players become aware of most games through descriptive ads and friend updates, many web gamers will randomly visit a game's site with little expectation. It's important that the game's theme (as conveyed in the art, title, music, and so on) always be conveyed, from the very moment a potential player visits the site.

Preece and Scott cite the example of Angry Birds (see Figure 8-1). Before Rovio's game launched, there were a number of other casual games involving projectiles and physics; however, most of them, such as Crush the Castle, were directed at a hardcore audience and were sold with screenshots that didn't make it clear that Castle wasn't strictly an action game, but in fact, a physics puzzle game.

FIGURE 8-1: Angry Birds' marketing and artwork

By contrast, every element of Angry Birds conveys that it's meant for a mass market, casual audience, with the basic physics mechanic of birds launched at pigs and the pigs' fortresses easy to understand in its marketing and artwork.

There's a related lesson to this, which can be found in Preece's breakthrough web game hit Desktop Tower Defense. Although it is fundamentally a tower defense strategy game, its artwork (with the background of a desk, cartoon monsters, and so on) suggests that it is a puzzle game.

> CROSSREF You can find out more about Desktop Tower Defense in Chapter 9, "Web Game Developer Profiles."

"My dad has never played console games," Preece tells me. "He doesn't play strategy games, but he played Desktop because it had just enough casual wrapping around the real-time strategy gameplay" to make it accessible.

Consequently, Desktop, like Angry Birds, became a crossover hit popular with both hardcore and casual gamers. This cross-genre wrapping is also a twist on the advice of matching a game's theme to gameplay. In the case of Desktop, it generated enough word-of-mouth buzz that players came to it with expectations. Hardcore gamers came expecting a challenging tower defense game, whereas casual players came expecting a fun puzzle game.

Create a Recognizable Brand That Unifies Your Games

As a web game developer, it's likely you're going to make many titles and that they're going to be hosted on numerous sites that you don't directly control. You can, however, control your brand, which you can promote within and throughout your game, to build player recognition—and hopefully, player loyalty. This was an insight that helped drive the development of Nitrome.com, a casual web game site that now counts three million monthly unique users.

"We make a lot more advertising money from someone playing the game on our own site than we do elsewhere," Nitrome's Matthew Annal tells me. "So a key aim is to attract users to our site. It is easy on other sites for your game to get lost among the sea of other games out there, and even if users enjoy your game, they are unlikely to check out your developer's site. If a user, however, realizes that other games they are enjoying are all made by the same developer, you gain their trust, and they are much more likely to seek you out to see what else you have produced." At this point, you not only attract site visitors—and earn revenue from them—but also you increase the chance of getting repeat visits and growing by word of mouth.

NOTE "[S]tart building your audience early on...it will take a long time and you may never get there, but you have to plant the seed if you want it to grow," says Matthew Annal.

For Nitrome, that meant building not only high-quality games, but also games that were recognizably from the same developer (see Figure 8-2). This meant creating consistent visuals (it's why all Nitrome games have a distinctive pixel style) and branding (see Figure 8-3).

FIGURE 8-2: Nitrome Games' distinctive look

"One of the most striking things is probably the intro we give to each of our games," says Annal, "where we show the Nitrome logo. Each one is different to get the player's attention, but the form of the logo is purposely easy to see through the extra decoration, and we keep the same chime [sound effect] at the point the logo is revealed, to help with recognition. We compared the approach to what they do at the start of *The Simpsons* episodes, where each time the family scrabbles to the sofa, but each time it is done differently."

Nitrome's distinctive logo

FIGURE 8-3: Nitrome Games' logo

DISTRIBUTING, PROMOTING, AND LICENSING YOUR GAME

Unlike Facebook and iOS, where games are accessible from the same source, web games are distributed far and wide, stretching out your potential audience and making them hard to find. Fortunately, there are some solutions, which are covered in the following sections.

Distribute on Multiple Platforms and Make More Distribution Even Easier

Like many successful developers, Nitrome's Annal recommends distributing your game on multiple platforms. "You want to spread your game as far as possible, which is actually easier than you would think," he says. He recommends sites like Newgrounds and Kongregate to start, which will lead to smaller sites that will also embed your game. You should do what you can to encourage this kind of distribution. You shouldn't just use this as a way to attract players, but to also drive gamers to install it on their own sites. "[A]dd a link into the game directing sites to a place they can get the game for their site, as this will increase the number of sites that take it further." Annal also recommends Mochimedia and Flashgamedistribution.com as good places to start this distribution wave.

But don't stop there. "When we started out, … I contacted over 100 sites in the beginning to see if there was any interest [in distribution]... you should contact as many people as possible, as you never know who might offer you the best deal," says Annal. This kind of direct promotion to actual site owners is better than simply uploading your game to an anonymous platform.

Alex Reeve, the lead designer at Synapse Games, describes a similar experience around Tyrant, the studio's collectible card game. Originally they launched it on Facebook and built some audience there. But "the defining moment for Tyrant's success," as he puts it, was when they ported the game to Kongregate (see Figure 8-4). Currently 4,000 of their players are on Facebook, but 15,000 of them are on Kongregate.

▶ "[P]ersonally I think you can't do better than direct contact for building a relationship with a games site," says Matthew Annal.

FIGURE 8-4: Synapse Games' Tyrant on Kongregate

"It's hard to build an audience from scratch now on Facebook without a big advertising budget, but it is still possible," Reeve says. "A much more reliable way for new developers to get their feet in the door is to work with a gaming portal—such as Kongregate—that already has a huge audience of players ready to jump on new games."

Consider Licensing before Advertising

Starting out, it's nearly impossible for a new developer to make significant money from advertising. "[I]n fact," says Annal, "I would say it is almost impossible to gain the amount of traffic needed to be worthwhile on the back of a single game." Instead, Annal recommends first pursuing licensing deals (sometimes called a "sponsorship deal") until you have built a substantial fan base. And while doing this is a good way to earn revenue early on, be sure that any deal you make lets you retain control over your games once the license expires—that way you can use them in future projects.

▶ In particular, Annal recommends Miniclip and Armor Games as potential partners.

OPTIMIZING YOUR GAME'S WEB PRESENCE

Although it's a good idea to build up an audience of fans on large sites like Kongregate, you'll probably want to draw traffic to your own site, where you can fully control the experience around your game, and better yet, collect much more of the money it earns. The following sections provide tips for optimizing your game's web presence.

Put as Much Thought into Your Web Page Design and Advertising Deployment as Your Game Design—and Track Changes!

This advice is especially important for web game developers who want to host their own games (which is why I spelled it out in such a long subtitle). It's not enough to have a site that can handle heavy traffic and displays well on all the major browsers. The site itself is the frame for your games, and how it appears on the site can impact how much money you make. Nitrome originally developed and published its games by instinct, but eventually learned to track how changes to their site layout impacted user behavior, such as click-through rates, which translate into more revenue.

"It is only by monitoring what you change that you can really see what works," says Annal. "For example, at one point we added a new tab to the website to link to all of the multiplayer games." (See Figure 8-5.) "That tab, which took minutes to add, ended up making us more money per month than our top game!"

▶ "It has been very surprising to us how much difference small changes on the site can affect the amount of money we make," says Matthew Annal.

FIGURE 8-5: Nitrome Games' current website

Changes to how ads are deployed on your site are also important. "When we first introduced an ad server rather than manually daisy chain the ads," says Annal, "we were blown away by the instant change in our revenue, which more than doubled over night." (In other words, Nitrome went from personally selecting the ads they planned to run to letting an automated server deliver them.) "Experimenting with the layout of the ads, too, has led to substantial increases in revenue."

> **NOTE** Desktop Tower Defense creator Paul Preece also told me he wishes in retrospect that he spent more time improving the website of the game, rather than improving the pathing system within the game itself.

Another important feature to include on the web is the Facebook widget. "We added a Facebook link to each page," Annal tells me, "and found ourselves getting 5,000 new people Liking our page a week, and a video box meant that we can easily get one million impressions of a video we want users to see now." Although these don't generate much revenue for Nitrome at the moment, they can also be leveraged to promote new developer content, such as some upcoming iPhone projects.

Seek "Force Multipliers" Outside the Game

Typically a game can gain only so much growth based on its quality; designers also need to consider "force multipliers" beyond it.

▶ *military term to ascribe attributes which, in combination, make a combat unit significantly more effective.*

Marketing is an obvious multiplier, but there are a number of others worth considering. Localization in other languages is one. As noted in Chapter 1, "Market Overview: iOS, Facebook, and the Web," web games are disproportionately popular in Brazil, Turkey, and other developing nations where English is not generally spoken as a primary language.

Grow a Community of Players

One force multiplier is so significant that it deserves a section of its own. Consider creating an online forum for fans, which generally helps boost retention, since it gives players a place to discuss game tips and brag about recent accomplishments. Reeve says the online community around Tyrant is the most important factor for increasing the game's retention and engagement.

To foster that community, Synapse created a Faction Wars game mode (see Figure 8-6). "Players group into teams of up to 50 players and battle each other to climb the Faction ladder. As groups of players battle each other, inevitably you will see some tight alliances and heated rivalries. This almost always leads to drama or intrigue on the forums, which is actually fantastic for the health of a community," says Reeve. "As soon as players begin interacting socially, either in a Faction or just posting on the forums, they are vastly more likely to stick with the game for a very long time."

▶ Good for the community; good for Synapse's bottom line.

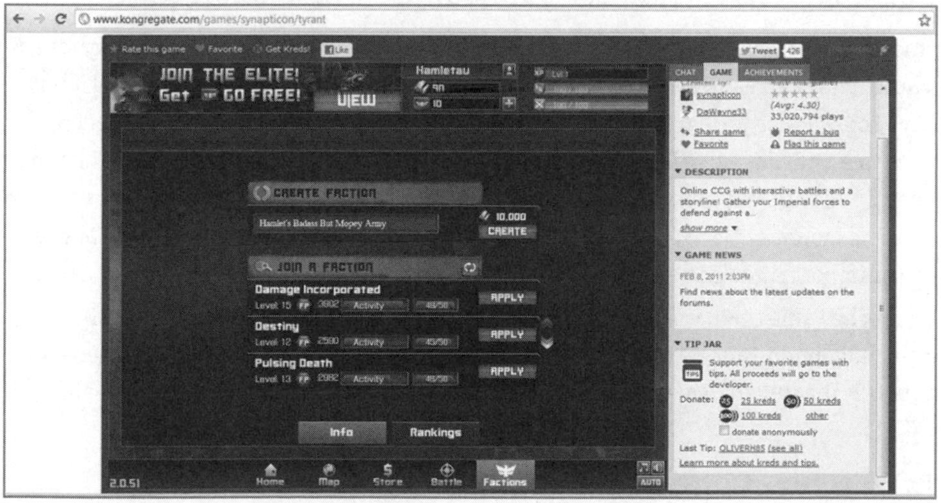

FIGURE 8-6: Tyrant's Faction Wars game mode

Besides game-related drama, of course, you also want to encourage players to post strategy guides, answer naive noob questions, and perhaps even develop a user-run wiki. Most of this activity will bubble up naturally through the passion of the players, but a developer can subtly enforce positive behavior with achievement badges and other virtual rewards.

But as Reeve points out, you don't just want players participating in the forum. "The best way to foster a positive community attitude is to have a strong developer presence on the forums or in the game," he says, "letting players know what updates are coming up, and listening to players when they bring up glitches or balance suggestions. It can be hard to do this with a large community and a small team, but it's extremely important to let players know they have a voice."

EARNING REVENUE FROM YOUR GAME

Most revenue from your web game will probably come from advertising, so the money you make from your players will be indirect. However, there are still opportunities to earn direct revenue from a fraction of your player base, via micro-transactions and virtual goods sales.

Build Monetization into the Game's Basic Design

▶ The trick is to reward players who buy premium content, without annoying free players.

This is a recurring point of advice for all three platforms in this book—in ecosystems where nearly all games are extremely cheap or free to play, monetization options have to be deeply integrated into the game's design, so that they're easy for players to notice and players will realize how paying will make the game more fun. "If nobody knows a feature exists," Reeve explains, "nobody will ever use it, so you have to make sure the monetization features are relatively obvious. If a feature isn't particularly fun or important to the game, no players will care about using it."

At the same time, it's also important to make it possible to play for free—that's especially important if your game is multiplayer or depends on leader boards or social network sharing to drive growth, which would only be slowed by a payment wall.

Take Advantage of Common Monetization Schemes: Monetizing Convenience, Collections, and Exclusivity

Three varieties of monetization are common in web games: monetizing convenience, collections, and exclusivity.

"One strategy is to sell convenience," says Reeve. "Allow premium currency to speed up progress or to earn items more quickly, while ensuring that these are all still available to free players as long as they're active." This includes most varieties of power-ups, boosters, and other enhancements to gameplay, because they tend to allow the player to accomplish in-game goals more quickly.

► KIXEYE, which is covered in the Facebook chapters, explicitly emphasizes the convenience factor by selling in-game "Speed-Ups."

"However, exclusive premium content is often a bigger motivator to convert players," says Reeve. This is true in many games, including Reeve's Tyrant. "We tend to offer exclusive items that are balanced at roughly the same level as or only slightly higher and more powerful than in-game items." This is to give paying customers an edge, but not one that totally overwhelms non-paying players.

"For example, in Tyrant, we offer a couple of full free sets of cards with a range of skills. We also have some premium exclusive sets that offer new skills but at roughly the same power level—a player with only free cards is still competitive with players who have purchased premium expansions." Many designers highlight an item's exclusivity by tying it to the player's social profile, with a visible achievement award or other highlights that make the paying player stand out among others. (Tyrant has an "Elite Membership" promotion with an exclusive card and a premium currency bonus.)

A good monetization option related to exclusivity is the sale of collectible items (see Figure 8-7). For that reason, says Reeve, "The collectible card game mechanic is an incredible monetization method because collection is such a powerful motivator." To help fuel that hunger, Tyrant displays the full set of cards early in the game. "[Then we] fade out all the cards you don't have. This makes it obvious to new players right away just how many cards you can collect.

► When visually appealing items are offered in a set, they tend to activate the acquisitiveness urge that seems to exist somewhere deep in the human brain.

FIGURE 8-7: Tyrant's collectible card game set display

Price High, Adjust Rates as Needed, but Don't Cap Spending

As discussed in Chapter 4, "Facebook Game Design: Basic Principles for Growth and Revenue," it's better to start by pricing virtual goods on the high side (say, $2–7 on average), and adjust with discounts or price cut announcements as needed. Finding the maximum number of players who will monetize in relation to the total amount they will spend on virtual goods usually takes some trial and error. "It's a delicate balance to figure out," Reeve says, "but constantly optimizing these features will greatly improve results over time."

▶ Setting a maximum amount of goods a player can buy at any one time.

Whatever rate at which you do price your virtual goods, it's generally a good idea to avoid capped spending. As Paul Preece of KIXEYE explains, it's nice to get a $5–15 monthly revenue hit from a subscribing customer, but if you give your game a subscription option, it tends to cap how much players can pay on any given month.

To be sure, some web games have earned impressive money through a freemium subscription model—the most notable case being RuneScape, an MMO that attracted more than a million subscribers at its peak. However, if you are building an MMO, taking on subscribers means taking on more costs in terms of billing and customer/technical support, which are probably not worth taking on until you've already attracted a large, regular player base.

▶ Some of your most devoted fans may want to pay more than you might imagine.

In any case, some of your most devoted fans may want to pay much more per month than what a subscription will cost them, while many (or most) players would rather pay less than a subscription minimum. It's important to monetize both types of players—those who want to pay hardly anything and those who want to pay a lot.

SUMMARY

Here are the key points we covered this chapter:

- ▶ Wrap the gameplay of one game genre in the trappings of another genre—if done well, you can attract fans of both genres.
- ▶ Create a recognizable brand that unifies your games, which helps build a fan base.
- ▶ Distribute on multiple websites and personally solicit sites that might host your game.

- ▶ Consider licensing your first games, since it's very difficult to make much revenue from advertising in the beginning.

- ▶ Put as much thought into your web page design and advertising deployment as you do into your game's design—and track changes, to see which of them earn you more money and users.

- ▶ Deeply integrate monetization options into a game's design. Make them easy for players to notice, and convey clearly how paying for them will make the game more fun.

- ▶ Keep in mind the three varieties of monetization that are common in web games: monetizing convenience, collections, and exclusivity.

- ▶ Price your virtual goods high, adjust rates as needed, and don't cap spending— some of your most devoted fans may want to pay more than your capped price.

CHAPTER 9

Web Game Developer Profiles: Kingdom of Loathing, Nitrome, and Desktop Tower Defense

IN THIS CHAPTER

▶ Taking lessons from Kingdom of Loathing, the indie cult RPG

▶ Knowing what to do when users "change" your game

▶ Learning from Desktop Tower Defense—including what its developer learned the hard way

▶ Preparing for your game's future success

▶ Turning hit web games into a hit web game factory, the Nitrome Way

This chapter draws from lessons learned by three web developers who launched successful games. The first developer managed to find success from relatively low user numbers, showing that it is possible to create a profitable game despite a small user base. This chapter also introduces you to a developer who did just the opposite. He attracted extremely large numbers of users, but failed to capitalize on that popularity. To your benefit, he has some hard-earned lessons to share so that you won't repeat these same mistakes. Speaking of which, we'll also talk with a developer who capitalized on the success of his first few hits by becoming a hit-generating factory.

LEARNING FROM KINGDOM OF LOATHING, THE INDIE CULT RPG

A deliriously wacky, free-to-play, turn-based Indie RPG that's also a parody of RPGs, where players choose character classes like Seal Clubber instead of warrior, Kingdom of Loathing launched in 2003 and is illustrated with stick figures (see Figure 9-1). Soon after its launch, the game steadily gained a cult following.

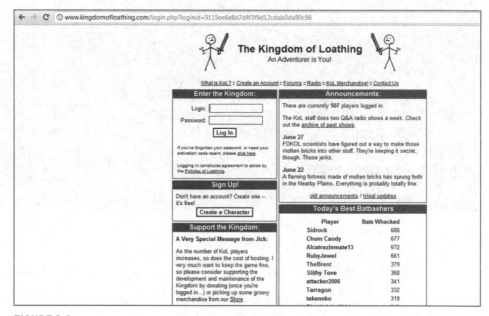

FIGURE 9-1: Asymmetric Productions' Kingdom of Loathing

▶ Despite its relatively small player base, the game remains successful.

Created by Asymmetric Productions, which was founded by Zack "Jick" Johnson and Josh "Mr. Skullhead" Nite, the company now employs five full-time workers.

According to a recent interview on Reddit with Nite, Kingdom of Loathing—known as KoL—has about 45,000 monthly players. "There have been over 2 million accounts created since the game began [in 2003]," he says, "so there are a lot of people who should be coming back." The game monetizes with donations and virtual goods sales. And, says Nite, the game is still "quite profitable."

Despite their success, KoL's creators learned two important principles of game design through trial and error. These lessons and more secrets are covered in the following sections.

Players Will Exploit Game Resources in Unintended Ways

"It never occurred to me that people would use an item or enchantment in any way other than the way I envisioned it," says Nite. "A good example from early in the game was the Purple Snowcone, which gave an enchantment that restored your Hit Points and Magic Points after every combat. There was no cap on the Magic Point restoration and, at that point, Magic Points were a controlled scarce commodity." With no cap on the restoration of a valuable game asset, you can probably guess what happened next (even though Nite didn't at the time).

"I intended it to be used casually, like I would use it—you get in a fight, cast some spells, and get your spell cost back afterward." However, after adding this item, the developers noticed their players using it in a totally different way: "[P]eople quickly started casting all of their out-of-combat spells, running their MP [or Magic Points] to empty, and then doing one combat to refill them." In other words, people were using the Snowcone in combat to generate MP to spend on non-combat spells. Or as Johnson puts it, "They were farming MP with it—an obvious strategy to everyone but me. So we had to change it after the fact."

Power Users Will Play against Your Intentions

"The other important lesson is that no matter how boring and joyless the most optimal way to play is, people will do it. A lot of people will do it and complain the whole time. So it's not enough to say that, as a side effect of this new mechanic, players can get an extra adventure if they slog through hours of crap—no one will do that." Once a developer makes it possible for players to optimize their game characters, a select number of power users will do so, no matter how time-consuming and difficult doing so is. Indeed, the very fact that it *is* difficult will actually be interpreted by some players as a challenge. "We have to consider the people who will stab themselves in the gut to play perfectly optimally and make sure to keep sharp objects away from them," explains Nite.

As for how KoL makes money, Nite shared some additional secrets, as described in the next section.

Secrets of KoL's Monetization Success: Enhanced Gameplay, General Coolness

"The ascension mechanic was vital," says Nite. Added to KoL in 2005, this feature enables players to "win" the game on various difficulty levels and gameplay choices.

▶ And it increased revenue by giving users a new way to pay.

Additionally, some rewards and other content can be gained only while playing in Ascension Mode (see Figure 9-2). The KoL developers also allowed players to speed up progress in this mode by sending them a donation. So this feature increased user retention by giving established players a new way to play.

Hardcore Ascensions

Hardcore, No-Path

- You receive a pork elf goodies sack containing 5 random gemstones.
- You receive a sparkling class tattoo in addition to the normal tattoo.
- You receive a filled-in roman numeral tattoo according to how many Hardcore ascensions you have done (up to XI+).
- You receive a disassembled clover.
- Upon defeating the Naughty Sorceress, you receive a stainless steel item from the Unblemished Uniform based on your current class:

	Class	Name	Power	Requirements	Item Type	Notes
	Seal Clubber	stainless steel shillelagh	90	30 muscle	1-handed club	Weapon Damage +20 4x chance of Critical Hit Muscle +15%
	Turtle Tamer	stainless steel skullcap	90	30 moxie	Hat	Maximum HP +30 Damage Absorption +60 Muscle +15%
	Pastamancer	stainless steel solitaire	-	30 mysticality	Accessory	-2 MP to use Skills +2 Adventure(s) per day when equipped. Mysticality +15%
	Sauceror	stainless steel scarf	-	30 mysticality	Accessory	Spell Damage +20 +20 to Monster Level Mysticality +15%
	Disco Bandit	stainless steel slacks	90	30 moxie	Pants	Combat Initiative +15% +20% Meat from Monsters Moxie +15%
	Accordion Thief	stainless steel suspenders	-	30 mysticality	Accessory	Damage Absorption +60 Maximum MP +40 Moxie +15%

FIGURE 9-2: Rewards in Kingdom of Loathing, from a KOL fan wiki

"[Ascension Mode] opened up the design space by turning the game from a single ongoing linear progression to a series of short challenges to see how quickly players could get through. That enabled us to offer real incentives for donating—stuff that would speed up each short challenge," says Nite.

In addition, for KoL's developers, *not* trying to make money at every turn has served them well: "I think we had success because we didn't take every opportunity to monetize," says Nite. "We didn't include a ton of micro-transactions; we didn't block off half the content we'd created until you donated; we didn't run ads or advertise the game on other sites. We started with a healthy wariness about selling out and being lame, and I think that caution paid off. People donate because they like us and like what we're doing, and they appreciate that we didn't try to trap them in a FarmVillian Skinner box." This donation-driven approach is especially valuable for developers making low-budget indie games as quirky as Kingdom of Loathing. Once players realize how unique and special it is, they are much more likely to donate in order to help ensure it keeps going.

Advice for New Designers Aiming for KoL's Quirky Success: Revive a Niche You Love and Launch Early

Nite's advice to developers who would follow Loathing's path: "Find a style of game you used to enjoy playing that nobody's making right now. KoL was in the style of old bulletin board system games like Legend of the Red Dragon, for example. The market for those games didn't go away, but the games did." As we've noticed in the last year, Kickstarter and other crowdfunder platforms have proven just how much players are willing to pay in order to revive a genre the industry has walked away from.

CROSSREF Read more about this in Chapter 15, "Is Your Game Ready to Get VC or Crowdsourced Funding?"

More counsel: "This one's harder to do, but it worked well for us—Zack put the game online before it was finished. It was playable, but it was the barest skeleton of what it ended up being. We had just enough game for people to enjoy playing it and make suggestions, and we were able to develop it with constant input rather than in a vacuum. That experience—including learning what feedback to ignore—was invaluable."

Related to this, many developers have pointed to the danger of not releasing early. It's easy to fall into an "it's not good enough yet" trap, spending extra weeks or even months tinkering on and improving a game, when it's generally better to tinker and improve *after* getting player feedback.

LEARNING FROM DESKTOP TOWER DEFENSE—AND WHAT ITS DEVELOPER LEARNED THE HARD WAY

When Paul Preece launched his Flash game Desktop Tower Defense in 2007 (see Figure 9-3), he was just a Visual Basic programmer with no professional experience in game development. Within three years, he'd become a co-founder of KIXEYE, one of the industry's most profitable social gaming companies.

CROSSREF You can read more about KIXEYE in Chapter 5, "Facebook Design Lessons from KIXEYE and 5th Planet Games."

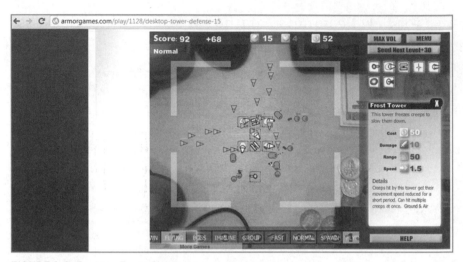

FIGURE 9-3: Desktop Tower Defense

 At peak popularity, the game was earning Preece high four figures a month, primarily through AdSense.

The game became phenomenally popular, played by upwards of 150 million people, but as noted in the beginning of this book, Preece considers it a failure, since it didn't earn the money it could have had he made some simple tweaks.

Ironically, KIXEYE went on to deploy Desktop Defender, a version of Desktop Tower Defense, on Facebook (see Figure 9-4). It wasn't very popular, but because it was far better monetized, it earned about as much money as the far more popular original version on the web.

FIGURE 9-4: Desktop Defender on Facebook

So if Preece could do Desktop Tower Defense over again, what would he do? Read on to find out.

Prepare for Success and Revenue

If he were to go back in time and design Desktop Tower Defense again, Preece says he would spend fewer resources working on unit pathing and more on developing the website. This might mean creating wrapper ads and other revenue streams, as well as direct revenue options, so that there'd be no way someone could play the game without earning him money, even if indirectly. The website would better promote these monetization elements, too.

▶ *The movement patterns of game characters.*

Preece would also sell a deluxe version of the game that could be played offline, with better graphics. "People like owning the stuff they really love," as he puts it. "If two out of every hundred Desktop Tower Defense players had purchased a deluxe version," he reasons, revenue would have catapulted into the tens of millions.

Design the Game to Be the Largest It Can Be

Preece experimented with creating different spinoff games to Desktop Tower Defense, but with "desktop" in the title. ("It's not like I could put it somewhere else," he says.) However, he was unsuccessful, perhaps because the game's setting on a desktop was not really significant. In any case, Preece's takeaway is this: Design with franchising in mind, so that a game's success can be multiplied through sequels/expansions and merchandise. "Maybe I could have given the creeps more personality," he muses now, "treat them like Angry Birds...like Angry Creeps." He recommends spending the extra few weeks of work to establish a franchise-able game, and one that can be portable and re-usable on other platforms.

Of course, planning with these ambitions in mind doesn't mean you'll get to capitalize on them—however, when one of your games finally does reach a high level of success, you'll be ready to expand.

TURNING HIT WEB GAMES INTO A HIT WEB GAME FACTORY, THE NITROME WAY

Created by just two people working in a spare room, Nitrome (www.nitrome.com) has become one of the most successful developers of web games, with 3 million monthly unique players and an enviable, advertising-friendly 50/50 gender split. Its biggest games, Rubble Trouble (see Figure 9-5), Icebreaker, and Skywire, have been played tens of millions of times. Their distributed games Flipside and Twinshot 2 have each been played around 100 million times across the web.

FIGURE 9-5: Nitrome's Rubble Trouble

And while it only earns revenue through advertising, the company, as co-founder Matthew Annal tells me, has been profitable from the first day. Now 10 years in business, the company currently has 15 employees and is operated from an office in London. "But," says Annal, "we still try to hold true to the values we had starting out, as we believe it is what makes us special." Unsurprisingly, Nitrome designs all its games and now has more than 100 in its library, the result of building one successful game after another, using the revenue from the previous hit to finance the next.

In the following sections, Annal shares some secrets that made Nitrome the hit-maker it is today.

Nitrome Games: Action Puzzle with a Novel Mechanic

"Most of our games would fall in the category of action puzzle games," says Annal. "We do, with each of our games, though, try to find a hook that will make the game stand out from what's out there. Usually that takes the form of some original idea or mechanic. We try to let the idea dictate the rest of the game, so the visuals get designed to fit the mechanic. [This is] possibly partly why a lot of our games are quite abstract in theme, because there is no other logical way to make it fit the mechanic. We also do a lot of sci fi–themed games for the same reason."

Nitrome Games's Key Design Feature: Unified, Identifiable Style

"We were very conscious early on that we would build an audience if we continued to put out quality games, but only if they realized that several games they liked were made by the same people," continues Annal. "To make that happen we had to make sure that all the games were of a high quality, but it was also important to build in some consistent hooks that would get the player's attention. The most obvious thing we did was get behind a consistent pixel style throughout all our games, but we did some more individual things, too. One of the most striking things is probably the intro we give to each of our games where we show the Nitrome logo. (More on that in Chapter 8.)

The Cost of Launching Nitrome, the Business

"I was very lucky in that the equipment and skills that we needed to be able to start were already there, and because all the work was done from home at first, there really were no startup costs. I knew I had enough money to support myself for six months saved up, so that was really the only safety net in place. But if it didn't work out there was always the option of doing work for hire or going back into the workforce and getting a job at an agency or games studio somewhere, so the risk was minimal," says Annal.

"The first game I produced made enough money to cover making it, so a second was made and made a slightly larger profit. By the third game, I struck a multigame deal with Miniclip to sponsor upcoming games, which made it more profitable and provided security to grow."

Nitrome's Turning Point: Big Partnership

"We had a pretty consistent deal in place with Miniclip, which would fund a new game to get produced roughly every four to six weeks," explains Annal. "One day we got a call out of the blue from MTV, and they basically said they wanted the same thing as we were doing for Miniclip for their arcade section on the MTV site. We didn't have the manpower at that point to do their deal as well, and we were happy with our Miniclip setup, but it was an offer too good to pass up.

"So we took the opportunity to take on two staff members to do the extra games. This led to us having games on our site a lot more often, and as some of the games weren't available on a single other site, there was finally a unique reason to visit our site, and we saw our traffic shoot up. Soon we were making as much money from the ads on our site as we were from the licensing/sponsorship money that we got from MTV and Miniclip and that gave us our independence, so I would say that was the turning point."

How Long It Takes to Produce a New Nitrome Game

▶ Still with just one artist and one programmer on each game.

"Starting out, the games had to be made in a month," says Annal. "We only got paid once a game was done, so working quite hand-to-mouth, it was really necessary to get it done in that time in order to make the money to keep it going. Nowadays the average game takes between two and three months."

"Some games take a lot less time, though, and some a lot longer. The games that took the most time were Steamlands [see Figure 9-6] and Nitrome Must Die, which were both around six months, [while] some of the smallest games have been produced in a couple of weeks."

Early Design Mistakes Nitrome Made—Lack of Hard Data in Design

"We are passionate about what we do," says Annal, "so from early on, we have focused on that, and led the company mainly by instinct, rather than using any hard data. This, I think, is fine for game development, as stats can get in the way of making something that is fun. But in terms of growing the site and making the most of it, I think it has held us back. So I would certainly change that if I could go back and apply what I know today."

FIGURE 9-6: Nitrome's Steamlands

SUMMARY

Here are the key points we covered in this chapter:

▶ Kingdom of Loathing, a cult parody of RPG games launched in 2003, still has about 45,000 monthly players and is profitable for its developer, Asymmetric Productions. The co-founder credits the monetization of special gameplay modes and a non-aggressive approach to making money for their success. He recommends that new designers revive a niche they love and launch it early so they can immediately incorporate user feedback.

▶ Desktop Tower Defense has been played by about 150 million people, but was poorly monetized. In retrospect, its creator, Paul Preece, says he would have invested as much time designing the game's revenue model and its franchise potential as in designing the game itself. He advises that other developers do the same, so when and if their game becomes a breakout hit, they'll be prepared to expand on it.

▶ Web game developer Nitrome has an audience of more than 3 million and makes most of its money through advertising. The studio's action puzzle games (more than 100 so far) come with a novel gameplay mechanic, generally take two to three months to develop, and all have a unified, identifiable style that makes the company's games recognizable. In retrospect, Nitrome developers wish their design decisions had been more data driven, which would have better encouraged user and monetization growth.

CHAPTER 10

Future Trends and Opportunities for Web Gaming

IN THIS CHAPTER

▸ Getting revenue from advertising-based payments and secondary markets

▸ Understanding the effect HTML5 will have on Flash

▸ Following the rise of hardcore on the web

▸ Seeing the blue ocean of opportunity: Twitter

▸ Developing for Google+ and Chrome

▸ Integrating asynchronous multimedia sharing

▸ Watching the continued growth of web-based app stores and the rise of indie development funds

As with Facebook and iOS, the web game market is evolving quickly, and if you're developing in this space you need to anticipate new opportunities that will likely emerge, not only in the next one to two years, but also in the few months after you buy this book. This chapter discusses several near-future trends to watch for, gathered from the wise minds of many gaming experts.

ADVERTISING-BASED PAYMENTS AND SECONDARY MARKETS

"I think advertising-based payments are going to be a major revenue stream in the next three years," says Billy Pidgeon, analyst with M2 Research. "It's been slow so far, but I think it is going to grow strongly, and advertising is already a major revenue stream in some countries, like China."

By advertising, Pidgeon means offers in exchange for virtual goods, long a common method of monetizing Facebook games, which he believes will gain traction in web games. "[S]o it's important to support all forms of advertising and tokening for payment for goods and services," he says. For instance, a consumer buys a soft drink that has an affiliate deal with a web game developer. The bottle contains a redemption code, which can be redeemed for the game's fancy items.

> Things like magic swords, virtual fashion with extra frills, etc.

Another variation of this, which Pidgeon also thinks will be big, is the brand-to-player payment. This is where companies "[r]un ads in one game for other games, offering virtual currency for other games." Pidgeon says, "Supporting ads for other games might sound counterintuitive, but there's money to be had in this play."(Chartboost and Kiip are two companies offering this service for mobile devices.) Although this kind of service is more applicable to in-app offers in mobile or in social games at this point, he adds that web-based games are likely to add support for things like this.

Beyond this, Pidgeon sees growing value in secondary markets, in which players can trade valuable items with others on a site hosted by the company (which typically takes a cut of the sales).

> Third-party service providers like Live Gamer already manage secondary markets for numerous games of various sizes, and it's likely that competitors will soon emerge.

Although this model has been popular with Asian games and niche online game worlds like Second Life and IMVU, it was recently given huge market validation by Blizzard Entertainment, which designed and integrated a secondary market for Diablo III, the latest installment of its epic franchise.

AS HTML5 RISES, DOES FLASH HAVE A FUTURE?

> To be sure, the graphics capacities enabled by HTML5 are indeed impressive.

Flash is near-synonymous with web games, but the rise of HTML5 as a development platform with rich 3D graphics has inspired some to believe Flash is dying, and soon won't be worth your time.

Facebook game platform developer Cory Ondrejka (formerly CTO of Linden Lab and co-creator of Second Life) recently told me he believes that HTML5 will make it possible for web games to catch up with consoles in terms of graphics by 2013. By "catch up," he means that by 2013, web-based game graphics will be a year or two behind console-based graphics, as opposed to 10–20 years, where they are now. His reasoning is that JavaScript (which runs in web browsers) can already get to 50 percent of the speed of C code (which runs on most console games), even if there's ultimately a threefold performance penalty. At that range, he argues, web-based game deployment is an appealing option for developers who might otherwise develop for consoles. (See Figure 10-1.)

FIGURE 10-1: Example of HTML5's current graphics quality from `schumann.elis.ugent.be/#`

With the growth of HTML5, many Flash game developers anticipate a near future when their platform will no longer be relevant. However, KIXEYE's Paul Preece is still bullish on Flash, and thinks it's worth developing on, at least in the near future. He points to the capability to import Unity to Flash, the platform's massive install base, and Stage3D, the latest version of Flash that enhances 3D content. (See Figure 10-2.) More than that, Preece plays up Flash's accessibility to new developers. From Preece's perspective, the fact that Flash is so easy to learn ensures that innovative new games will continue to emerge from Flash.

▶ Unity is a very popular authoring tool for high-quality 3D graphics that can be deployed on the web.

FIGURE 10-2: Example of Flash running Stage3D, Yellow Planet game at `flare3d.com/demos/yellowplanet/`

> **NOTE** "The best thing about Flash is people are able to code games in their bedrooms," says Paul Preece. That spirit went away in the 80s with the advent of consoles, but Flash development's barrier to entry is so low, it's practically non-existent.

Preece believes that HTML5 is not yet a mature system, and still has technical concerns that make it vulnerable to piracy and hacking. Although Flash has its own vulnerabilities in that regard, it's been around for so much longer that Flash coders have a knowledge base to address those problems. "It's definitely the future," Preece says of HTML5, "but in order to make games, you need the tools, the platform, and the wide reach, and [you need to] be able to do it in a secure manner." HTML5 doesn't have any of that yet, and to boot, it has a small install base in comparison to Flash. What's more, HTML5 is not consistent across platforms, and it plays differently on different browsers.

Nitrome Managing Director Matthew Annal also thinks Flash has a strong future, especially with the late 2011 addition of Stage3D, which also allows export from the 3D engines Unreal and Unity. "[Which] means," says Annal, "that games can look just as good within the browser as they do on consoles or other formats. I don't think this means that online games will all start to look like console games, but I think it is causing a perception shift in what an online game can be—it can be a serious gaming platform. For years, Flash games held a stigma that they were cheap, because of all the amateur-level games that flooded the market." A rise in the quality of Flash-based graphics will likely lead to increased development of web games aimed at the hard-core market.

Much of the Flash versus HTML5 debate rides on what Apple will do. At the moment, iOS only runs HTML5. (A couple of years before his death, Steve Jobs publicly rejected the idea of making iOS Flash-compatible, probably at least in part because allowing iOS users to access Flash-based programs would threaten the monopoly of the App Store.) The strong growth of tablet computing (primarily the iPad line) suggests a time in the next few years when developers will largely shift their focus away from laptop and desktop programs and concentrate on tablets. At that point, Flash may be in jeopardy.

There are industry rumors that Apple may ultimately cut a deal with Adobe to allow Flash on iOS, but even if that happens, my personal sense is that HTML5 will become the de facto standard in five or so years. However, that's a whole generation away, in Internet years. Until then, it's best to follow Paul Preece's advice—"If you're making a game for the web, then yes, use Flash."

Whatever the dominant platform is that drives the web in the next few years, in any case, the most important principle for developers is to develop with an eye toward multiple platforms. "The main thing to consider is to be platform-agnostic and always on the lookout for new opportunities," as gaming analyst David Cole of DFC Intelligence puts it. "The beauty of web games is they work on all kinds of platforms and platforms can pop up at any time. Five years ago there was no iOS opportunity; two years ago there was no iPad; Android is still young, and ditto with Facebook. A company like PopCap was successful because they quickly moved to new platforms... Angry Birds became a success on iPhone, but its true success was going multi-platform. That cross-platform play is the key to success. I think too many developers get locked into one platform."

Fellow analyst Billy Pidgeon concurs—"On technology, it's important to support the broadly distributed formats, such as Flash, while considering support for other platforms (PHP, Java) and emerging tech such as HTML5," he says. "Always consider support for a new platform with big-spending backers. Independent developers may see far smaller distribution through new platforms, but may gain big money for exclusive deals. Smart TV, including Apple TV and Google TV, is also going to be a major platform and is a natural migration for web games." (By SmartTV, sometimes called *Hybrid TV*, Pidgeon means the next generation line of Internet-connected, social media–integrated televisions.)

THE RISE OF HARD-CORE ON THE WEB

Given the rise of Unity deployed in Flash and other 3D-friendly platforms on the web, Spark Capital's Nabeel Hyatt believes the web may trend more and more toward a hard-core audience over time, especially since it's not as ideal a channel for casual games as Facebook. In the next few years, he says, "Consumers will start to see [web] graphics getting close to consoles."

At the same time, Hyatt notes, the audience for web games seems to have peaked. This has happened even with the growth of graphics quality in web games. (From my perspective, that's probably because hard-core gamers already have the graphics power on their PCs to run high-end games on Steam, or via downloadable clients—so why would they shift to core-focused games on the web?) "But," Hyatt suggests, "that may change with some new thing I can do on the web that I can't do elsewhere."

Which takes you to Hyatt's next prognostication, covered in the following section.

> ▶ For the hard-core audience, however, the ultimate question is whether they want to play on the web or on the next-gen console.

TWITTER: A BLUE OCEAN OF OPPORTUNITY ON THE WEB

Hyatt believes Twitter remains a great—if unexploited—opportunity for promoting and interacting with some specific types of games on the web. For example, he notes that much of Draw Something's growth was fueled by drawings posted and shared on Twitter. (See Figure 10-3.)

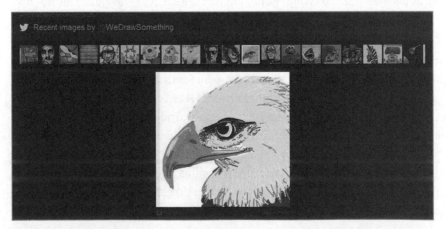

FIGURE 10-3: Draw Something shared on Twitter via @wedrawsomething

"[W]e have yet to see those [Twitter-integrated] games, though Draw Something is a hit in that direction," Hyatt says. For that reason, Twitter, which continues to grow in user numbers and engagement levels, remains a "blue ocean" of opportunity that has hardly been explored. Not only does it currently attract nearly 175 million monthly visitors (according to Google Ad Planner), but also its content is not walled off or stove-piped as Facebook's is.

▶ Consider a look at Blue Ocean Strategy, the influential book by W. Chan Kim and Renée Mauborgne, which argues that businesses should expand in an uncontested market space.

With that in mind, let me add a thought experiment here—if the Pictionary-like Draw Something can go viral through image sharing, why can't a Mad Libs–like web game go viral through text sharing on Twitter? Also keep in mind other social networks beyond Twitter, such as China's huge Sina Weibo (300 million users) and mobile social apps, like Foursquare, which could emerge as potential gaming platforms.

GOOGLE+ AND CHROME: A SECONDARY MARKET WORTH WATCHING, ESPECIALLY IN SOUTH AMERICA

In the next couple of years, Google will almost certainly expand its reach and selection of games featured on Google+, its social network, in a bid to compete with Facebook. As of this writing, it's still doubtful they can meaningfully catch up with Mark Zuckerberg's social network as the best platform for web-based games, but the search giant has a number of trump cards to play, including:

- ▶ Increased Google+ interconnectivity to its Android line of phones (important to integrate when porting your game to Android!)

- ▶ Expanded promotion of Google+ features through its popular Chrome browser

- ▶ Services like YouTube

- ▶ Chromebooks, Google's new line of laptops

- ▶ Any or all of these features could expand Google+'s reach and importance as a web game platform.

▶ Nexus, a Google tablet, will also appear just before this book goes to print.

What's more, according to an April 2012 report by the UK web-hosting company Pingdom, Chrome dominates the market in South America (48 percent). As discussed in the last chapter, the audience for web-based games is notably and disproportionately strong in South America. Moreover, the old Google-owned social network Orkut still dominates in the continent's largest country, Brazil. For those reasons, Chrome-based web games aimed at the South American market are probably a very worthwhile opportunity.

▶ Frankly, it's still my own favorite social network—it's pretty much designed like a real-world MMO!

That aside, as discussed in Chapter 6, "Future Trends and Opportunities for Facebook Games," it's highly unlikely Facebook will lose its prominence as the web's main social network. By the time you read this, it will have one billion monthly users, and the sheer gravitational force of so many users will keep it the main market for social games on the web for quite some time. This is a pity in a certain sense, because Chrome/Google+ has the potential to become a better platform for games. But unless Google is interested in cutting a special deal for you, it's probably best to devote your primary attention to Zuckerberg's walled kingdom.

ASYNCHRONOUS MULTIMEDIA SHARING INTEGRATED INTO GAMES

Draw Something's success as a user-created content game is probably only the beginning of a trend in user-generated content-driven games. I touched on the reasons for this in Chapter 6 (short version: it's crazy viral), and you are likely to see more games in that genre appearing on the broader web. Among these could be Creatarr (www.creatarr.com), a game developed a couple of years before Draw Something launched, which now seems poised to push out into this cresting wave. Like Draw Something, Creatarr shares the virtue of being based on asynchronous multimedia sharing, which makes it a natural fit for how most people use the Internet on a daily basis.

Lead designer Jim Purbrick says, "[T]here's a big opportunity for games to work around web ideas of social objects like images, music, and video, which is something that Creatarr is doing—building small nuggets of gameplay that produce social objects on the web that can be shared and commented on, but that also become input to someone else's game later. It avoids the problems of lobbies, appointments, events, critical mass, dropped connections, and differing participation levels that you get with synchronous gaming and provides the social elements required to build community. All this without having to force downtime into a game design just to stop people playing for a moment so they can hang out."

THE CONTINUED GROWTH OF WEB-BASED APP STORES

The unprecedented success of Apple's App Store will influence other major players to launch similar offerings of their own on the web, which will mean new markets for game developers there.

"I think the emergence of app stores is the new trend that will increasingly take hold over the next few years," as Nitrome's Annal puts it. "Already iOS and Android are big business for some online devs that port their games there, but I think there is a wider trend about to take hold, as the big players push to capitalize on that App Store experience on the desktop. Online we already have the Chrome Store [see Figure 10-4], and on the desktop, the Mac store is already growing, and Microsoft's Windows-based store is coming in the next version of Windows. Developers could see huge amounts of profit there if they took advantage of that."

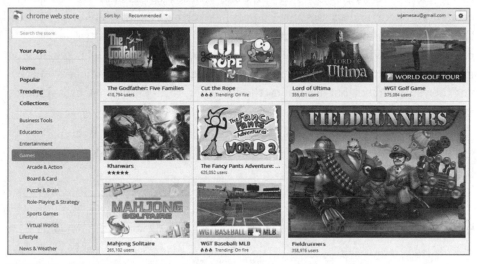

FIGURE 10-4: Google Chrome Store for games

This is definitely true, although in the short term, the biggest beneficiaries of this move will probably be the established developers. To grow these new app markets, the major players (Google and Microsoft, for starters) will continue turning to the Angry Birds of the world, offering them exclusive or preferred deals. (This has already happened with the Chrome Store.) For that reason, it's quite possible that the web game market will generally resist this trend toward web apps, because it adds several additional steps to the gaming process, which they've come to expect to be seamless and friction-free. In addition, much of the web game market audience is made up of minors, so any kind of pay wall may meet extreme resistance. Although Annal is right that app stores are a major opportunity, the converse is also probably true. Competing against app stores—offering similar games with less friction—is a great opportunity for web game developers too.

THE RISE OF INDIE DEVELOPMENT FUNDS

"Many publishers and investors see huge talent potential in independent developers," Pidgeon says. "Nearly every large publisher has publicly announced millions in funding regularly available for small developers."

He notes that major publishers like Nexon are providing office space and other resources for indie folks, whereas "Electronic Arts and Ubisoft are first investing in independent developers with work for hire and then buying indies and giving them creative autonomy and accesses to resources [marketing, IT, and so on] to enable the rapid scale necessary to support a small game going big." Add to this the rise of companies like Swiss-based Digital Capital with a new publishing model, "where investors pay an indie developer's creative overhead for a game or a number of games and then share profits, but often allow the developers to maintain control over their intellectual property."

To say it another way, as Pidgeon puts it (and this should be up in lights):

"Independent developers have more power now than ever, and this is a trend likely to become commonplace."

SUMMARY

Here are the key points we covered in this chapter:

- Advertising-based payments, in which players take a real-world company offer in exchange for virtual goods in a game, will probably emerge as a strong revenue source for web games, as will secondary markets in which players can exchange game goods with each other.

- HTML5 and WebGL may supplant Flash as the leading development platform for the web in three to five years, but thanks to new features in Flash, such as accelerated graphics rendering, it will probably enjoy its prominence for quite a while. Whichever platform succeeds, it's important for developers to be as platform-agnostic as possible.

- The growing quality of high-end graphics in web games will probably lead to growing interest from hard-core gamers, but they will probably need to see products different from what they are accustomed to on Steam or on their consoles.

- ▶ Twitter is still a "blue ocean" opportunity for web game developers that's yet to be exploited, but has excellent potential as a gameplay mechanic and channel for viral promotion.

- ▶ Users of the social networks Google+ and Chrome are an important market worth developing for, especially in South America, but overall Google+ will probably remain secondary to Facebook and the broader web.

- ▶ Draw Something's success is probably just the beginning of a trend in user-generated content-driven games, in which content can be shared asynchronously on Facebook walls, Twitter, and the web.

- ▶ The success of Apple's App Store is influencing other major players to launch app stores of their own. This is a good opportunity for game developers, although it may mainly benefit established brands (at least at first.)

- ▶ Major players and investors are actively courting indie developers with resources and money. Independent developers have more power now than ever.

Part IV

IOS

CHAPTER 11

Quick Survey of the iOS Game Market

IN THIS CHAPTER

▸ Surveying the iOS market: finding out what players spend and what developers earn

▸ Purchasing revenue from in-app payments

▸ Pitching to and working with publishers

The audience for games on the iPhone, iPad, and iPod is vast and growing vaster every day. However, while many developers have found huge success on the App Store with their games, far more wind up floundering in a market that's saturated with competitors. As a starting guide into that fiercely competitive terrain, this chapter contains a brief sketch of the iOS game market—who buys and spends money on those games, how most of the money is made, why advertising is necessary, plus the pros and cons of distributing your game using a publisher.

SURVEYING THE IOS MARKET: WHAT PLAYERS SPEND, WHAT DEVELOPERS EARN

The current market for iOS gaming is about 110 million (as discussed), with rough gender parity. By mid-2012, just over half of consumers with an iOS system owned an iPad, as opposed to an iPhone, with just a small sliver of owners with an iPod (according to a Technology Tell report). This is important data to keep in mind, because of the iPad's much larger screen/playspace and better graphics. And because it has the largest share of iOS gamers, it's important to design your game so that it optimally runs as well on the iPad as on the iPhone/iPod.

▶ This especially includes strategy, MMOs, and RPGs, which are suited well to the iOS platform.

Games directed at the hard-core market monetize particularly well (see Figure 11-1), as do casino/gambling games, as well as games in the casual/social quadrant, which includes disparate hits like Angry Birds, Draw Something, and Fruit Ninja.

FIGURE 11-1: Global Attack, a highly monetized strategy game from Spyra.

Mobile Game Spending Patterns (iOS and Android)

Mobile analytics leader Flurry is an immensely important resource for data on mobile game spending patterns. While the company's data aggregates information about iOS and Android gamers together, the numbers included in the following sections generally apply to iOS gamers in particular.

▶ Read the company's blog at blog.flurry.com.

HOW FREE-TO-PLAY STACKS UP AGAINST PAID DOWNLOADS

As of late 2011, freemium games on iOS and Android accounted for more than 65 percent of total app revenue.

HOW LONG IT USUALLY TAKES FOR A FREEMIUM MOBILE PLAYER TO MONETIZE

"The rule of thumbs says that if your user has not showed the money within two weeks," says Flurry's Patrick Minotti, "she probably never will." However, he adds, this can vary widely depending on genre.

WHAT IOS MODELS MONETIZE BEST: IPAD GOOD, IPOD BAD

"iPod doesn't monetize very well," says Minotti. "The more expensive/recent the phone the better the monetization will be (but less volume). iPad monetizes the best because it is a better gaming device."

HOW MUCH MONEY A HIT FREE-TO-PLAY IOS GAME CAN MAKE

"A hit game across most free-to-play game genres typically ranges between $500k to over $1 million per month," Flurry's Peter Farago tells me.

WHO PLAYS AND PAYS FOR IOS GAMES

According to Flurry reports, iOS owners play games more than twice every couple weeks, on average. Retention rates are extremely high, with nearly 70 percent of iOS owners returning to play a game they've downloaded.

Gamers between 25–34 spend the most money on freemium mobile games (this group accounts for 49 percent of total freemium revenue), even while accounting for just 29 percent of total playtime. Gamers between 35–54 have the second highest monetization rates (accounting for 28 percent of total revenue) while accounting for even less (14 percent) total playtime. Notably, while the 18–24 bracket are avid gamers (32 percent play), revenue from this group amounts to just 16 percent of the total. By gender, men between 25–34 spend the most (accounting for 29 percent revenue), while women between 25–34 spend the most among females, accounting for 20 percent of total revenue.

HOW MUCH MOBILE GAMERS SPEND ON FREEMIUM MOBILE TITLES—AND ON WHAT

In 2011, Flurry reported that consumers spent an average of $14 per in-app payment transaction in games; 71 percent of transactions were for items costing $10 and under, 16 percent of transactions were between $10–20, and 13 percent were more than $20. Sixty-eight percent of in-app purchases were for consumable items (for example, one-time power-ups), while 30 percent were for durable enhancements (for example, permanent equipment), and only a 2 percent sliver were for personalization (for example, custom names).

In a late 2011 survey of 252 iOS developers conducted by Streaming Colour Studios (www.streamingcolour.com), about 63 percent of respondents reported lifetime revenue from their games as being $10,000 or less, whereas some 15 percent reported lifetime revenue between $100,000 to $10 million. A 4 percent sliver reported making between $1-10 million. See Figure 11-2.

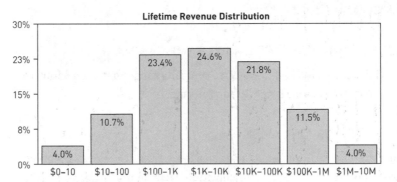

FIGURE 11-2: Lifetime revenue earnings for game developers survey. Copyright Streaming Colour Studios (www.streamingcolour.com).

To look at this data another way—of the developers surveyed, 20 percent were earning 97 percent of the total revenue. What's more, in Streaming Colour's survey, revenue correlated to the number of developers in a given studio. See Figure 11-3.

With two or fewer developers, the median per month revenue was around $100 or less. With six or more developers on the team, median monthly revenue was between $4,500–61,700 (with teams of 10–19 earning the most on average). Further, only 25 percent of developers surveyed reported more than $30,000 in lifetime total revenue from App Store sales.

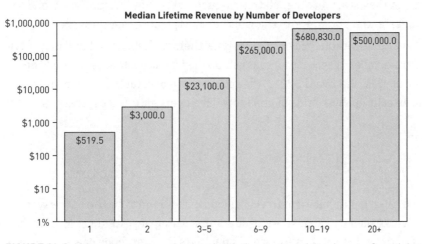

FIGURE 11-3: iOS game revenue correlated with the number of developers. Copyright Streaming Colour Studios (www.streamingcolour.com).

In other words, it's very unlikely you will earn a living as an indie iOS game developer. However, the odds suggest a substantial side income is plausibly in reach. (And a goal of this book is make those odds even better.) What's more, as you'll see later in this chapter, it's important to realize that independent developers as a group still dominate the iOS space (see Figure 11-4).

Indie Games Dominate Consumer Usage

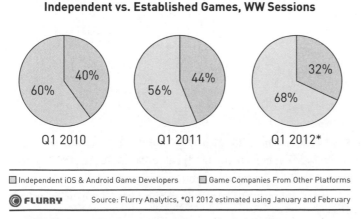

FIGURE 11-4: Mobile game market share. (Copyright Flurry.com.)

As the chart in Figure 11-4 by Flurry Analytics indicates, independent game developers not only dominate the market (68 percent in 2012), but also their share of the market has been strongly growing over the last few years. By contrast, game companies that got their start on other platforms (such as Electronic Arts, Zynga, and so on) have a substantial but minority share of the smartphone game audience.

In 2011, notably, established companies grew their market share, but Flurry attributes that to a number of acquisitions, as established game companies bought their way into the market. But by mid-2012, the small growth of established companies in 2011 has been eclipsed by a surge of new indie developers entering the market.

▶ In 2011, for instance, Electronic Arts bought Chillingo, whereas the Japanese mobile game giant DeNA bought ngmoco and Gameview.

PURCHASING REVENUE FROM IN-APP PAYMENTS

As discussed, in-app purchases for free download games tend to be the best way for developers to earn money. "Paid downloads are something of yesterday," as Michael Oiknine, CEO of mobile analytics service Apsalar, puts it. "Everybody or almost everybody has moved to a freemium model."

He doesn't even recommend charging 99 cents. "You may think, 'What is a dollar?'... but when you have so many games out there, the end user doesn't have the time" to investigate whether it's worth paying for when they can just play a slew of free iSO games before they find one they like. "Perception is reality, and they'll think 'I can get this download for free.'" Oiknine recommends selling your game as a paid download only when you're going after a niche market.

Still, this does mean only a small percent of your players will pay to play: According to Oiknine, anywhere between 1–5 percent of players will make in-app purchases, depending on the game.

▶ The United States, Japan, and Korea have the most highly monetized markets for free-to-play payments, followed by Western Europe.

PURCHASING ADVERTISING AND THE NEGLIGIBLE BENEFIT OF OFFER-BASED ACQUISITIONS

The best and cheapest way to acquire players is through organic downloads—a good game that generates positive word of mouth and media attention. But in such a saturated market, says Apsalar's Oiknine, you can't completely rely on this—even when your game is awesome. "At some point you need to go out there and acquire users."

▶ That mainly means through advertising.

At the moment, however, with so much competition in the iOS market, especially from major publishers, the cost per install (CPI) for a game has increased quickly to nosebleed heights. A year ago, says Oiknine, a developer could expect to spend about 30–50 cents in advertising and promotion to acquire a new user. Now CPI has grown to $1.50 per download. Actually, this is a bargain rate, because CPI can cost some developers as much as $5.

An alternative to straight-up advertising is going with an offer service, or what are often called *offer walls*. In these, gamers are given the opportunity to gain some kind of benefit (usually virtual goods and currency in the iOS game they play) if they install and launch a designated game at least once. (For example, "Download and play Obstreperous Aviaries once and get a free armor upgrade to use in Moebius Sword.")

"The problem," Oiknine points out, "is these are the worst downloads you can get." According to his analytics service, 90 percent of people who opt to download a game will typically launch (but not necessarily play) it just once. The remaining 10 percent will typically just play the game a few times. "And that is the curse of engagement."

Instead, Oiknine recommends acquisition campaigns that carefully target the kind of player who's most likely to play your game. "If you have to spend a lot of money," as he puts it, "go and spend it on someone who matters."

> CROSSREF You can find out more about advertising strategies in Chapter 12, "iOS Game Design: Basic Principles for Growth and Revenue."

PITCHING TO AND WORKING WITH PUBLISHERS

There are a number of reasons to get your game picked up by a major publisher. Among them are expanded cross-promotion to the company's large user base of players and expanded technical and server infrastructure support.

Then again, there are at least a few reasons not to go with a publisher. Publishers usually expect to take a significant cut of the revenue (on top of the 30 percent Apple's already getting), for instance, and they may demand creative changes you're not comfortable with. Because there are trade-offs when going in either direction, it largely depends on your larger goals for a given game—and for your career.

"Some indie developers are well connected with other developers and bloggers in the community, and have a knack for self promotion," Phill Ryu of Impending Studios says. "If that sounds like you, self-publishing is the way to go. If not and you're able to get favorable interest and terms from publishers, that's probably a mutually beneficial partnership." Although no publisher can turn your game into a hit, "ones that know what they are doing can improve your odds a lot."

Roxanne Gibert, founder of Spyra, a mobile game company whose latest game, Global Attack, hit the Top 10 in Strategy Games in the U.S. App Store, recommends publishers for indie developers, with some qualifications. "It really depends on the purpose of developing," she says. "If it's strictly for artistic reasons, then it might not be a good fit. However, if an indie is trying to grow a business, then I think working with publishers is strategically sound." Here's why: "A publishing agreement is a great way for indies to leverage use of [the] publisher's user distribution networks and tools, while reducing personal risk and obtaining development funding."

Publishers will offer various levels of revenue sharing for developers, which can go from anywhere from 10 to 80 percent. Which is subject, Gibert says, "to the level of involvement on the publisher's end, the funding provided, and the added benefits such as user distribution."

There are some red flags to watch for when negotiating with a publisher. "The main thing to understand is what type of relationship you want with your publisher," as Gibert puts it. "Do you have creative ownership? Who owns the intellectual property? What are the terms and limitations?"

From my own perspective, characters are the most valuable kind of intellectual property, so if you've put a lot of time and passion into making them unique and appealing, you should be very careful about giving ownership of them away to a publisher, because you're giving away the potential to do spinoffs, sequels, and merchandising.

In developing his next game Hatch (which you'll read about soon), Phill Ryu and his team have invested enormous effort in creating game characters that are appealing, memorable, and ripe for merchandising (see Figure 11-5). In cases like theirs, it's best for the developers to zealously protect their intellectual property (IP) rights.

If, on the other hand, the main appeal of your game is the overall gameplay (which can't be copyrighted or trademarked, at least not without difficulty), and it's not deeply original, it may be worth letting the publisher control the intellectual property in exchange for more revenue.

FIGURE 11-5: Characters in Hatch, a game with great merchandising potential.

In any case, when you do negotiate with a publisher, be prepared to bring a lawyer. "I would never sign an agreement with a publisher without going through a lawyer," Smith says, "which we reserve for only the most important things such as this. A good lawyer will be able to spot red flags. Heated topics may include owner-ship over the IP [and] whether the publisher is required to support the product or can opt to bail if they change their mind. Ditto for the developer—whether and how the publisher can suggest and enforce changes, and complicated and conditional revenue share formulas that leave various loopholes under weird conditions. I prefer agreements that put everyone in the same boat, succeeding if the game succeeds and failing if it fails. Watch for contracts where the publisher can let your game fall down without any risk or cost to themselves."

When you do approach a publisher, advises Smith, bring "a prototype that dem-onstrates both the promise of the idea you want to create and your team's capability of delivering it. These will put you in a much better position to discuss and negotiate than a slide presentation that supposedly describes an idea they should put their pre-cious weight behind."

And finally from Smith (but probably most importantly): "When looking for a pub-lisher, I personally would seek out a small company where face-to-face individuals have authority, not just impersonal policy and shareholders. I would look for people who seem genuine, invested, and moral—people you would be happy to have lunch with or help out if they needed something. There are lots of people out there who are sincerely helpful, and lots of them work at publishers. I would sign with those publishers."

If you do decide to try working with publishers, many of the top iOS publishers have an open-door policy for indie developers interested in publishing their games. The following sections describe a sample of the market leaders.

ngmoco (DeNA)

Launched in 2008 by longtime Electronic Arts game developer Neil Young, ngmoco was acquired in 2010 by Japan mobile giant DeNA for $400 million. Most of their games, such as Rolando and We Rule, focus on highly casual, light play. However, they also release games for the hard-core market, such as Eliminate Pro, a multi-player FPS that the company ceased developing, and Star Defense, a sci-fi themed tower defense strategy.

DeNA accepts queries from indie developers at the e-mail address `gamemakers@ngmoco.com` and encourages them to register to use the DeNA-owned development platform Mobage at `developer.mobage.com`.

Chillingo (Electronic Arts)

Publisher of epic iOS hits like Cut the Rope and the first Angry Birds game (after which, developer Rovio parted ways with the company), the UK-based Chillingo was acquired by Electronic Arts in 2010 for just under $20 million. Their site features a number of endorsements from successful indie developers who've been published on Chillingo. See `www.chillingo.com/developers/`.

To submit your idea, you need to fill out a submission form at `www.chillingo.com/about/submit-your-game/`.

GREE

A Japanese mobile game publisher with more than 230 million registered users, GREE acquired OpenFeint, the United States-based social platform for mobile games, a clear bid to enter the Western market (just like its Japan rival, DeNA, indicated with the purchase of ngmoco a few months earlier). GREE has its own robust platform with an iOS SDK for indie developers who want to publish games on the OpenFeint network. This network is connected to registered users around the globe, including Japan, which has one of the best ARPUs in the world.

> **CROSSREF** Read more about it here at `developer.gree.net/en/`.

And now, iOS game developer, you have a rough idea of who your potential audience is, how much they'll typically pay to play your games, and the publishers who can help you reach them (if you want to go that way.) In the next chapter, we'll focus on the design principles that will encourage them to do more paying *and* playing.

SUMMARY

Here are the key points we covered in this chapter:

- ▶ The current market for iOS gaming is about 110 million, with roughly half owning an iPhone and half an iPad.

- ▶ Most iOS game developers earn less than $10,000 in lifetime sales/in-app payments from their games; about 15 percent will earn a lifetime revenue between $100,000 to $10 million. This means that about 20 percent of iOS game developers earn 97 percent of the total revenue.

- ▶ Independent game developers dominate the iOS market (68 percent in 2012) and continue expanding their share.

- ▶ In-app payment from free games is the best and most reliable way to monetize iOS games. Genres that generate the best in-app payment revenue tend to be hard-core games, such as MMOs and RPGs.

- ▶ Because of the platform's heavy competition, advertising is becoming more and more necessary. Cost-per-install is now about $1.50 per download and is growing.

- ▶ When deciding whether you want a publisher to distribute your game, carefully consider how important creative control and ownership of intellectual property are to you. Always bring a lawyer to work out the final terms of the publishing agreement.

- ▶ Publishers offer various levels of revenue sharing for developers, which can range from 10 to 80 percent, depending on support, promotion, and other factors.

CHAPTER 12

iOS Game Design: Basic Principles for Growth and Revenue

IN THIS CHAPTER

▶ Starting advice from successful indie designers
▶ Making money in free-to-play iOS games
▶ Starting out: a smorgasbord of miscellaneous final advice

As you might have noticed when looking at any list of top downloaded iOS games, many of the games aren't there due to high-quality design. As veteran designer Randy Smith of Tiger Style studio notes, some are likely there for questionable reasons.

"I've heard that you can hire *download farms* that pay thousands of people to download your free game to give it a boost on the charts, which sounds dirty but may be common practice," he says. "And on the revenue charts, some of the highest earning games do so by designing game mechanics and flow strongly for compulsion, getting players to spend a little at a time for a long time without noticing that they're doing so, not unlike how slot machines are designed."

Despite these dubious designs, games like these often get to the top of the iOS charts, especially when they're published by large social game companies that cross-promote and advertise from their existing titles. "If you're only in it for the money," adds Smith, "these are the types of things you should be thinking about, and I wish you bad luck."

If, however, you want to develop a good game that can succeed on its own terms, you're reading the right book.

GETTING STARTED: SOME BASIC CONCEPTS

This section contains some starting advice from Smith and a couple of other successful indie designers on creating an iOS game that you can be proud of *and* that stands a better-than-average chance of being successful.

Design for Short Play and Socialization; Market Effectively

Just as Tiger Style's Smith has a lot of ideas on how not to make a popular iOS game, he has much advice about the features that help a good game succeed, including short play sessions, social sharing, and a visually compelling design. These ideas are described in detail in the following sections.

SHORT PLAY SESSIONS WITH EMERGING COMPLEXITY

"It's important to be aware of the types of games that are already succeeding on iOS," says Smith, "because that will give you some insight into how this demographic uses devices and what types of play patterns to design for." One common element is play session length.

> **NOTE** "Most of the successful games can be played and enjoyed for just a minute or two while standing in line at the grocery store," says Randy Smith of Tiger Style.

"Their design is very immediate, dropping you straight into the play experience with minimum overhead," says Smith. "These games tend to be casual, focusing on one mechanic that is simple to understand, but in the most successful games the core mechanic is often something new you haven't done before, with depth and complexity that unravels over time before you get bored with the basics."

Apply that observation to iOS's biggest hit: Angry Birds. It's relatively simple to complete level challenges in Angry Birds (and often a matter of dumb luck). However, to succeed while earning multiple star ratings, the player must learn through experimentation the game's subtleties—how different bird types interact with various environmental barriers and physics, and so on. See Figure 12-1.

FIGURE 12-1: Angry Birds' deceptively simple gameplay.

GAMES DESIGNED WITH SOCIAL SHARING ASPECTS

According to Smith, the best advertising on iOS is word of mouth, so game designs that lend themselves naturally to socializing have a big advantage. This socialization component is why asynchronous, turn-by-turn multiplayer games like Words With Friends and Draw Something are such big hits—existing players help recruit new players.

You can also encourage players to use Twitter, Facebook, and other social networks from within the game to communicate about their experience, connect with new players, or brag about achievements and leader boards—all functionality provided by Apple's Game Center.

VISUALLY COMPELLING DESIGN AND STRONG PRESENTATION

"[D]esign your game to be shown off," says Smith, "or to draw attention when seen over someone's shoulder, and to be intriguing enough to start conversations between strangers." See Figure 12-2.

"Along similar lines, the packaging of an iOS game is crucial. Your icon needs to be eye-catching enough to pop out of the crowded field in the App Store and communicate something compelling when combined with the game's name. Similarly, your app description and screenshots are on the front lines of reaching potential customers. It makes a lot of sense to design all of this stuff up front and then design your game to fulfill the promise those packaging materials are selling. Lastly, especially if your game isn't free, supply a video trailer so people can preview your gameplay before buying."

▶ Name, icon, app description, screenshots, and so on.

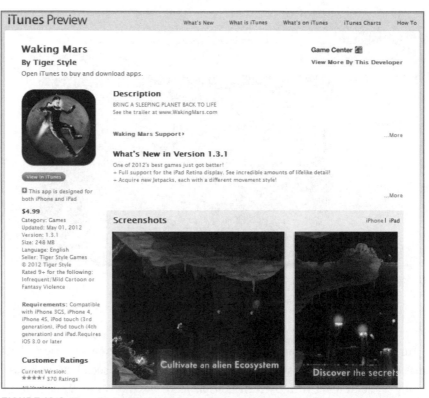

FIGURE 12-2: Tiger Style's Waking Mars presentation in the App Store.

CROSSREF Chapter 13, "iOS Game Developer Profile," describes more about Smith's iOS game design approach. Chapter 13 also includes a talk with Phill Ryu of Impending Studios, developer of The Heist, an iOS game that sold nearly a million downloads in its first month. Ryu has a holistic approach to creating good and popular games, as discussed in the following sections.

Design for the Medium and the Market, and Create Pop Music-Style Hooks

Says Ryu: "I like to think of hit apps a little bit like popular singles on the music charts—they share some traits. Like great pop songs, I think a successful iOS game needs a strong hook (or two, or three) to really stand out in the crowd, make an immediate impression, and spark buzz and word of mouth."

NOTE "[The hook] could be a delightful and unique control method or gameplay mechanic, novel genre experimentation, an amazing art style, or your team's impeccable pedigree. You just need something that jumps out at people and lets their imaginations latch onto it and run wild. It needs to be catchy, " says Phill Ryu.

"For a song, that means you can't get it out of your head, and you might find yourself humming it throughout the day, have friends inquiring what the tune is, things like that," continues Ryu. "For a game, it's how fun and addictive it is, and how strongly it compels you to spread it to your friends or rave about it on Twitter, and how long it remains on your home screen."

Ryu shares two additional tips.

DESIGN TO TAKE ADVANTAGE OF IOS' UNIQUE STRENGTHS

"You get big bonus points if you design for the medium and consider how your audience interacts with it. Play to the touchscreen's strengths instead of designing around its failings—onscreen buttons and D-pads, yech."

▶ Line drawing, direct manipulation, and so on.

A great example of this principle is High Noon, a popular combat MMO with a unique gameplay twist. The game uses the iPhone's position-detecting accelerometer to simulate "quick draw" of the player's gun and also for aiming. See Figure 12-3.

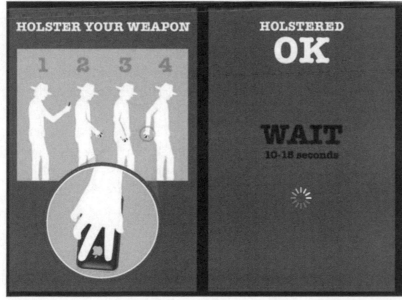

FIGURE 12-3: Happylatte's High Noon MMO uses the iOS accelerometer to simulate "quick draw" gun fighting.

Also, adds Ryu: "Think about the way people play games on their phones. It's in little bites throughout the day, so design your game to embrace that natural rhythm."

DESIGN FOR THE IOS MASS MARKET

▶ Think The Dark Knight squeaking by PG-13 with some minor edits and cutaways.

Ryu's final tip: "[N]ever forget who you're designing for. If you have a big App Store hit in mind, you're trying to design a game that a sizable chunk of the planet will find compelling. There might be opportunities to make some smart design decisions and broaden the audience without compromising a more hard-core vision."

Design for Unique Familiarity; Respect Your Players But Gently Guide Them

This section includes some final thoughts about getting started from Robert Thomas, Chief Creative Officer of RjDj, a studio founded by Michael Breidenbruecker that developed the official immersive entertainment iOS app for the movie *Inception* (which attracted millions of downloads) and the upcoming iOS augmented audio game Dimensions.

BE DIFFERENT *AND* BE FAMILIAR

Thomas says, "I believe that people are basically bored with the same old game forms. They will always consume yet another physics-based puzzler, to a certain extent. But if you give them something exciting and different to spark their imagination, it will make you stand out and give them exciting new experiences. On the other hand, if it is too different, you will be faced with a product that is impossible to describe. This can be tricky, so hitting a good balance between innovation/surprise and familiarity/understandability is key."

"Fruit Ninja is a good example. It's different in that it takes full advantage of the unique capability of the device touchscreen, but it's familiar in that it's an accuracy-based time trial with a bit of luck thrown in. There is a familiar basis to the game which is easy to grasp but also is an exciting new twist." See Figure 12-4.

RESPECT YOUR PLAYERS, BUT GUIDE THEM WITH CARE

"I believe that trying to pull a fast one on your users backfires. People are so aware of anything that smells of manipulation to achieve goals that are not oriented around benefit for the user. Align their benefit with yours," says Thomas. "Equally, it is important to guide them carefully to all the good fun stuff in your game. It always surprises me how much guidance they will need to do things you consider to be obvious and how little guidance it will take for deep gamers to find the things you thought nobody would ever find."

FIGURE 12-4: Fruit Ninja: familiar... but different.

> **NOTE** "A game like Game Dev Story does a good job of guiding the player through the 'relatively complex' ways they can play the game, prompting them with things they need to do, as well as explaining optional strategies and the 'good stuff' that might be hidden in there," says Robert Thomas.

"In Dimensions, we had a tough job of having to guide the player through some very unusual types of gameplay." (See Figure 12-5.) "[This included] exploring augmented sound and accessing different Dimensions by doing things in their life. This is both the hardest type of guidance and the most necessary."

Design for Fun (and Growth) Through Analytics

Although it probably sounds counter-intuitive, analytics services can be a boon for designers who want to optimize their games for fun. (In this context, I'm referring to companies that collect and categorize iOS user behavior from a number of sources.) Of course, analytics can't tell you when a player is *having* fun, but it can tell you, say, how many players completed your game's tutorial, or the third level, or when users first press the Pay button. Analytics tell you the kinds of things people do when they're enjoying the experience.

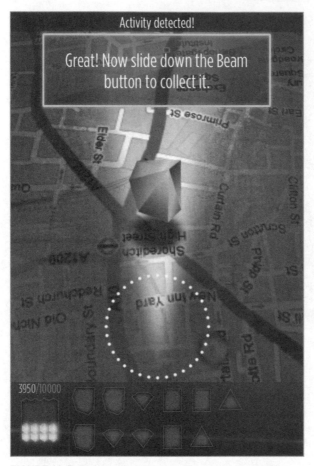

FIGURE 12-5: Guiding the player in Dimensions.

In the following sections, Michael Oiknine, CEO of leading iOS analytics service Apsalar (www.apsalar.com), which tracks the app-related activity of 150 million iOS gamers, shares some general advice on leveraging analytics services like his.

START SMALL AND LEARN AS MUCH AS POSSIBLE FROM CUSTOMERS

According to Oiknine, it's important to release an early build of your game to a few hundred or a few thousand users, capture their gameplay information, iterate, and then release to a few hundred/thousand more. Then make your game available in the App Store of a smaller country; for instance, many developers first launch only in Canada, which allows them to further iterate and improve the game at a larger scale than they did in beta.

Also, you should encourage your early users to give you good user ratings and concentrate on the product's basics—minimizing crashes, while making sure users are flowing naturally through the game, and staying engaged with it. This is an important process, because once you're ready to launch the game in the U.S. App Store, you'll have a very short time cycle to identify issues and address them.

▶ Michael Oiknine calls this "organic juice," since it's based on players' natural enthusiasm for your game.

TRACK BETA USERS BY COHORTS

It's a good idea to have beta players playing slightly different versions of your game (some with one particular gameplay feature, such as a new level or gameplay mode, others without it) in order to test how these differences impact retention and engagement. Often called *A/B testing*, the basic strategy is a more-or-less scientific way of measuring whether a new feature or feature improvement makes an overall difference to player behavior (good or bad).

TREAT ANALYTICS AS PART OF THE GAME DESIGN PROCESS

Successful developers carefully plan the aspects of the game they want to test with analytics and then incorporate the feedback into the design. What analytics questions do you want to address? What events and user actions do you want to tag? Which actions allow you to answer these questions? (See Figure 12-6, for an example of how this game behavior is tracked by Apsalar.)

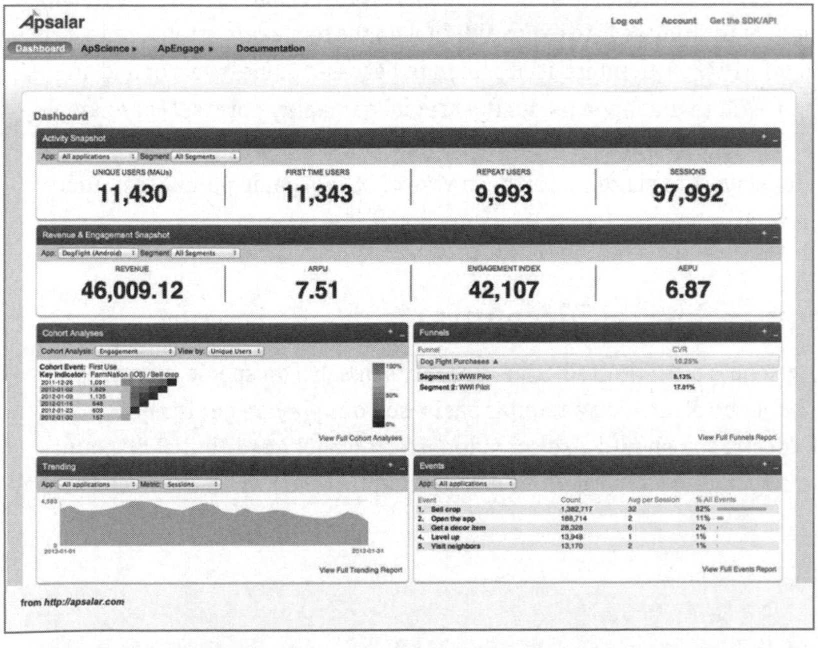

FIGURE 12-6: Tracking app game user behavior with Apsalar.

To create Dimensions, the latest iOS game from RjDj, the team led by Robert Thomas and company founder Michael Breidenbruecker honed it through the analytics process. "In Dimensions we used analytics to monitor many aspects of the game—always anonymously," says Thomas, "including players' engagement, retention, loyalty, and more detailed statistics related to tutorial completion, their purchasing patterns, and game progress. Being able to understand the key aspects of the game's performance in various areas can be a very powerful development direction tool."

MONETIZING FREEMIUM GAMES: DESIGN CONSIDERATIONS

Although some developers with an established reputation can still succeed via the paid download model (see the profile of Tiger Style in the next chapter), you'll probably want to give your game away for free and monetize through in-app payments. Here are five design tips for making money in free-to-play iOS games.

Get Your Goods in Front of the Player As Often As Possible:

▶ A developer with OpenFeint, the iOS-based social network, told me that developers saw virtual goods' sales rise when players could see each others' virtual items displayed in their profiles.

Your game should frequently display the virtual goods the players can buy and give them frequent opportunities to buy them. Many developers I spoke with emphasized the importance of finding ways to expose virtual goods to players often. For instance, display such offerings in an interstitial screen in between game levels or add an in-game pop-up message that appears during crucial gameplay points. (For example, "Running low on health? Buy regeneration boosts from Dr. Bob's pharmacy!") Also, create ways for players to make each other aware of in-app game purchases, such as with social media updates.

Offer Regular Special Discounts

▶ This is especially true on the weekends, when most players have the leisure to buy and play.

Many iOS developers offer limited-time discounts or sales on special items. Ideally, these should be offered on a regular basis, so your players get in the habit of checking for deals. You should also consider offering packaged "bulk" discounts, whereby the player gets more items (or more valuable items) when they buy them all at once.

Make Some Free Goods Better Than For-Pay Virtual Goods

Although this is another point of advice that might seem counter-intuitive, many designers of freemium iOS games make sure that some of the free in-game items are better than the ones players can buy with in-app purchases. There are at least a couple of reasons for doing this: It reduces complaints by players that buying virtual items constitutes "cheating," for one thing. For another, it encourages players to stick with the game in the hopes that they'll earn these fabulous items through gameplay. If you keep them playing, you can at the very least make indirect revenue off them via advertising. The longer they play, the more likely they are to eventually make in-app purchases. For instance, in the iOS cowboy dueling game High Noon, players can pay for special upgrades to their characters' weaponry and armor, but they can also randomly win these items when they're successful in a duel.

Try Selling Virtual Currency Instead of Virtual Goods

Rather than selling virtual goods and items, many developers prefer to sell their own virtual currency for in-app payments (which players can then use to buy the game's virtual goods). That way, you can easily adjust item prices and avoid the time-consuming process of getting new sale items approved by Apple.

Be Sure Your Virtual Goods Make Sense to the Game

Time and again, iOS designers emphasize the importance of selling virtual goods that are connected to a game's storyline and theme; this makes them seem less like a "give us money" interruption and more like a part of the game experience. If it's a Mafia-themed game, for example, why interrupt the experience with a generic message from the developer about in-app payments when you can have a mob boss tell the player, "Kid, you're too light in the wallet to run with the big boys—better get some cash, quick!"

Of course, none of this advice will matter much without a compelling game with frequent updates and outreach to your player community. Connecting with your hard-core base of players keeps them engaged with the game and encourages them to evangelize it to their friends.

On the flip side, the next sections cover two problems you should avoid when designing your freemium iOS revenue strategy.

▶ Updates encourage current players to keep playing and former players to take a look at what's new.

AVOID WORDY COPY AND LOW PRICES

Verbose descriptions of virtual goods are often unappealing, especially when they take up more than a single screen. Players will often tire of the description and exit before buying. Better to be concise as possible. Related to that, it's better to price your items too high than too low. You can always decrease the price of updates to encourage more sales. Better that than increase the price of an item after the fact. You'll incur the wrath of your user base as a result.

AVOID PAY-TO-PLAY VIRTUAL GOODS

No matter how good your game, the reality is that most players will not make in-app purchases, no matter what. Don't compound that challenge by designing virtual goods that must be bought in order for the players to progress. By and large, players will take that as a cue to move on to another game.

An even worse design move is to sell items for in-game currency and real money in the same place without any clear indicator of which is which. That just makes it easier for players to accidentally spend real cash on virtual goods they weren't planning to buy. Then you run the risk of players not only hating your game, but also sending complaints about it to Apple.

Instead, it's far more important to design an experience that free players enjoy without having to pay at all and want to share with their friends. As mentioned elsewhere, this is why it's a good idea to consider selling game boosts and other optional enhancements. That way, a player can still complete the entire game without ever having to pay—or better for you, will finally opt to pay in order to enjoy the experience that much more.

CLOSING THOUGHTS AND ADVICE FOR STARTING OUT

To close this chapter, the next sections contain a smorgasbord of miscellaneous final advice for iOS developers starting out.

Consider Developing Games Smaller Than 50MB for Impulse Downloads

At the moment, Apple and its carrier partners prohibit app downloads via the 3G/4G network that are more than 50MB. This, as Phill Ryu points out, limits the potential market for impulse downloads that don't require an iOS owner to be connected to a wireless network (see Figure 12-7).

FIGURE 12-7: A 25-minute wait for the bus. No wireless connection. A perfect impulse download customer!

Typically, a phone owner with a sudden craving to play a game is, say, at a train stop or a doctor's waiting room and nowhere near an open wireless connection. So if your game client is just above 50MB, it's very much worth trimming it down to size.

Be Careful Who You Reveal Your iOS Game's Special Features to Before Launch!

The App Store is notorious for carrying knockoff titles that are more or less cloned from existing hit games. It's not uncommon for a knockoff to show up in the store just days after a new title starts to show traction on the charts. For that reason, while you're developing your game, it's a good idea to be cautious about revealing what makes your game unique.

"If you've invested heavily into novel gameplay or an innovative concept," as Impending Studios' Ryu puts it, "you have incentive to keep the development secret, both to protect the ideas from being stolen but also because you can generally depend on more buzz and general interest when you do reveal it. It's really the Apple playbook and it works if you're onto something genuinely new and great."

▶ Or to put Ryu's advice another way: Think WWJD—What Would Jobs Do?

Follow the App Submission Guidelines Carefully!

Although this point may seem like common sense, enough developers complain about Apple's app submission process to point it out: Read the App Store guidelines and adhere to them carefully.

"Compared to other distribution channels and publishers," says Tiger Style's Smith, "Apple has few guidelines, but it's very important to follow them. Follow the rules about search tags, mature content, rating your app, and so forth, and you should have no problem. If you mess up, you'll have to resubmit, which essentially starts the process over from the beginning."

Go After New and Existing Players with Carefully Targeted Ads

As good as your game is, the app market is so large, and the competition for attention so fierce, you'll probably want to launch an advertising campaign to increase downloads. Apsalar's Oiknine recommends a highly targeted and carefully managed campaign.

▶ *Remember, revenue is not the same as downloads, and lots of downloads do not always translate into lots of in-app payments.*

Successful developers often create different links to different kinds of campaigns (emphasizing different features and artwork in the game, for example) so they can test to see which kind of ad works best, thus bringing in the most revenue.

Then you can optimize your acquisition costs in relation to the lifetime value of your targeted players. This is especially important for indie developers, for as Oiknine puts it, "You have less money to waste than a [giant mobile game publisher like] DeNA".

Oiknine brings up another point related to advertising: It costs less to retain existing users than to acquire new ones. In other words, find the folks who've already installed your game (especially if they've made in-app payments in it) and try to entice them back. Segment out your whales, as opposed to highly engaged users who didn't monetize, and go after the former.

Oiknine recommends an ad campaign that's triggered by a period of inactivity, such as a week, and sends lapsed players in-app virtual goods offers and other special deals. These kinds of campaigns can be costly over the weekends, when the big publishers are advertising their own iOS games like crazy, but Oiknine says it's typical that a re-engagement campaign directed at existing whales can bring back 10-30 percent of them. "Even bringing back 10 percent of these guys could have a huge impact on your bottom line," he says.

SUMMARY

Here are the key points we covered in this chapter:

- ▶ Design for short play and socialization. Most people play iOS games a few minutes at a time, so design like they play. Many like to share their fun gaming experiences with friends; make that possible and easy.

- ▶ Design for the medium and the market, and create pop music-style hooks. Design for the touchscreen, the accelerometer, and all the other features that make the iOS unique and great; design for catchy gameplay that hooks people who want to share the experience with others.

- ▶ Design for unique familiarity; respect your players but guide them. Create new spins to well-known genres and gameplay features; make it easy for your players to discover all the cool things about your game.

- ▶ Design for fun (and growth) through analytics. Ask yourself what kind of gameplay behavior you'd expect to see if players were enjoying your game, and then use analytics to determine if your beta testers are doing so.

- ▶ Monetize freemium games. Offer regular special discounts, especially in bulk and on the weekend, make some free goods better than for-pay virtual goods, try selling virtual currency instead of virtual goods, and make your virtual goods make sense to the game.

- ▶ Consider developing games smaller than 50MB for impulse downloads. iOS users can download a 50MG game pretty much anywhere they have 3G/4G connection.

- ▶ Go after new and existing players with carefully targeted ads. Test different kinds of ads to find the market that not only wants to play your game, but pay for it. But remember, rather than always chasing after new players, it's often better to re-engage your existing players who once paid for goods in your game and might do so again.

CHAPTER 13

iOS Game Developer Profile: Tiger Style and Hatch

IN THIS CHAPTER

▸ Learning from the style of Tiger Style: Innovative iOS games made with a Hollywood studio model

▸ Preparing to hatch: Lessons learned from designing a virtual pet iOS game

Now that you've surveyed the iOS gaming market and learned some basic design principles, it's time to spotlight two case studies. The first is Tiger Style, a successful iOS game studio run by veteran designers originally from the traditional game industry. The second is Phill Ryu of Impending, a relative design newcomer who has spent several years and more than $250,000 trying to succeed with an innovative new game that could (in my view) become the next Angry Birds-level hit.

LEARNING FROM THE STYLE OF TIGER STYLE

Tiger Style, the game studio behind the paid download iOS hits Spider: The Secret of Bryce Manor and Waking Mars, has a long and legendary history in game design—and with me. The studio was founded by Randy Smith and David Kalina, both of whom worked on Thief, the groundbreaking PC/console franchise. Smith was lead designer for the first three games, whereas Kalina was the AI programmer on the final installment, Thief: Deadly Shadows (see Figure 13-1).

FIGURE 13-1: Thief: Deadly Shadows (Eidos).

Masterpieces of immersive and emergent gaming, the Thief series convinced me over 10 years ago that games could be an art form, and they're a chief reason why this book exists.

With Spider and Mars, Smith and his team have been adapting some of the core principles that made Thief so great on the PC and consoles, and translating them to the iOS. And in the process, they prove you can create thoughtful, artful, genre-defying games for the platform and do quite well.

▶ Spider still earns more than $5,000 in a good month.

In Spider (see Figure 13-2), you play an arachnid, jumping and spinning your way through an empty mansion with the flick of your finger, discovering the mysteries of the family who once lived there along the way. As of mid-2012, the game has sold more than 360,000 copies and grossed more than $1,000,000.

FIGURE 13-2: Tiger Style's Spider: The Secret of Bryce Manor.

In Waking Mars (see Figure 13-3), you play a lone, stranded space explorer with a jetpack, lost in the caverns of Mars recently discovered to be full of life—specifically, a living, breathing ecosystem of alien life forms. Mars, which launched in March 2012, has so far sold about 55,000 copies, grossing more than $240,000. "Both games have a long tail," Smith notes to me, referring to their small but steady sales months or even years after launch, "and as of this writing Waking Mars is still in the beginning of its sales lifetime."

The sales numbers are even more impressive when you consider how much these games took to produce: Smith estimates it cost $15,000 to develop Spider and $38,000 for Waking Mars. This is possible because Tiger Style doesn't really have an office or investors, and operates, as he puts it, with a business model that's "more like a film production company or a cooperative, perhaps."

FIGURE 13-3: Tiger Style's Waking Mars.

Smith shared extensive details on the development style of Tiger Style with me, which many Indie developers should consider drawing from for their own projects. The following sections describe these details.

How Tiger Style Budgets and Produces Their Games

Smith estimates the budget of Spider to be about $15,000. That's a number that includes the purchase of all equipment, licenses, and legal support. It also includes $10,000 in royalty advances paid to the team. That sum, however, doesn't include any salaries or benefits. For example, during its eight months of development, Smith lived off of his own money.

"We're all essentially unpaid contractors during a project; then we all collect life-time royalties when the game is released," says Smith. On top of that fact, consider that Tiger Style is a distributed company without an office; the company employees work over the Internet, and the company doesn't have investors. That's about as low of an overhead as companies can get.

Waking Mars operated under the same model. It was a two-year development cycle that was supported by the income of Spider, according to Smith. They paid out $38,000 in advance royalties and about another $5,000 in other expenses.

NOTE According to Smith, he and co-owner Kalina lived off the income from Spider during the two-year development of Waking Mars. While they were developing Spider, they lived off their savings. Now they're living off of Spider plus Waking Mars' income to develop their next projects.

"The rest of the team is more like a film production company," says Smith. "They are contractors who work with us when we have projects for them to work on and find other income the rest of the time. We provide royalty advances to those who need it during production."

How Tiger Style Increases Sales: Quality Design and Apple Promotions

"There's no substitute to making a high-quality game that people play willingly, enjoy, become impressed by, and tell their friends about," says Smith. "Since we've earned a reputation for doing that, we get plenty of attention from the press when we release our games, and that definitely helps us." Some press sources, like Yahoo!, Wired, and Touch Arcade, can even cause a noticeable bump in Tiger Style's sales graph. However, on iOS, nothing beats support from Apple, especially getting featured with an App Store banner. Waking Mars was blessed with a "Game of the Week" banner for both iPhone and iPad, and that helped with sales tremendously.

Spider had a similar story. In both cases, they worked hard to make a game that was native to the platform, made good use of the hardware, was beautiful, original, and compelling, and showed that iOS was a great home for high-quality content. They believe that impacts Apple's decision making about whether to feature them.

Premium Downloads versus In-App Payments—The Pros and Cons

Both Spider and Waking Mars were developed with a "traditional boxed-goods mentality," as Smith describes it. However, he acknowledges this revenue model is being replaced on the iOS by the free-to-play, games-as-a-service model. For him, this approach will make sense for future games his studio develops.

▶ meaning they were sold as relatively high-priced paid downloads.

"The try-before-you-buy aspect of free-to-play makes a lot of sense in a market flooded with products, many of which, let's face it, are low quality. And games-as-a-service is often a better match for the usage patterns of this demographic and hardware." This means moving away from the retail model he's been accustomed to, after working for so long in the PC/console side of the game industry. On the iOS, as he puts it, "[W]e want to be in alignment with our platform, not fighting its trends and evolutions."

The challenge ahead, then, is to create new games that maintain the same level of ambition, while also being free-to-play. "When the App Store first started to take off, we saw an opportunity to stand out by offering something higher quality, which resulted in Spider," says Smith. "We're eyeing the latest trends with the same consideration."

Promoting Tiger Style Games with Social Media: YouTube to Illustrate Gameplay; Facebook/Twitter to Share It

According to Smith, the trailers for both Spider and Waking Mars were definitely key instruments in selling the games to players who had heard of them but wanted to see more before spending their money. For example, Spider had a feature that let you brag on Facebook that you were playing it or that you solved one of the quests (see Figure 13-4).

▶ The adoption rate of that feature was eleven percent.

new high score!
186580
my name is
geminiradio

Logged in as:
Randy Smith   f Logout

stats   ok

FIGURE 13-4: Facebook update option in Spider.

"We consider the trailer to be the single most important piece of promotion that we can do," says Smith. "We choose to show gameplay footage while also communicating the fantasy and story that was being offered."

Waking Mars did something similar (with social media promotion), allowing you to Tweet to your friends back on Earth when you had completed research on one of the species. Fewer people Tweeted from Mars than Facebooked from Spider. Smith says, "Our goal was to encourage players to reach out when they'd just accomplished something and were feeling good about the game. I think the Spider solution was better integrated into the game flow at an appropriate moment compared to the Mars solution. The Mars Tweets were also a bit more mysterious. Sharing with your friends that you just solved a mystery in a video game is probably an easier sell than posting something cryptic like [a Waking Mars Tweet] 'Larians prefer to eat mobile life forms but are also able to derive some nutritional value from Zoa seeds.'"

Design Lessons: Updates to Increase Installs; Extensive Testing; Discrete Levels; and Leaderboards to Increase Engagement

Spider had a very significant update called the Director's Cut that added 10 new levels for a total of 38 (see Figure 13-5). These new levels patched some holes in the story that players were confused about and contributed to fun new gameplay.

FIGURE 13-5: Spider's Director's Cut level.

"The Director's Cut was such a significant update that it attracted new players, more attention, and some additional press," says Smith. "The iOS market likes to know that developers are listening to them and keeping their games updated and fresh. Updates also increase the chances of a promo spot in the App Store and draw attention from your existing install base."

> NOTE   According to Smith, "Some developers go so far as to release a game with only the bare bones that make it enjoyable, and then update continuously, targeting improvements and extensions to the aspects of the game that seem to satisfy players the most."

▶ Casual gamers who were new to some of the deeper features Tiger Style was attempting.

"For both Spider and Mars we did very extensive play-testing before shipping the games," continues Smith. "We really refined this process for Mars, having players focus on the iPad in front of them while the rest of the team was watching on a big screen. Fellow developers often had great insights, but the highest-quality data came from play-testers who were most like our target audience. Sometimes it was really depressing to watch these players get tripped up on designs that we thought made learning the game easy."

"We refined the opening levels of Spider and Mars over and over and over again until they were as tight and economic as possible while still easing casual players into an exciting, new experience. This all happened before we shipped the game, so we can never be sure how it impacted sales, but our guts tell us this emphasis on reaching the casual audience is one of the major contributors to our success on iOS."

Waking Mars originally featured a seamless world that would stream in as you explored (see Figure 13-6). This made the caves seem vast and rambling and very believable. It soon became evident that the trade-off was player clarity. Players didn't know when one experience was starting and another was over. It was hard for them to tell if they were winning or losing; instead, they just kept stumbling forward into new things. By contrast, discrete levels that you have to finish one at a time helped with pacing and clarity. It gave players the sense of accomplishment and an understanding of the game.

Spider was a simple game based around the one core *action-drawing* mechanic for building webs. To provide more dimension, Tiger Style added leaderboards, achievements, and different game modes. "Waking Mars was a much larger game with more gameplay variety, so we felt those would be unnecessary additions," says Smith. "In retrospect we were probably wrong. Some players really got attached to the leaderboards, and most players had fun questing after the achievements. Without them, the game feels akin to a movie that you watch once. With them, the game feels more like a hobby that's worth coming back to."

FIGURE 13-6: Cave exploration in Waking Mars.

Strategies for Remote Development: Convey the Concept to All; Delegate the Solutions to the Team

As mentioned earlier, Tiger Style doesn't have a traditional office location, and all of its developers work remotely. "I don't think being a distributed company has impacted our final products, but it does change the processes we use to create and communicate design," says Smith.

As the creative director, one of Smith's most important jobs is to get everybody seeing the same end goal so that their efforts align nicely into a cohesive, unified work. Smith worked for years at game studios where people saw each other every day in the office, talked often about the game they're designing, and looked at each others' screens to review and collaborate on their work. You'd think that kind of direct, high-bandwidth communication would increase clarity, and to some extent it certainly does, but Smith also found that there's a tendency to take for granted that people understand each other when sometimes they don't.

"Comparatively, at Tiger Style," continues Smith, "I don't see everyone face-to-face, so I rarely assume they're picturing the same game I am. This puts pressure on me to provide effective direction. I find myself creating more evocative documents to communicate the vision and design."

> CROSSREF See Chapter 16, "Game Design Document: Tiger Style's Spider and Waking Mars," for Waking Mars concept art.

> NOTE "I work hard to find photos, concept art, and other reference materials that capture the correct vibe and tone. I write short stories that help establish the universe. I draw more complete sample screenshots," says Smith.

"If I have to design something, I often focus more on how it should feel and how it should impact the player experience, but I omit details, painting the actual mechanics in broad strokes only," says Smith. "And really, this is exactly the right way to give creative direction. I am not tempted to micromanage, because doing so requires high-bandwidth channels. Instead, I'm forced to emphasize how the game should feel and what it should accomplish without specifying the details, instead trusting those to my team's interpretation."

"Sometimes things get tricky when we're attempting to solve a design problem, say something that's not working in the gameplay. Ideally, you'd like to converge on a whiteboard to sketch out your thoughts. Editing diagrams collaboratively in real-time is a great way to brainstorm possible solutions. When that hasn't been available to us, we've at times just individually taken ownership over the problem for a few days until we can present a potential solution that's interactive and running in code. It's essentially like prototyping your answers instead of trying to talk through them. Again, it takes extra effort but is more likely to produce clarity."

PREPARING TO HATCH: LESSONS LEARNED FROM DESIGNING A VIRTUAL LIFE iOS GAME

In the beginning, Phill Ryu of Impending wanted to make an iPhone game that could teach people about themselves; in the process, he learned a lot about the iterative nature of game design.

His first game, Heist, used the iOS touch control to simulate safe cracking and attracted about a million paid downloads (see Figure 13-7). Hatch, his follow-up, was conceived while developing Heist. It uses all the unique functionality of the iOS to create an artificial pet game (see Figure 13-8).

FIGURE 13-7: Safecracking in the iOS game Heist.

FIGURE 13-8: Hatch's fugu pets.

With Hatch, your pet, called a *fugu*, is fed by dragging fruit from the trees with your finger into the creature's mouth. To help keep it happy, you pet your fugu by stroking your finger across the screen (see Figure 13-9).

FIGURE 13-9: Petting your Fugu in Hatch.

If you're playing music on your phone, your fugu will dance. Incorporating the iPhone's new face-recognition software, Hatch even allows you to play a minigame of peek-a-boo with your fugu.

Perhaps most clever of all, and unlike other artificial creature games, your fugu is directly linked to your phone—as your iPhone's battery loses energy, your fugu starts getting tired too (see Figure 13-10).

FIGURE 13-10: Your Fugu Losing energy as your phone does.

If all goes as planned, Ryu will launch Hatch shortly before this book goes to print, as a free-to-play iOS game monetized with virtual goods sales, employing a clever marketing strategy that you'll read about later. With amazingly evocative and adorable artwork and character designs by David Lanham (co-founder of Ryu's software studio, Impending), Hatch has a decent chance of becoming a hit. It could quite possibly be a major hit on the order of Angry Birds or the Tamagotchi digital pets that were so popular with kids in the 90s. Whether or not that happens, Ryu learned a lot about the nature of iOS design in the creation of Hatch, which fellow designers can likely draw from.

Consider the Marketing and Community Building Potential of Kickstarter Apart from Fundraising

If all goes as planned, Ryu and his team will announce the game's launch by August 2012 on Kickstarter. This is not so much for raising money, but for using Kickstarter's social and promotion tools to create a supportive community around Hatch, which will in turn become evangelists for the game and help Impending promote it.

> **CROSSREF** Chapter 15, "Is Your Game Ready to Get VC or Crowdsourced Funding?" covers basic advice on using Kickstarter for game development. However, always keep in mind the publicity and community-building aspect of the service and of crowd-funding platforms like it.

Develop a Monetization Plan That's Natural to the Game

Free-to-play Hatch will monetize with virtual goods sales—essentially, items players can buy for their pet.

> **NOTE** "With freemium you need to build a relationship with the player," Ryu argues, "that's when the money starts coming in."

By design, this monetization is organic and natural to the game, because Hatch will be about building a relationship with your fugu and starting to care about it.

If the game successfully creates that bond, players will naturally look for toys, treats, and other items they can buy to spoil their fugu, same as they would with an actual pet (see Figure 13-11).

▶ Unsurprisingly, Ryu and his team may also merchandise real fugu dolls.

FIGURE 13-11: Hatch virtual pet supplies for (real) sale.

Product Testing: Start with Fellow Designers and then "Civilians"

Ryu found some frustrations with the testing process of Heist, his first game. Initially he gave it out to 20 beta testers who were basically friends and fans. But many of their reactions were not substantial or constructive enough to help the iteration process. Instead, Ryu recommends showing your game to fellow designers first, because they better understand how different game features fit into the larger whole. After fellow designers offer their feedback and you implement it, you can then bring in the "normal players" to try out your game. Have them test the game for bugs and glitches.

Remove Abstraction from the User Interface

▶ Seriously!
Game for Cats,
by Nate Murray,
is a highly rated
iOS title.

A lot of design thought went into the user interface of Hatch, Ryu's goal being the removal of abstraction. In other words, he wanted to remove anything like the directional pad control from traditional handheld consoles, in which, as he puts it by example, there's an "arbitrary onscreen button to push something to move to the right." These kinds of controls aren't organic to the iOS's touchscreen experience, which is so intuitive and natural, even cats can play an iPad game.

With that in mind, Ryu went beyond the finger-petting mechanic; instead of getting info on your pet through a floating HUD (as would typically happen in most games), game info is contained in a little notebook that you "drag up" from the bottom of the screen. It's this design philosophy that also informed the connection of the fugu's energy with the iPhone's battery and the integration of a peek-a-boo game with the iOS camera—a virtual pet experience that's fully merged with the phone.

In future updates, Ryu plans other features that will layer the virtual pet experience with the phone. For instance, these features will reflect the real-life weather (as detected by the iPhone's weather app) in the fugu's game world and include a "pet walking" feature that will incorporate the game's accelerometer and compass.

Innovation Takes Time, Money, and Managing Good Ideas

Although Hatch was conceived as a virtual pet game from the start, Ryu began with a grander vision: in the original conception, the player's fugu would mirror your real life in instructive ways. If you ate a cheeseburger, for example, your fugu would start to get fat. In this way, the fugu would illustrate the costs of taking short-term pleasure versus working toward long-term rewards. At the same time, Ryu was frustrated to see hundreds of virtual pet games in the iOS store, with only a few that were (to his mind) good or even unique. (Most were ports or imitations of existing games.)

"No one was putting in that R&D effort," as he puts it. "My frustration with that was on a low boil for years." One reason for that, he learned, is that innovation costs money. To develop Hatch, he first borrowed $75,000, and all told, development may wind up costing $250,000 total. Much of that money went into creating high-quality assets (he spent $10,000 for the sound design, by someone who worked on BioShock), legal fees to trademark the game, and an animated short that accompanies the game (which turned out to be the biggest expense).

As you might have noticed, this is quite a different budget from Tiger Style's first two games, which cost $15,000 and $38,000 to develop, and were also very innovative in their own right. Much of the expense making Hatch had to do with working on and ending up with an over-abundance of good ideas. At the same time, he found value in starting with a hundred cool ideas, and winnowing them down to a handful that made sense and worked well together. Only by coming up with so many great ideas is it possible to stumble on the handful that will truly be magical. "It's important to have all the options and explore the entire space," as he puts it now. However, Ryu learned, "you need to edit it well in your head and have an idea how these [features] work together."

Among the casualties of this editing process is the "gamification" aspect of having the fugu teach the player about life choices, which in the end, detracted from the game's development. Still, Ryu adds, "Even if we're not trying to consciously improve people's behaviors, the DNA of incorporating [the game] into people's life is still there."

The result of Ryu's efforts, in any case, should be evident in the App Store, shortly after this book reaches print. Download Hatch and see how well he's managed to match his ideas and design aspirations to the end product available there.

SUMMARY

Here are the key points we covered in this chapter:

- ▶ Tiger Style operates like a film production company, with the founders financing themselves on revenue from their previous games, and contractors paid through royalties and advances on royalties for the next game.

- ▶ Media coverage and Apple promotion are significant ways to increase sales.

- ▶ Trailers depicting gameplay are important for game promotion, especially with paid download apps.

- ▶ To increase installs, make frequent (and substantial) new content updates.

- ▶ To increase engagement, add leaderboards and achievement systems.

- ▶ When working with a remote team, convey the design concept through art, writing, and other assets, and delegate specific solutions to individual team members.

- ▶ Consider leveraging the potential of Kickstarter apart from fundraising, as a platform for promotion and community building.

- ▶ Develop a monetization plan that's natural to the game.

- ▶ During the game-testing process, consider first showing the title to fellow designers, implementing their feedback, and then testing it with non-developers.

- ▶ Remove abstraction from the game's user interface, so it feels as organic as possible to the iOS.

- ▶ It is sometimes true that only by coming up with a lot of great ideas—most of which will ultimately be discarded—is it possible to stumble on the handful that are truly magical.

CHAPTER 14

Future Trends and Opportunities for iOS Gaming

In 2012 it became increasingly clear that the future of gaming platforms would be dominated in great part by tablets, a category ovewhelmingly owned by the iPad. According to a *Business Insider* forecast from February 2012, by the time we reach 2015, tablet unit sales will reach nearly 500 million, while sales will grow at an approximately 50 percent compound annual growth rate. The PC market is too large to go away any time soon. But the iPad and its smaller iPhone cousin will increasingly influence the direction of game development. It's likely we soon won't even think of "Facebook games" or "web games" as separate categories, because those games will be made to work on and with the iPad's web browser and iOS's Facebook connectivity. For this reason, it's especially important to consider the future of games on iOS—even if you don't develop for that platform.

SURVEYING UPCOMING iOS TRENDS: EXPERTS WEIGH IN

As earlier chapters did with the other two platforms, this chapter takes a 1–2 year look ahead at likely trends in iOS that game developers should consider when working on projects today. The following sections describe these upcoming trends in detail.

Free-to-Play Will Remain King

Echoing the opinion of many experts, Tiger Style's Randy Smith believes the free-to-play approach "will continue to dominate for some time." For someone like Smith, who came from the PC/console world, he adds, "I have mixed feelings about that. There's always been a degenerate approach to making money in entertainment media across time, but that doesn't mean you have to follow the trends and cash in. Instead, you can be inventive about how to improve the experience players are having and thereby open a niche to design into."

However, he suggests a way for developers to approach this new model. "It can be depressing as a designer to think of giving away the elaborate creation you slaved over, but that's probably not the right way to think about it." Instead, "think of gathering a huge audience of players who can support and enrich each others' experiences, who will return to your game day after day, and although many of them won't ever wind up paying anything, the ones who care the most will."

The Entrance of Facebook into Mobile Will Be a Challenge to Game Developers

"Facebook is aggressively moving into mobile," notes M2 Research's Billy Pidgeon, "and this will have a significant impact on phone game developers working in iOS or Android." The upcoming iOS 6 operating system will come with deep Facebook integration, while the iOS Game Center will let users import friends from Facebook.

This is a challenge for developers, observes Pidgeon, because "[a]s Facebook works to improve the social network's mobile experience, consumers will begin to spend a greater portion of their 'out and about' leisure time on Facebook." This will probably not only cut into the time iOS owners usually play iOS games, but also draw them toward Facebook games that run on iOS. "If Facebook is successful in gaining momentum on mobile—and there is a good chance they will be—games on Facebook will also be optimized for mobile and will compete more directly with pure play phone games."

Pidgeon advises developers get ahead of this trend now by working with a large partner with a broad user base. "I'd suggest partnering with a publisher such as ngmoco or GREE that incorporates a game-focused social networking architecture and building in their own game-focused social networking architecture to connect gamers for co-operative and/or competitive group play," he says.

Rising Acquisition Costs Will Benefit the Biggies

"The most obvious current trend is the increasing CPI," says Flurry's Patrick Minotti. "As the market gets more competitive, it is getting more and more expensive to acquire users. This means that it is going to be more difficult for small companies to sustain their game. It will allow publishers with big pockets—Zynga, GREE, DeNA, Electronic Arts, and so on—to regain some dominance in the market that is currently being ruled by indies." Given that, small developers should consider two possible strategies.

Cost per install.

 "Find ways to integrate user acquisition with game mechanics," says Minotti, citing Draw Something and its Facebook/Twitter-player matching as an excellent example of that (see Figure 14-1). But even then, for most small developers, it will probably be time to consider the second strategy: get on the consolidation train.

Flurry's Minotti explains, "It is probably better for developers to focus on what they are good at (making games) and let a publisher deal with the user acquisition and game discovery side of things."

This rise of acquisition costs will probably give rise to another trend, discussed next.

FIGURE 14-1: Draw Something integrated new user acquisition through social sharing into its gameplay.

Game-of-the-Week Games

Noting that games that appear toward the top of Apple's game charts enjoy a huge sales/download boost, Spark Capital's Nabeel Hyatt believes we'll see companies that play on that assumption and become, as he describes them, "Game-of-the-Week" companies. In other words, the developer will begin to turn out a single app per week, such as the latest installment of an episodic game, in a bid to hit the charts. This also means we'll see games with a lot of design features intended to achieve chart placement.

> ▶ Developers could do well to think about how they might expand their games into a weekly franchise.

This prediction leads to yet another likely trend:

Anticipate Changes in App Store Discovery

Discoverability remains a pressing and persistent problem with the App Store, so it's probable Apple will change the way games are categorized and displayed there. Two likely possibilities to consider, courtesy of Flurry's Minotti, are as follows.

First is social network integration, whereby the App Store displays games that your friends are playing (yet another reason to add social media integration to your game).

Second is categorization cleanup. At the moment, developers can designate the genre of their game; consequently, many of them list the same title under Strategy and Arcade *and* Roleplaying, and so on, no matter how much a stretch it is to do so. (And if you're a developer reading this who does that—dude, enough with it already.) As Minotti notes, "In a bookstore, it's not the publisher who decides on what shelf his book should be." At some point, it's plausible that Apple will address this categorization problem.

> ▶ If Apple finally fixes its App Store categories, my guess is that games designed with strong genre trappings will benefit.

iPad Will Go Hard-Core

With an increase in graphics quality and cloud-deployment options (among other factors), the iPad will probably become a hard-core gaming platform (see Figure 14-2).

Flurry's Minotti points to two hard-core genres that will benefit from this change: "As a human interface, tablets are especially well-suited for MMORPGs [as are] any strategy/resource management games with lots of selecting and moving things around."

> NOTE "Expect the next version of World of Warcraft to be played as much on a tablet as on a PC," says Patrick Minotti.

For game developers, the implications of iPad as a hard-core platform are pretty clear—start thinking about MMOs and strategy games in relation to the iPad.

FIGURE 14-2: Selection-heavy strategy games like Battleheart are an ideal fit for iPads.

The Rise of Location-Based iOS Gaming

With the success of location-based services like foursquare and Glancee (which was recently purchased by Facebook), you're likely to see more interest in games based around that functionality—an interest game developers would do well to tap into.

"[A] few years in the future," argues Tiger Style's Smith, "it will be a lot more common for people to share their current location, such that you will routinely look at a map to see where your friends are, what they're doing, what their status message is, and what photo they've posted from there. I think there will be opportunities to take advantage of this data stream to make some really interesting game experiences."

The biggest gaming beneficiary for location-based services? Quite probably, the game genre that already largely takes place in the real world. "I've always been fascinated by the potential of Alternate Reality Games—ARGs—in which you, for example, look through your mobile device to see another world overlaid on the real world, since these games cross the fourth wall to merge a structured fantasy with reality, and the player has to respond to both," says Smith.

However, Smith thinks these ARGs won't be the esoteric exercises we've come to expect from the genre. "I think the locational games that will really take off will be much more casual in nature—just fun little games you can play with strangers pertaining to the places you've both visited, whether that's your local supermarket or famous international landmarks. I can imagine leaving markers, traps, notes, and pictures for other people and being worked into a game where these real-world locations are relevant."

On this point, RjDj's Robert Thomas concurs. "I also think more and more of the virtual will become overlaid and interwoven into our daily experiences using every possible trick developers can think of with these devices," he says. "It's all going to be about who provides the best and most useful experiences." (See Figure 14-3.)

FIGURE 14-3: Location-based gameplay in RjDj's Dimensions.

The Death of the D-Pad

Phill Ryu of Impending Studios has a bold prediction about the console-style directional pad that is still fairly common in many iOS games. "I don't think the onscreen virtual D-pad is going to exist in any of the top 50 popular iOS games in two years," he says. His reasoning as a designer and a market observer: "If you want a great user experience for your players, direct manipulation in your interface and controls is huge. There's already been a developing allergy of games with onscreen controls crowding the screen and complicated HUDs, and this backlash is going to grow."

> **NOTE** "People are going to expect native experiences on their devices, and they have a right to five years in," says Phill Ryu.

If I can add to Ryu's point (I am the author after all): children who first experienced the iPhone at 5 years old in 2007 are now 10, and in the next few years, they will become a major sector of the gaming market (see Figure 14-4).

FIGURE 14-4: *This* is who you're designing future iOS games for. Do you think he wants a D-pad? (Pictured: Author's nephew Henry Oesterle.)

Not only are kids likely to have little sentimental affection for old school, handheld game console-style controls, for many of them, the iOS has been their *only* handheld game console.

Now that we've covered some of the trends likely to impact the iOS market in the West, let's move on to a far larger trend that's already changing the world of iOS gaming: the rise of smartphone gaming in China.

UNDERSTANDING THE FUTURE OF IOS GAMES IN CHINA: OVERVIEW AND ADVICE FROM YODO1'S HENRY FONG

Chat with Henry Fong, founder and CEO of Yodo1 (www.yodo1.com), a Beijing-based company that has helped many leading Western game studios launch their mobile games in China, and you'll realize just how different the market for iOS gaming is in that country. Different in *every* sense. Courtesy of a conversation with Fong, here's some data from Spring 2012:

► By volume and free downloads, China is already the second largest market for iOS games in the world.

► At the end of 2011, China had approximately 80 million smartphone owners, around 35–40 percent of which were iOS. By the end of 2012, that market should increase to 180–200 million.

► As of February 2012, monthly activations of iOS devices in China exceeded those in the United States.

► Up until January 2012, China Unicom, the second largest mobile carrier, was the sole provider of iOS devices to their subscribers. China Telecom, the third and smallest mobile carrier, announced that it would carry iOS devices that month. China Mobile, the country's largest carrier by far, with more than 670 million subscribers, has yet to announce it will officially sell iOS devices, but already hosts more than 15 million gray market iOS devices on its network.

► Casual gamers will typically buy 1–2 iOS games every two weeks, spending $1–2 in the process, whereas hard-core gamers can spend hundreds of dollars a month for their gaming and spend on the same game over a long time frame.

These are all data points pointing to the fact that the future of iOS gaming will soon be dominated by China. However, as Fong explains, the Chinese gaming market has some key differences from the market in the West, the most major one likely being this:

"Chinese gamers are very different in nature to Western gamers," Fong explains. For MMO players in the West, for example, "The last you thing you want to do is admit is you're spending a lot of money" to gain advantage by paying. Indeed, as you'll notice throughout this book, designers consistently recommend making it possible for players to advance in a game without paying and removing any impression that paying players are "cheating." This advice, while valid in the West, doesn't apply as you go East. "Chinese gamers are totally different," says Fong. "Many like to flaunt the fact that they're spending a lot of money... so that tips the game monetization mechanics on its head."

To dramatize that giant difference, Fong tells the story of a property developer in China who wanted his MMO guild to win. He wanted it so deeply that he spent $800,000 on a single online game. But he did more than that. "He went as far as to fly his entire guild to Shanghai to have guild meetings," says Fong. "He paid for his team members to level up and pay other people to keep his character leveled up." It's difficult to compare that extreme level of monetized passion to anything we've seen

► Assuming Apple maintains its market share in China, as we go into 2013, there could be about 80 million iOS owners in China alone.

in the West. But, says Fong, "Though extreme, that's the kind of gamer mentality that you're dealing with in China. These kinds of gamers give a whole new meaning to the term 'whale,' used by gaming companies to describe high revenue customers."

> **NOTE** The Chinese perspective on virtual goods can probably be attributed to the country's hyper-consumerist economy, where it's considered a sign of success to spend a lot of money in a very visible way, flaunting wealth and spreading it around. Big spender, big ego, and big social status.

That's a fascinating cultural difference in itself, and it also leads to the first bit of wisdom Fong has to offer Western game developers, when it comes to how they sell virtual goods in their games.

"Don't be shy about encouraging gamers to pay to gain a competitive advantage," says Fong. Not only that, design cool ways for players to show off to other players how much they spent in your game. "Chinese people like showing off their achievements," says Fong. He suggests a passport page that displays a player's in-game awards on their social network profile pages.

> For example, via leaderboards, badges, medals, customized avatars, and other prominent displays of virtual goods that fellow gamers can see.

That's just one reference point Western game developers need to consider when launching their games in China. The following sections describe several others.

Free-to-Play Dominates China's App Store

Free-to-download iOS games are popular in the Western App Stores, but far more in China. The country's gamers, as Fong tells it, are simply not used to the pay-for-download model. In 2011, for instance, only one premium pay for download game, Infinity Blade, consistently sustained top grossing rankings in China. Instead, Chinese players are accustomed to downloading a number of games before deciding on one or more that are worth paying for in micro-transactions. Despite this reluctance to pay up front, Chinese gamers *do* pay to game.

> In 2011, the country's overall gaming market was $6 billion, and for 2012 was on track to exceed $8.8 million.

Casual and Female Gamers Dominate iOS, But the Hard-Core Market Is Growing

Within the first couple years of the iOS launch in China, most of the phone's purchasers were new to gaming, skewing to young women and male white-collar workers in the 23–35 year old range. Consequently, casual and puzzle titles like the Angry Birds and Talking Friends franchises are very popular on iOS in China, as are Plants vs. Zombies and Fruit Ninja.

> Indeed, Chinese developers will often clone popular Western games, although the versions from the West tend to be better in quality.

This casual market is huge and Fong adds, "Chinese people like high-quality eye candy," noting that the hidden-object game Mystery Manor was very popular in China at launch, largely due to the high quality of graphics.

All that said, the traditional gaming audience is growing on the iOS. It's now about 20 percent of the total iOS market, but is growing faster than the casual segment. As in the West, the per-game spend for hard-core games on the iOS is also higher. In-depth simulation/strategy/MMORPG games like Hoolai and Three Kingdoms expanded from the PC to the iOS, and did extremely well. Hoolai, in fact, started a cross-platform trend for MMOs, which Chinese gamers are embracing.

But again, the market for hard-core on iOS is just starting to grow. Hard-core games for the PC are quite huge in China (it's not uncommon for Chinese MMOs to have tens of millions of active players), and there's every reason to think this market will continue moving to the iOS. The challenge for Western developers is to properly localize their products for the China market and succeed in the same way that Microsoft's Age of Empires and all of Blizzard's games have. "RTS and RPG will do very well in the upcoming 6–12 months," predicts Fong, "assuming they're adapted properly."

Android Market: Huge, But Hard to Monetize

It's worth noting that the Android has also experienced a massive explosion in China, especially versions of the smartphone that are now sold in China for under $100 (and consequently, do not display high-end graphics.) Much of this growth in the Android market is coming from outside major cities like Beijing and Shanghai—in 2011, half of Android's revenue came from second- and third-tier cities. According to Fong, it's typical for Android owners in these regions to earn $300–400 dollars a month, *and spend half of that on gaming*.

However, despite this enthusiasm for Android, the market is extremely fragmented and, therefore, difficult to monetize. In China's Google Play, gamers cannot pay for games; Amazon doesn't even have an app store for the local market. Instead, there are more than 70 Android app stores that divvy up the market. For now, then, the primary monetization channel for Android games in China is through advertising. Over time, Fong believes, this market will consolidate and payments will get easier. Until then, Android is more or less the Wild East for gaming.

To Avoid: Western Social Media Integration

China already has its own local social networks, like Sina Weibo, RenRen, and Tencent's social networks, and the West's leading social networks, Facebook and Twitter, are blocked by the government. This painful political fact reverses another common design consideration for game developers: it's better *not* to have core game features for an iOS title that depend on Facebook and Twitter, because doing so will cripple or even ruin the game experience for Chinese gamers. If your core game mechanics depend heavily on social network integration, as part of the localization process, Western developers should work with local publishers like Yodo1 to integrate their games with China's social networks.

Avoid Designing Locally (Just for Western Audiences)

This point is what Fong dubs the "Who the hell is King Arthur?" problem. In other words, as he puts it, "The Chinese audience has no idea why a guy who pulls a sword out of a stone will be the King of England."

In other words, avoid adding specifics to your game that assume knowledge of Western culture. Instead, since Chinese culture contains a lot of myths and folklore that have strong thematic overlaps to well-known stories from the West, it might be worth marrying aspects of these themes to your existing story. (By example, *The Romance of The Three Kingdoms*, a classic beloved in China, contains stories of heroic chivalry and battle that Chinese audiences can easily relate to.)

This leads to a related point.

Avoid Verbal and Written Elements Essential to Gameplay

Even though words and voiceovers can add impact, warns Fong, "try to remember you're designing for a global audience." While some Chinese are bilingual, you're giving up a high proportion of the gaming population if you make English literacy a prerequisite for enjoying your game. Therefore, don't put game-critical information into screen text or English-language voiceovers.

Instead, it's better to use verbal and written cues to enhance the experience; players should be able to discern game objectives and information through visual and non-language audio cues. This is an especially important rule for a game's opening cut scenes. If you bombard Chinese gamers with a lot of English text and voiceovers early on, warns Fong, "they're going to jump to the next game."

Design Globally (for Everyone)

Designing globally is the counterpoint to designing locally (which you should avoid). As Fong notes, major hit games like Angry Birds, Fruit Ninja, and Plants vs. Zombies don't require a lot of social context or cultural background, nor do they require language skills to play. Hollywood learned this lesson decades ago, crafting film projects that would be about as appealing to the overseas markets as local U.S. theaters. Now that games also have a mass market and an international audience, designers need to start thinking about the universal themes and storylines that translate across cultures and bind us together, not separate us.

▶ Good advice for promoting world peace; pretty good strategy for selling games, too.

Consider Adding Chinese Elements Organic to Localized Games

When Yodo1 worked with the game studio Robot Entertainment to launch their award winning iOS title Hero Academy to China, they worked extensively with the developer to co-design and develop a new race of characters themed around popular Chinese fantasy heroes such as the Shaolin monk, Taoist, and other roles that have been widely popularized in Chinese TV dramas and movies (see Figure 14-5).

FIGURE 14-5: Chinese-themed content from Hero Academy (Jiang Hu Heroic Team) for China.

Rovio took a similar tack when introducing Angry Birds to China, adding Moon Festival levels, and timing the game's release for that holiday. As a Chinese gamer, says Fong, "That draws my attention immediately." And gaining attention in China translates into game downloads from tens of millions of players, which in turn translates into in-game payments from hundreds of thousands of them—a potentially huge revenue stream that should draw Western developers' attention.

SUMMARY

Here are the key points we covered in this chapter:

- ▶ Free-to-play will remain king on iOS, so commit to designing games with in-app payments, virtual goods, and other alternative revenue models besides paid downloads.

- ▶ Rising user acquisition costs will benefit the big publishers—small developers should consider joining them or find ways to integrate user acquisition with their game mechanics, such as with Draw Something.

- ▶ It's likely that Apple will change the way games are categorized and displayed and will add even more social network integration in the near future.

- ▶ iPad will become popular with hard-core gamers, with MMOs and strategy games benefiting most from this move.

- ▶ Interest in games with a real-world location-based function will likely grow.

- ▶ By 2014, no game with an onscreen virtual D-pad will be in any of the top 50 popular iOS game charts.

- ▶ China already has the second largest market for iOS games in the world and will soon become number one. To make your games popular and successful there, encourage Chinese players to spend more via in-app payments to gain a competitive advantage. Additionally, design games with universally recognizable stories and elements and consider adding Chinese elements that integrate well with the existing gameplay.

Part V

FUNDING YOUR GAME

CHAPTER 15   Is Your Game Design Ready to Get VC or Crowdsourced Funding?

Is Your Game Ready to Get VC or Crowdfunding?

Many indie developers assume they'll need to fund their first game projects with their own money. Often, that's true, and the easiest way to get started. However, with the right design and "elevator pitch"—Silicon Valley jargon for a short, punchy, compelling summary of the game you're working on—even small developers stand a pretty good chance to get external funding. That money might come from a venture capitalist or angel investor, if you can convince them you have the talent and track record to deserve their cash. And increasingly, it can also come from a group of people across the Internet, through a process called "crowdfunding." This chapter will introduce you to these forms of funding and give you advice on going after both.

WEIGHING THE PROMISES AND PERILS OF FINANCING YOUR GAME THROUGH VCS OR CROWDFUNDING

Game developers can gain a lot of money through well-designed monetization, but they can also acquire cash through two other means:

- ▶ Venture capital (VC) funding from an established firm or angel investors
- ▶ Crowdfunding from a large group of supporters

Of course, both of these routes come with promises and perils.

On the plus side, a venture capitalist may offer you six, seven, even eight figures in capital, and a chance to earn far more by setting you up to go public or selling to a larger company. Just the act of getting funding confers credibility to your company, in the tech/gaming industry, because it's clear proof that some major players think you're worth backing.

However, all this also means that they get a stake in your company, and usually, a say in its management and even design decisions. Add to this the pressure of an investor who expects returns and has a right to expect that you deliver them, usually sooner rather than later. And of course, one way or another, they'll usually take a large cut of your revenue, too.

Meanwhile, crowdfunding has proved to be a great way for indie developers to raise enough money to make their games, while staying true to their original vision. However, most successful game crowdfunders only manage to raise total pledges in the four- or five-figure range, and it's very likely the market for crowdfunded games will soon reach a saturation point. Further, even if you do raise enough, you're then under the collective pressure of your supporters to complete the game (no matter what problems or delays emerge). You still probably need the game to turn a profit, so you'll have enough to finance your next title.

Assuming these basic cautions don't stop you, the next sections describe the advice of two venture capitalists who can tell you what comes next, whether you decide to go the VC route or opt to launch your own crowdfunding campaign.

UNDERSTANDING HOW TO SELL VCS ON YOUR GAME, PART I: NABEEL HYATT, SPARK CAPITAL

Nabeel Hyatt, a venture partner with Spark Capital, is in a unique position to understand game design as a VC, because he first began his career as a developer himself.

▶ And you may not like what they tell you to do.

▶ So you probably won't be able to quit your day job.

▶ Zynga paid around $200 million for OMGPOP.

Founder of Conduit Labs, a game studio acquired by Zynga in 2010, Hyatt then became a general manager at the social game giant, where he led development of Adventure World. Hyatt joined Spark just in time to be there when OMGPOP, a game company backed by Spark, was acquired by Zynga for around $200 million.

Notably, Spark stuck with the company even after struggling with a string of unsuccessful titles, so he was there when the company finally hit its stride with the cross-platform iOS/Facebook game Draw Something (see Figure 15-1). When it comes to hearing developers pitch him their ideas for a game company, "I'm always happy to hear from folks with a dream," says Hyatt.

▶ E-mail Nabeel Hyatt at nabeel@sparkcapital.com.

FIGURE 15-1: OMGPOP's Draw Something, funded by Spark Capital.

What Interests Hyatt in a Gaming Startup

Besides user growth and revenue, Hyatt's number one metric for games that interest him as investment prospects is the day one retention. This refers to new users coming back the next day to play again. This is an especially important way for Hyatt to evaluate games he might not personally "get." His rule of thumb: anything below 13 percent day one retention is bad, and a great target is toward the 60 percent range.

▶ If a game remains below 13 percent day one retention after a couple of months despite several attempts to grow this number, it may be time to kill it.

Hyatt also looks for teams to invest in who understand why their game is succeeding along various metrics—why players are rating the game highly, why day one retention is strong, or even something as simple as why people smile while playing the game. "That tells me a lot about their thought process," Hyatt says. "The game companies in this new ecosystem that are doing better and better are the ones asking why."

It used to be that games would evolve every few years with the launch of a new console; now, however, game evolution cycles are happening on a near quarterly cycle. For that reason, Hyatt says, "It doesn't matter how analytical you are or how cutthroat you are; it comes down to measuring those results to figure out how to get better."

The Best Points Developers Can Make During a Pitch Meeting

As discussed in Chapter 4, Hyatt puts a lot of stock in the long-term goals a game creates for its players: "What's the aspiration of a player? What's the thing they're trying to build in the future? How would they imagine themselves playing the game in a year? What's the moment-to-moment experience in order to meet the aspiration?" This isn't just a high-minded design goal, but good business sense. His firm invests in games as a recurring service, not games enjoyed for a day or two and then discarded.

For the company pitching to Hyatt, they need to answer two key questions:

1. Why now?

2. Why you?

"We invest in areas where there might be an opportunity for explosive growth," he says. Most companies aren't likely to realize such growth, so the developer must explain to him why they're the exception.

Know Your Strengths and State Your Weaknesses

"What I want to see is an entrepreneur who understands their biggest strength and their biggest weakness and be able to talk about both honestly," says Hyatt. Some developers in search of funding may obscure their shortcomings, but he would prefer if they say something like: "If you're not going to invest, this is the number one reason you're not going to invest." Not only does this demonstrate that the developer truly understands their business, it also opens up an opportunity for the VC to offer suggestions and help the startup.

There's a corollary to this advice: Developers should know what they're best at and be able explain why and how. "A small company can't be good at one hundred things," says Hyatt. "They can only afford to be number one in one area."

UNDERSTANDING HOW TO SELL VCS ON YOUR GAME, PART II: JEREMY LIEW, LIGHTSPEED VENTURE PARTNERS

A managing director with Lightspeed Venture Partners, Jeremy Liew has invested in a number of successful gaming companies, including Playdom (acquired by Disney), Serious Business (bought by Zynga), and KIXEYE. Liew is always interested in pitches from game developers, in the form of a two-page executive summary—although, as he explains in the interview that follows, user activity numbers matter more to him than design. "You're better off when you have the user engagement and monetization data," as Liew puts it.

▶ E-mail Jeremy Liew at jeremy@lightspeedvp.com.

What Interests Liew in a Gaming Startup

Besides user growth and revenue, your game needs *repeatability* and *discoverability*, and a long-term *strategy of discoverability*. Or as Liew puts it, for repeatability, "How do you build a hit factory?" Although not every game will be a hit, a startup should have some kind of native advantage that makes their games more likely to be a hit. That could be due to a built-in audience created by a series of sequels, or a hit niche game genre with real complexity and a passionate user base. As an example of that, he cites KIXEYE, which focuses on core gamers who are under-served by Facebook games. At the time of company launch, most Facebook games were highly deterministic and predictable.

NOTE "You can write the game design document just by playing the game," Liew says of most Facebook games.

By contrast, KIXEYE's real-time strategy games came with randomness and unpredictability driven by the game's artificial intelligence, which makes gameplay quite different and difficult for competitors to copy (see Figure 15-2). "Frankly that's why the best real-time strategy games are still published by KIXEYE," Liew told me. "Only [KIXEYE] can see the internal logic and AI, and see the implications for user numbers."

For discoverability, Liew describes the current playing field this way: whereas in the past, game distribution used to be the bottleneck (that is, selling games in boxes on shelves), now most games are available online, so distribution is free, easy, and democratic, and development on the larger platforms is relatively inexpensive (as compared to AAA console games).

FIGURE 15-2: War Commander RTS from KIXEYE, backed by Lightspeed.

▶ This is even more true for the library of iOS games, which grows exponentially on a weekly basis.

However, this very fact makes discoverability quite crucial. "In a world where there are tons and tons of games," says Liew, "how do you get [your game] to be the one people try and are talking about?" It's not enough to create a great game, because, "There are so many great games that are sitting out there languishing."

▶ Quite a number of popular physics-based puzzle games were on the market before Angry Birds, but few could have guessed the game would not only dominate that category, but would also become a mainstream phenomenon.

The Biggest Mistake Developers Make During a Pitch Meeting

What is the biggest mistake many developers make during pitch meetings? Talking about how good the game is going to be, to the exclusion everything else. Liew tells me this is a common mistake, with developers insisting, in the face of his skeptical questions, "Yeah, but the game is going to be awesome... that's why it's definitely going to work."

The hard user data shows that this prediction is almost always wrong. Instead, show Liew the data. He makes a point that may be hard for developers to swallow: "Game design is not predictive... user engagement is predictive."

Instead, Liew generally looks for games with good user retention, over a second-day, seventh-day, and 30-day period. Monetization rates are also important, but can greatly vary, based on the type of game and its monetization strategy. He cites the example of an iOS company that produces extremely casual games/entertainment apps with little replay value, but that attract tens of millions of free installs. Because the apps are produced for extremely low budgets, it's sufficient that only a small percent of users spend money on upgrades and other freemium payments.

Liew's Closing Advice for Developers

Here is Liew's closing advice:

- ▶ Instead of launching late, launch in another market.
- ▶ Find new niches; revive old genres.

Let's discuss the first item. A common mistake developers make, says Liew, is waiting too long to launch the game, in the hopes it can be perfect when it comes to market. Instead, he says, "You gotta start getting user feedback as soon as possible." One way of doing this is launching the game in a smaller market—for instance, the Philippines, which is English-fluent (and thus doesn't require localization) and has an audience that is fairly predictive of a game's chances in the broader markets. This strategy helps the developer make changes and fixes as needed, before going to the "big leagues."

Also, rather than compete directly with a platform's major developers, find new niches. Liew advises, "Try to find a genre or an audience or a style that hasn't been exploited." By way of example, he cites the rise of old genres that have been repackaged for the digital age: Zynga's Words with Friends is a variation of Scrabble, whereas "hidden object games," long popular in many mediums (including books and board game puzzles), are currently enjoying a renaissance on Facebook. Following the principle of "everything old is new again," consider the vast library of existing games for previously popular game types that are in need of being re-born to a new era.

UNDERSTANDING BEST PRACTICES OF CROWDFUNDED GAMES, PART I: OVERVIEW AND GENERAL ADVICE

As of Summer 2012, about $30 million out of a total $230 million in pledges to Kickstarter, the leading crowdfunder service, have been made to video game-related projects (see

Figure 15-3.) There have been more than 1.5 million unique pledges to all Kickstarter projects (some individuals pledge more than once), with more than 200,000 distinct pledges going to game-related projects.

FIGURE 15-3: Double Fine's successful crowdfunder on Kickstarter.

Far more people, it's worth noting, have considered *making* pledges to Kickstarter projects. According to Compete, Kickstarter gets about one million unique visitors per month. Earlier this year, the company added social network features (connections, messaging, and so on) to Kickstarter, which will probably grow the site's user base.

Although every Kickstarter campaign is different, some basic guidelines (shared with me by an insider) generally apply to all of them.

Be Clear, Be Compelling, Be Concise—Be Video

The first best practice is to hone your project into a story that establishes the premise of your project, the journey and struggle you've made to develop it, and what you need to complete it. (This ends the story on a cliffhanger and makes Kickstarter users the hero of the story who ride in to help save the day.) Clearly articulate what you're trying to accomplish and package your presentation in a compelling way. This almost certainly means video—nearly all successful Kickstarter projects include a video.

▶ Many videogame-related Kickstarters have offered the pledger a chance to name the game's villain or a hero.

Create a Common Sense and Communal Reward Structure

Pledge rewards should be fairly priced and have a logical and consistent structure, so that it's clear how pledging more money will lead to better rewards. They should also narrow the gap between creator and fan. For example, a reward could provide the

209

Understanding Best Practices of Crowdfunded Games, Part II: Advice from Adrian Hon, Developer of ZOMBIES RUN!

pledger exclusive access to the developers' behind-the-scenes process, or the chance to be listed as a patron on the completed work. At the same time, even if you need a lot of money, you still need to provide a good value in exchange for backing—keep in mind consumer price points and what would be a fair retail cost if the pledger went into the store to buy a similar item. (For instance, a sensible reward at $20 could be a custom T-shirt... not a ballpoint pen.)

Promote, Share, and Be Transparent

Don't be shy about getting word of your Kickstarter out to inspire your network to promote it to their network ("Please share/retweet!"). Once your project is funded, remember that this is just the beginning of the process. It's best to share your progress, because the people who pledge like to follow the project's development. Be sure to provide regular updates to your pledgers.

The project will probably evolve along the way, so update pledgers on these changes as often as possible, too. This is doubly true if something is blocking the project's progress: be transparent with your backers about any delays.

> ► Remember that the Kickstarter process is about much more than funding: It's about building an audience, engaging them, and making them part of the process.

UNDERSTANDING BEST PRACTICES OF CROWDFUNDED GAMES, PART II: ADVICE FROM ADRIAN HON, DEVELOPER OF ZOMBIES RUN!

ZOMBIES, RUN! is an indie game project for iOS and Android that successfully used Kickstarter to raise nearly $75,000 from 3,464 backers, well above a target goal of $12,500 (see Figure 15-4).

FIGURE 15-4: Concept art featured on ZOMBIES, RUN! Kickstarter page.

A highly original and innovative game, ZOMBIES, RUN! uses the smartphone's stereo sound capability to create an immersive, post-apocalyptic world depicted with sound effects, music, and dialogue, while the phone's location-aware capability tracks the distance a player runs and incorporates it into the game's map.

By the time this book hits the shelf, co-creator Adrian Hon tells me, the Android version should be out, along with starter content, "plus a whole new website that will sync player's data online and make the game much more social. So, quite a lot!"

Notably, Hon and his co-developer Naomi Alderman raised this funding without advertising or paid PR. They sent a few e-mails and tweets to get the Kickstarter rolling. "The rest was done by the community."

How? Hon explains in the next section.

The Secrets to ZOMBIES, RUN!'s Success: Clear Explanation, Good Presentation, and Rewards

"There are a few things you need to get right if you want to have any chance of success," says Hon:

- ▶ A video showing as much of the gameplay or intended experience as possible.

- ▶ A clear, concise project description that shows why the game is genuinely unique and deserving of funding, with good graphics and photography.

- ▶ Well-structured reward tiers that offer something good for $10, something better for $20, and physical goods for $40+, plus some super-tiers for the very keen people at $200 and above.

"That'll get you pretty far," says Hon, "But then you still need a good idea, ideally one that can be summarized in a single tweet, and 'An iPhone game where you run away from zombies in the real world' is pretty simple—and I think that's what made it go really viral."

Be Careful with Physical Rewards

"We were a little optimistic on how quickly we could ship the physical rewards," Hon tells me. "If you haven't printed, packed, and shipped hundreds of T-shirts and posters internationally before, well, it's not a picnic and can easily consume a lot of time and money." See Figure 15-5.

"I've actually sold posters online before, and this was still more complicated than I thought. It would have been better to promise them coming a couple of months later, so we weren't trying to do too many things at once."

The T-Shirt!

FIGURE 15-5: T-Shirt rewards for ZOMBIES, RUN!

For New Developers: A Truly New Idea and a Playable Demo

Hon has an established game company, Six to Start, and co-creator Alderman is a seasoned writer for Perplex City and other relatively well-known games. Their experience probably made it easier for them to raise funds. For those without a professional track record, Hon has this advice:

"[I]t's crucial to wait until you have the right idea—the one that you *all* think is fantastic and you can't wait to get started on. If you aren't well-known, it's also very useful to have a unique idea and an alpha that you can show off, to demonstrate that you're serious."

SUMMARY

Here are the key points we covered in this chapter:

▶ Venture capital funding can generate a lot of capital for game development, but at the cost of developers losing some control of their product. Crowdfunding is also a viable option, but usually raises small amounts, and the market for crowdfunders may soon reach a saturation point.

▶ VC Nabeel Hyatt commented on what developers should know, when pitching to him: day one retention is the most important metric (aim for 60 percent), and good developers know why their game is working. A game should create a long-term aspiration for its players, and a good developer should know his or her strengths and weaknesses, and be able to state them to a VC.

▶ VC Jeremy Liew discussed what developers should know, when pitching to him: developers worth funding have the ability to make several hits, and a strategy of discoverability, so their games are easy to find. Game design is not predictive, compared to user engagement. Instead of launching late in the U.S. market, launch early in another market. And instead of competing with the game developer giants, find a niche genre and audience that hasn't been sufficiently entertained on Facebook, the Web, and iOS. Old genres often have the chance to enjoy a second life on new platforms.

▶ To increase the chance you'll have a successful crowdfunder for your game, be clear, compelling, and concise about the game you intend to make— and shoot your pitch on video. Create a common-sense reward structure for pledgers, and be transparent and shameless in your promotion of the crowdfunder.

▶ When running a crowdfunder, it's best to have a good, easy-to-understand pitch. In your Kickstarter video, include as much gameplay footage as possible, but avoid giving out physical item pledge rewards. If you're a new developer, consider showing off as much gameplay as possible, to prove how serious you are.

Part VI

GAME DESIGN DOCUMENTS AND FINAL THOUGHTS

CHAPTER 16

Game Design Documents: Tiger Style's Spider and Waking Mars

IN THIS CHAPTER

▶ Excerpts from Spider's Design Document
▶ Excerpts from Waking Mars's Design Document

Randy Smith, co-founder of Tiger Style, shared his game development strategy in Chapter 13, "iOS Game Developer Profile: Tiger Style and Hatch." In this chapter, I'm very grateful that he's also offered to share selected excerpts from the game design documents for Tiger Style's first acclaimed hit, Spider: The Secret of Bryce Manor, and the studio's latest, equally well-received hit, Waking Mars. (I highly recommend downloading and playing both games before reading further!)

Although both games were developed for the iOS, the basic design concepts that Smith explains in this section apply to games on the web and Facebook as well. This is particularly true when (as he explained in Chapter 13) the team is working remotely and needs a clear point of reference to maintain the game's overall vision.

EXCERPTS FROM SPIDER: THE SECRET OF BRYCE MANOR

"This document [see Figure 16-1] is the 'treatment' of a brainstormed game concept," says Smith. "Its purpose was to develop a one-sentence idea into a potential game design that everyone could envision. This was written quickly, as we were considering several concepts simultaneously.

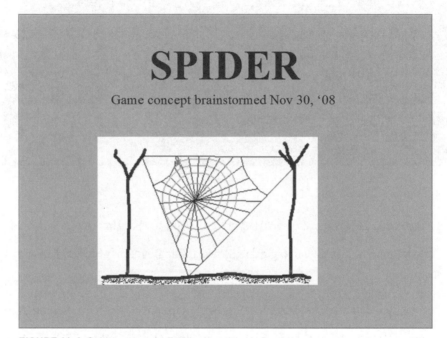

FIGURE 16-1: Spider game design document

"It's important that you be able to boil the essence of your game down to a small number of very succinct bullet points." (See Figure 16-2.) "This helps you identify what is most important so you can focus on it to the exclusion of potential distractions and embellishments.

"In this case, we already see right away that this document describes a different version of Spider than what we shipped." (See Figure 16-3.) "We started with this concept but let the software speak to us once digital prototyping began, evolving it into a more accessible, casual game. There was never any need to redo this documentation, but if I had, the second bullet would probably say something about the core 'action drawing' mechanic and the third would reference the environmental storytelling that quietly invites players into the mystery of an abandoned mansion.

Focals

- Live the life of a spider: walk on walls and ceilings, catch and eat bugs, and pick the best place to build your web

- Unique web-building mechanic lets you craft your custom web step by step

- Eat your way to greater strength and obtain your goals to progress through the story

FIGURE 16-2: Gameplay focus of Spider

Summary

Spider is a 2D, side-scrolling action/simulation game where the player takes on the role of a spider. The player moves around a cut-away 2D view of an "open world" (really just 1-3 levels which represent rooms of a house or barn) by walking on walls and ceilings or using webs for shortcuts. Once they find a suitable location, the player can use a cool, gravity-defying, touch- and tilt-based mechanic to design their own web by building it one thread at a time. The world is populated only by insects and you, so the next step is waiting or better yet actively luring insects into your web. Get up close and personal to suck the life out of your prey, which replenishes your resources and grows your size. Different types of insects have different behaviors and movements, which means you'll have to build different webs in different places to catch them. It's not hard to maintain a baseline level of survival, but you have to prove your capabilities to grow larger, progress through the story, and win.

Story – you weren't always a spider. One day you were in the wrong place at the wrong time and become the victim of a horrible curse. Um... let's say you were making a good faith house call to a reclusive neighbor rumored to be a witch. Now you're a spider, and once you figure out how to survive, you can start figuring out how to get yourself out of this mess and maybe even exact your revenge.

Game design focals:
- Use the abilities of a spider: walk on walls, eat insects, build webs, live it up.
- Express yourself with your web design: make a crazy web, make the most realistic web, make one that says "some pig" etc..
- Gaming the system in terms of web design, placement, resource management, and other mechanics to obtain insects (or equivalent goals), grow in strength, and progress through the story

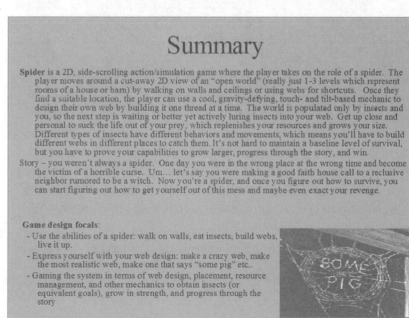

FIGURE 16-3: Spider game summary

"On this slide [Figure 16-4] I'm attempting to establish the tone that informed Spider: hip and realistic, not cartoony and goofy. In the end, we abandoned photo-real for an Edward Gorey–inspired illustrated art direction, but the tone set forth in this slide still helped to distinguish Spider."

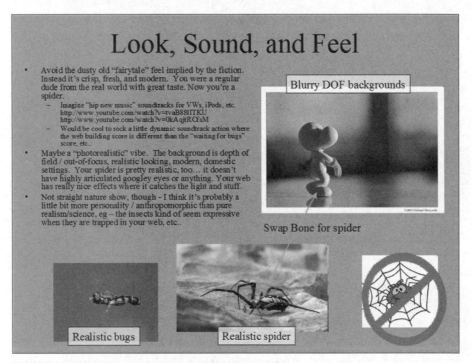

FIGURE 16-4: Gameplay look and feel of Spider

"[Figures 16-5 and 16-6] describe a way to walk by tilting the device. The idea was to be as native to the iPhone's capabilities as possible. During prototyping, we abandoned this because it was disruptive to play in a way we couldn't design around to our satisfaction. Instead we developed the 'touch to walk' control, which was more playable and equally native. (Two of four slides from the document are featured in Figures 16-5 and 16-6.)

"This describes a mechanic for building a web one thread at a time." (See Figures 16-7 to 16-10.)

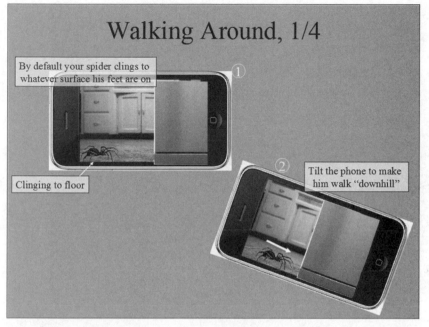

FIGURE 16-5: Initial design for Spider user interface

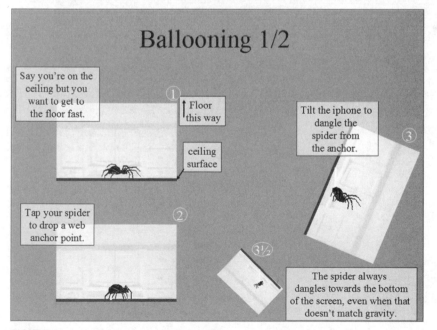

FIGURE 16-6: Initial design for Spider user interface, continued

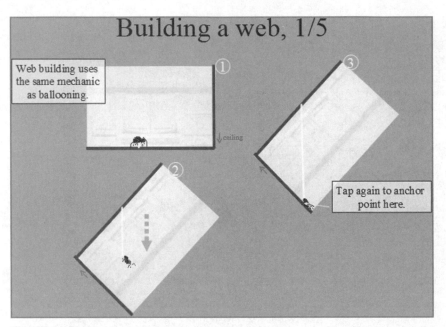

FIGURE 16-7: Initial design for web building

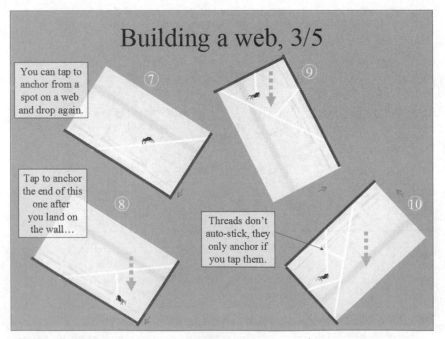

FIGURE 16-8: Initial design for web building, continued

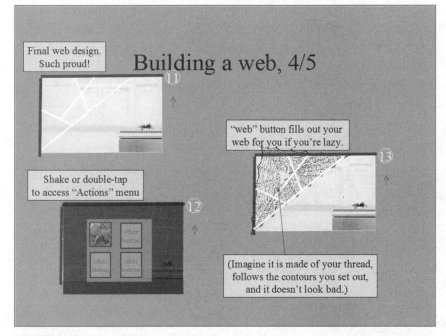

FIGURE 16-9: Initial design for web building, continued

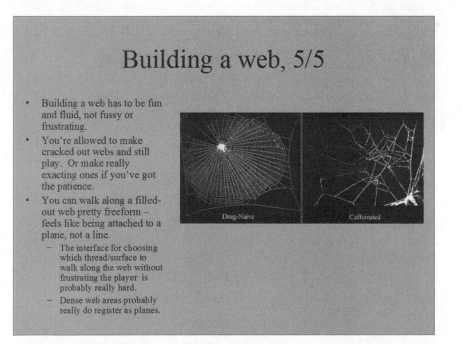

FIGURE 16-10: Initial design for web building, continued

"The original version of the game was a 'spider simulator,' where you would also wait patiently for bugs to fly into your webs. Most of these slides were replaced by the 'swipe to jump' mechanic, which was central to Spider's action drawing. However, even in this document you can see the seeds of the 'tap to anchor' and 'webs fill in automatically' mechanics, which evolved into the faster, more immediate web-building we shipped."

The next four images (see Figures 16-11 to 16-14) from Spider's design document cover the insect-catching mechanic.

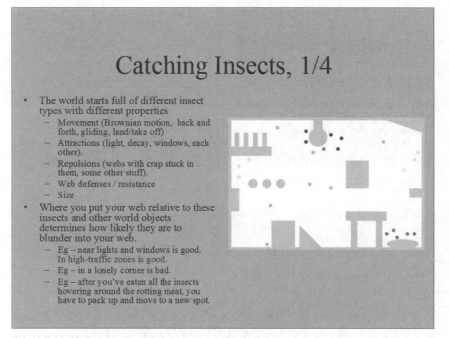

FIGURE 16-11: Design for insect-catching in Spider

"Eating bugs was originally planned to be pretty grody and personal in a Nickelodeon/fifth grade boy/gross-out way, but we were always skeptical of this idea, both for its fringe appeal and its modal interruption of play flow, so in the end we went with something very simple and abstract. There are a few more brainstorms on [Figure 16-15] about using the vibration to signal that a bug is in your web or spinning your finger on the screen to spin bugs into cocoons, but many of these wound up being cut because they were peripheral to the central experience."

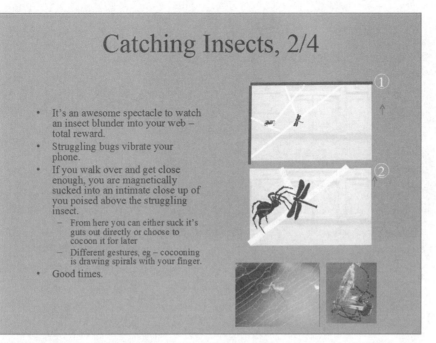

Catching Insects, 2/4

- It's an awesome spectacle to watch an insect blunder into your web – total reward.
- Struggling bugs vibrate your phone.
- If you walk over and get close enough, you are magnetically sucked into an intimate close up of you poised above the struggling insect.
  - From here you can either suck it's guts out directly or choose to cocoon it for later
  - Different gestures, eg – cocooning is drawing spirals with your finger.
- Good times.

FIGURE 16-12: Design for insect catching in Spider, continued

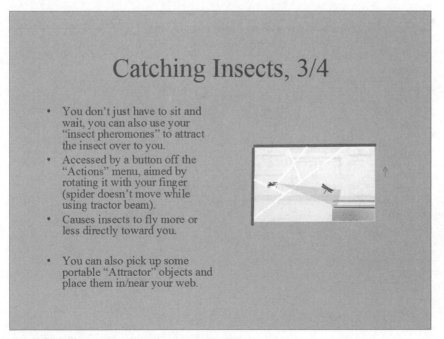

Catching Insects, 3/4

- You don't just have to sit and wait, you can also use your "insect pheromones" to attract the insect over to you.
- Accessed by a button off the "Actions" menu, aimed by rotating it with your finger (spider doesn't move while using tractor beam).
- Causes insects to fly more or less directly toward you.

- You can also pick up some portable "Attractor" objects and place them in/near your web.

FIGURE 16-13: Design for insect catching in Spider, continued

Catching Insects, 4/4

- Rules about whether an insect gets stuck in your web or flies through without touching it.   These rules exist:
  - To avoid degenerate web design (eg – one line from floor to ceiling) – your webs need to have density or most insects won't get caught.
  - To map different expressions of web design onto catching different insects. Not sure exactly how to do this – average distance between threads? Parallelism of threads? Overall shape/size? Length of spine threads?
- If a large insect winds up in your web and you're a small spider, there is a time limit before it rips itself out, which damages the web.

- Sometimes random crap like leaves falls into the web, which repel insects (they see the web). You can walk over to the crap and attach to it. The insect-killing view in this case maps onto cleaning the crap out of the web.

- Some environmental affordances, eg – you can do things that open windows or turn on/off lights, thereby changing the parameters of insect behavior.

- You can maybe build a web, then stop playing and log on later to see what landed in your web. Ie – time passes while you're not playing.

FIGURE 16-14: Design for insect catching in Spider, continued

Web Resource

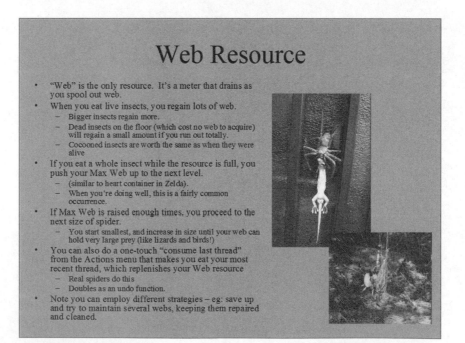

- "Web" is the only resource. It's a meter that drains as you spool out web.
- When you eat live insects, you regain lots of web.
  - Bigger insects regain more.
  - Dead insects on the floor (which cost no web to acquire) will regain a small amount if you run out totally.
  - Cocooned insects are worth the same as when they were alive
- If you eat a whole insect while the resource is full, you push your Max Web up to the next level.
  - (similar to heart container in Zelda).
  - When you're doing well, this is a fairly common occurrence.
- If Max Web is raised enough times, you proceed to the next size of spider.
  - You start smallest, and increase in size until your web can hold very large prey (like lizards and birds!)
- You can also do a one-touch "consume last thread" from the Actions menu that makes you eat your most recent thread, which replenishes your Web resource
  - Real spiders do this
  - Doubles as an undo function.
- Note you can employ different strategies – eg: save up and try to maintain several webs, keeping them repaired and cleaned.

FIGURE 16-15: Design for resource generation related to insect capture

Figure 16-15 includes "[s]ome speculation about more granular game design issues, such as resources and capture mechanics," says Smith. "We provided some suggestions but left the prototyping process to answer them definitively, which is appropriate."

The next four images (see Figures 16-16 to 16-19) from Spider's design document consider the market and franchise potential of the game.

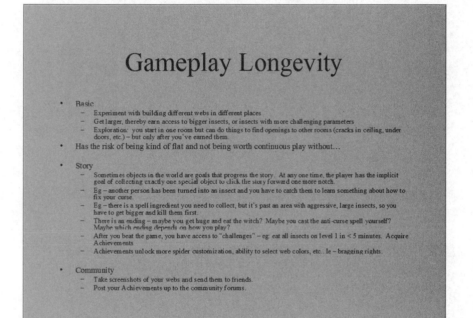

FIGURE 16-16: Market and franchise considerations for Spider

"Here we're thinking explicitly about Spider's potential as a commercial product. What makes players come back to it, or tell their friends about it? Can we build a larger IP out of it? Is there anything else like it already in the App Store? Does the demographic want it? The details mostly changed, but pushing these topics in our documentation made them active throughout development."

These slides illustrate how Spider evolved from its original conception to its execution, with extraneous or unfeasible elements discarded along the way, while the developers adhered to the core concept. In Waking Mars' design document you'll see a similar process.

iPhone Demographic Speculation

- The powers of a spider are pretty interesting – building webs, clinging to walls, cool.

- But spiders are creepy! People are put off by them. And does anyone really want to eat insects? Gross!

- Not sure if this skews old/young, male/female?

- Worth noting that as described (with rotating/accelerometer, especially) this game could only exist on the iphone. Adds appeal?

FIGURE 16-17: Market and franchise considerations for Spider, continued

IP Opportunities

- The story can be a new IP or attached to a Universe that several of our company's games are set in.
  - Eg – if we made a wizard apprentice game, then the witch could be a character in that.

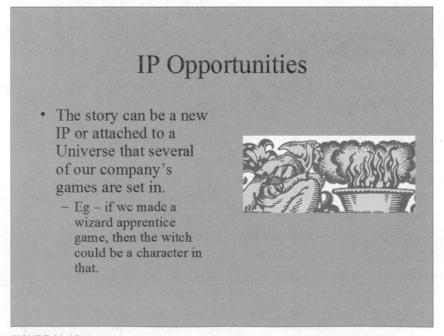

FIGURE 16-18: Market and franchise considerations for Spider, continued

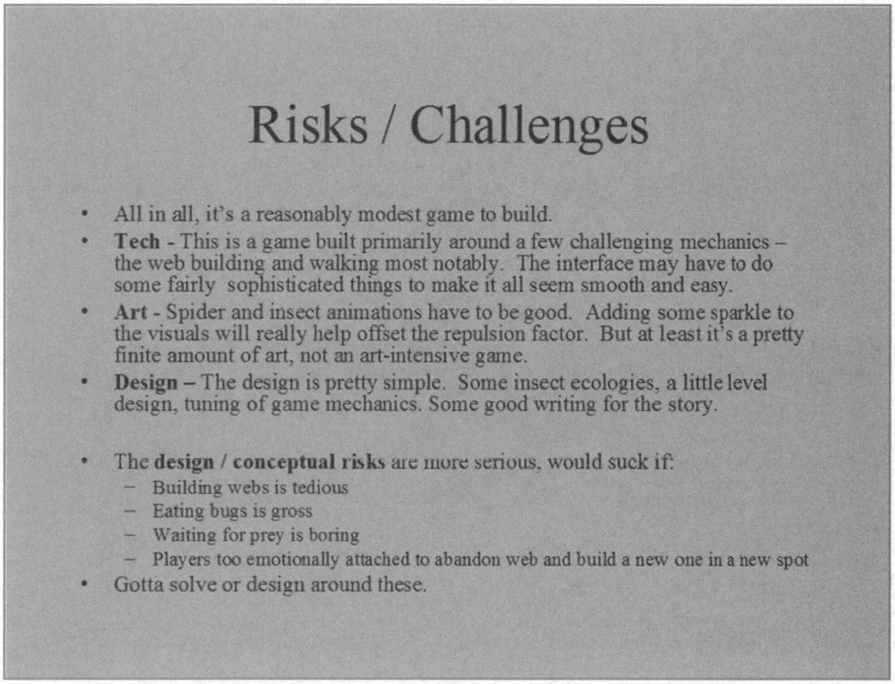

Risks / Challenges

- All in all, it's a reasonably modest game to build.
- **Tech** - This is a game built primarily around a few challenging mechanics – the web building and walking most notably. The interface may have to do some fairly sophisticated things to make it all seem smooth and easy.
- **Art** - Spider and insect animations have to be good. Adding some sparkle to the visuals will really help offset the repulsion factor. But at least it's a pretty finite amount of art, not an art-intensive game.
- **Design** – The design is pretty simple. Some insect ecologies, a little level design, tuning of game mechanics. Some good writing for the story.

- The **design / conceptual risks** are more serious, would suck if:
  - Building webs is tedious
  - Eating bugs is gross
  - Waiting for prey is boring
  - Players too emotionally attached to abandon web and build a new one in a new spot
- Gotta solve or design around these.

FIGURE 16-19: Market and franchise considerations for Spider, continued

EXCERPTS FROM THE WAKING MARS DESIGN DOCUMENTS

Randy Smith of Tiger Style next explains the studio's design document for Waking Mars. "This document sets out the highest level direction for Waking Mars. Similar to the Spider concept document, it describes the focals of the project and goes into each with some additional depth and explanation. [See Figures 16-20 and 16-21.]

"It has a 'pitch' that in this case is an evocative summary of the high-level story (which is actually somewhat different than what we shipped)." (See Figures 16-22 through 16-24 in the next section.)

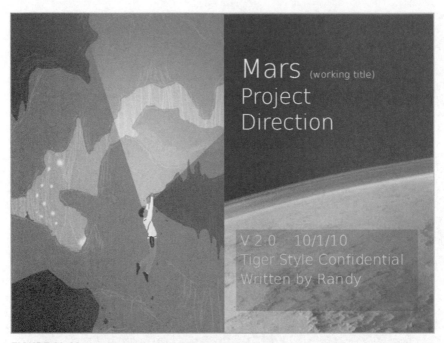

FIGURE 16-20: Waking Mars overall direction design doc

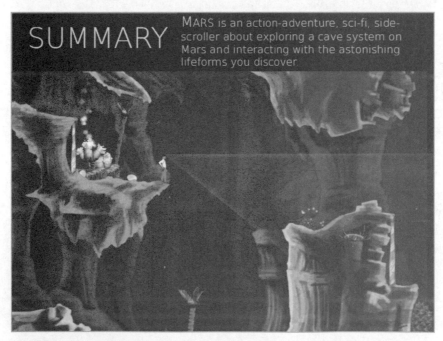

FIGURE 16-21: Waking Mars overall direction design doc, continued

Waking Mars Story Premise (from the Original Design Doc)

From the original design doc:

> *In 2093, the colonization of Mars is just beginning. Several expeditions around the planet are tasked with inspecting sites of scientific interest. You are a member of such a team investigating one of the many lava tube caves. This cave happens to be along the slope of Valles Marineris. An unexpected dust storm causes a horrible accident. The outpost is destroyed and you are the sole survivor. You are forced into the cave system to survive the disaster.*

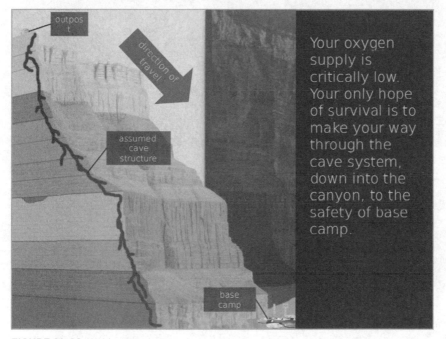

FIGURE 16-22: Waking Mars gameplay summary

"[About] 'Cave Diving On Mars,' [see Figure 16-25] the original version of the game focused on ground movement such as spelunking, jumping, and rock climbing." (See Figure 16-25.)

"We ultimately eliminated the cave-diving focal in favor of the simpler jet-packing movement model in order to put the emphasis on the ecosystem and its interactions." (See Figures 16-26 to 16-31.)

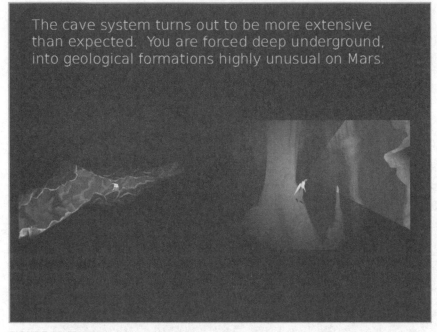

FIGURE 16-23: Waking Mars gameplay summary, continued

FIGURE 16-24: Waking Mars gameplay summary, continued

FIGURE 16-25: Waking Mars design focus points

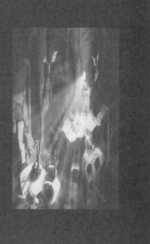

FIGURE 16-26: Waking Mars design focus points, continued

FIGURE 16-27: Waking Mars design focus points, continued

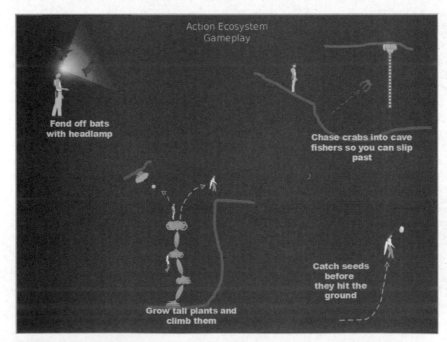

FIGURE 16-28: Waking Mars design focus points, continued

Action Ecosystem
Gameplay
Throw rocks to dislodge explosive seeds
Daring raids on bat nests
Use headlamp to grow plants in custom shapes
Toss food to distract crabs

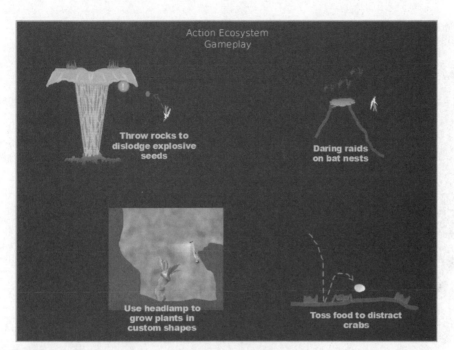

FIGURE 16-29: Waking Mars design focus points, continued

FOCAL #3
Story of Discovering Life on Mars
Play an adventuring scientist who unearths gradually unfolding discoveries of utmost historical importance:
Conditions for Life
Lifeforms
A Thriving Ecosystem
Extraterrestrial Sentience
Lightweight adventure / research gameplay with a serious, immersive, NASA-esque tone
Dynamic moments of "first contact" with a variety of creatures
Reawaken a long-dormant ecosystem
Unlock the purpose of a complex created by an ancient civilization
Different conclusions depending on how much mystery you solve and what actions you take

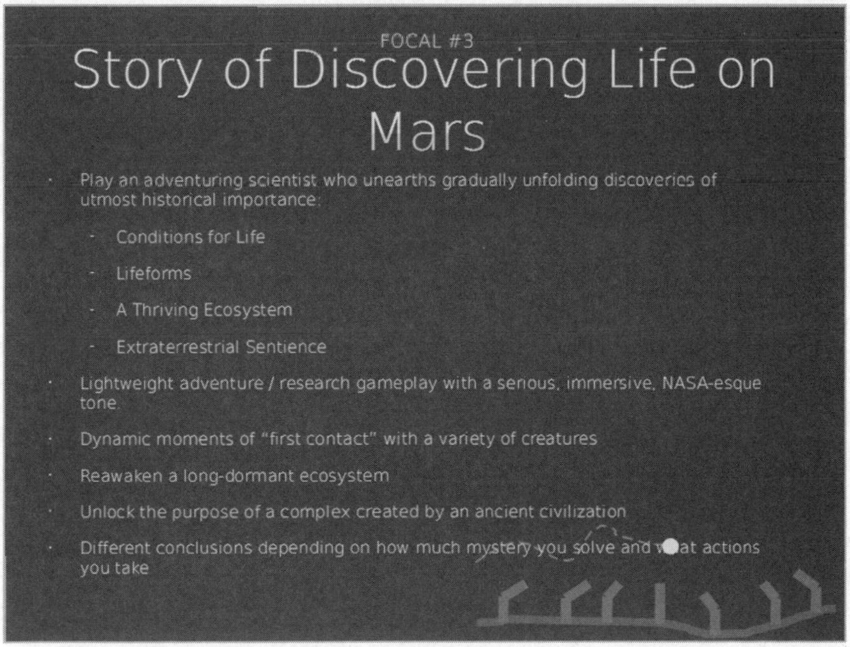

FIGURE 16-30: Waking Mars design focus points, continued

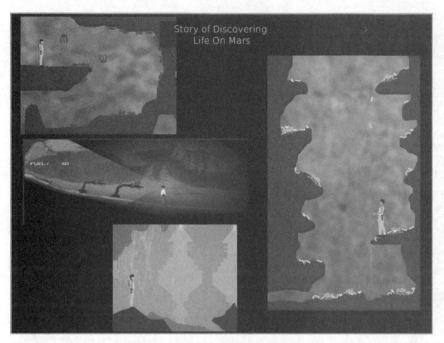

FIGURE 16-31: Waking Mars design focus points, continued

"For instance, it wasn't as fun to climb to the top of a cliff just to toss seeds to feed creatures. It was faster and more immediate to be able to jet-pack up there instantly, which meant you could perform more ecosystem actions more quickly without worrying about falling to your death.

"[Many slides refer] to the headlamp, which was a major player tool for many months of iteration. Similar to the cave-diving mechanics, we eventually cut this to keep the emphasis of the game in the right place and to keep the controls simple. However, we held onto it for a long time, so lots of our documentation attempts to describe ways to make the tool valuable as a central aspect of gameplay—growing plants with light, or repelling flying creatures, and so forth."

The next slides from this Waking Mars Design document (see Figures 16-32 to 16-36) depict the gameplay throughout the course of the game and the intended feel of the core game mechanic (see Figure 16-36, "Action Gardening").

FIGURE 16-32: Waking Mars gameplay description

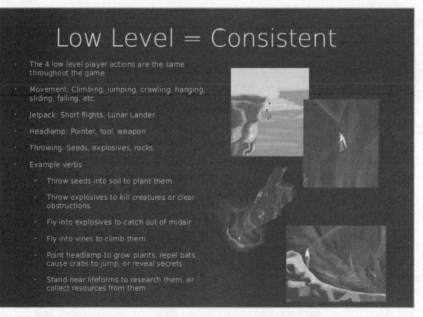

FIGURE 16-33: Waking Mars gameplay description, continued

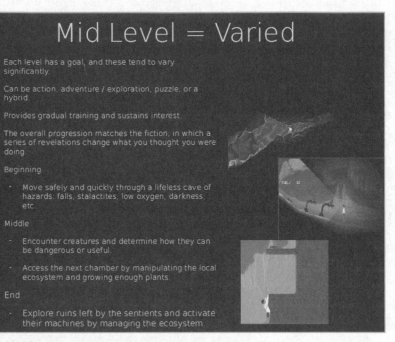

Mid Level = Varied

- Each level has a goal, and these tend to vary significantly.

- Can be action, adventure / exploration, puzzle, or a hybrid.

- Provides gradual training and sustains interest.

- The overall progression matches the fiction, in which a series of revelations change what you thought you were doing.

- Beginning

  - Move safely and quickly through a lifeless cave of hazards: falls, stalactites, low oxygen, darkness, etc.

- Middle

  - Encounter creatures and determine how they can be dangerous or useful.

  - Access the next chamber by manipulating the local ecosystem and growing enough plants.

- End

  - Explore ruins left by the sentients and activate their machines by managing the ecosystem.

FIGURE 16-34: Waking Mars gameplay description, continued

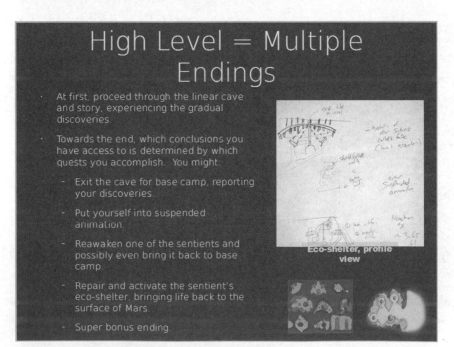

High Level = Multiple Endings

- At first, proceed through the linear cave and story, experiencing the gradual discoveries.

- Towards the end, which conclusions you have access to is determined by which quests you accomplish. You might:

  - Exit the cave for base camp, reporting your discoveries.

  - Put yourself into suspended animation.

  - Reawaken one of the sentients and possibly even bring it back to base camp.

  - Repair and activate the sentient's eco-shelter, bringing life back to the surface of Mars.

  - Super bonus ending.

Eco-shelter, profile view

FIGURE 16-35: Waking Mars gameplay description, continued

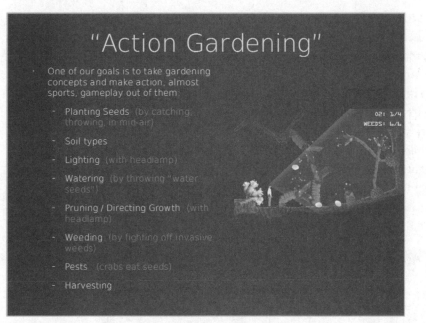

FIGURE 16-36: Waking Mars gameplay description, continued

Ecosystem Gameplay Design Notes

This section describes designs and brainstorms about the ecosystem interactions in Waking Mars, which were crucial tools for communicating and evolving ideas and theories about how to turn the words "action gardening" into fun gameplay (see Figure 16-37).

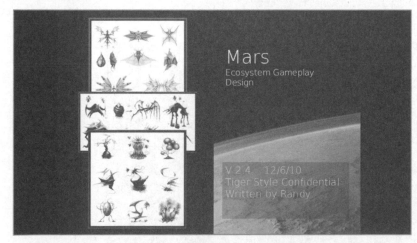

FIGURE 16-37: Waking Mars Ecosystem Gameplay Design doc

Figures 16-38 through 16-41 describe a few "mid-level gameplay" possibilities that attempt to answer the crucial questions, "Why are you growing plants?" and "Why does it matter where you choose to plant a particular seed?" Smith explains, "So for example, in Figure 16-41, you see that Light plants must be planted where they can shine on Oxygen plants, weeds must be planted where they can toss seeds back and forth to each other, and so on. This interaction encourages the player to think carefully about where to plant and then respond accordingly as conditions evolve. There is an alternative possibility expressed in Figure 16-40, a complicated (but thematically appropriate) mid-level system that measures various environmental conditions impacted by the life forms you've grown. Your goal would be to get each condition within target ranges by growing or destroying life forms, making sure you'd hit a minimum amount of biomass.

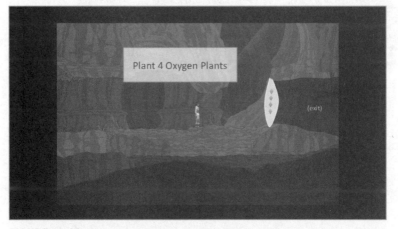

FIGURE 16-38: Mid-level gameplay ideas for Waking Mars

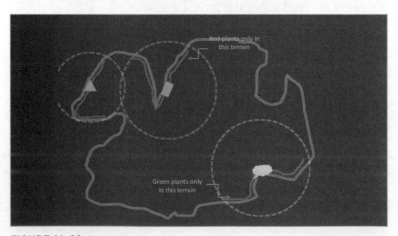

FIGURE 16-39: Plant life distribution in gameplay areas

FIGURE 16-40: Ideas for environmental conditions changed by player interaction

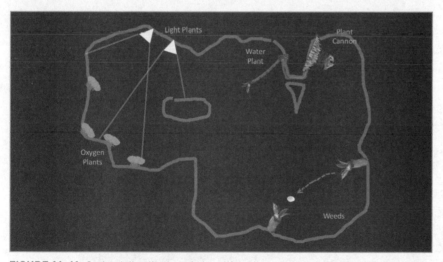

FIGURE 16-41: Optimal distribution of plant life to improve cavern biomass

"Interestingly, in the end, we went with something incredibly simple: The player's goal is simply to raise biomass high enough in each level," says Smith. "The mid-level complexity turned out to be a red herring for our project goals, driving the game more in a strategy/puzzle direction, when we really wanted an action game. Keeping the mid-level simple put all the emphasis back on the action gameplay and the ecosystem interactions between the life forms. The more life forms you create, the more dangerous or valuable the interactions in the world are, making Waking Mars a sort of 'design your own level, then survive it' game.

"Figure 16-42 shows a design for a complex life form we didn't ship. We had lots of ideas that didn't work.

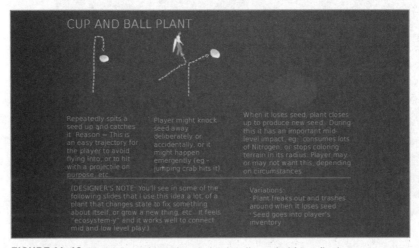

FIGURE 16-42: Idea for complex plant behavior discarded from final game

"Figure 16-43 describes 'bat nests' that wound up being the Cycot life form in the game that shipped. I like how this figure describes the mechanics in terms of what they are meant to accomplish, as opposed to a bunch of specifics that add up to the larger goal. It keeps the document clean and leaves room for the team to figure out whether and how to make it happen.

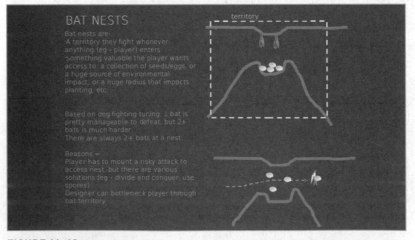

FIGURE 16-43: Smith's description of bat nest behavior for Waking Mars's development team.

"Another interesting observation is that we assumed players would want to raid bat nests to collect seeds, but in practice it's a more effective emergent strategy to feed Cycots as many seeds as possible so they will reproduce and increase biomass. In emergent systems, it can be very hard to predict how everything will come together, and in this case we felt the emergent strategy was appropriate to the game's themes, so we didn't attempt to return it to our original intentions.

"Figure 16-44 describes an interesting idea for a dangerous alien plant. Despite minor differences, we ultimately felt it was too similar to the cave fisher (known as Larians in the game we shipped) in terms of how it contributed to gameplay.

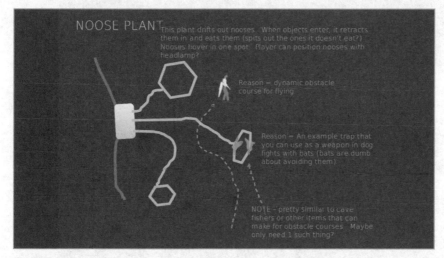

FIGURE 16-44: Discarded idea for dangerous plant in Waking Wars

"In Waking Mars, it was often a tough process to whittle our ideas down to the smallest set of life forms that would have very orthogonal features with respect to each other, creating the widest range of possible interactions without overwhelming the player with too much weird alien information to remember.

"Figures 16-45 and 16-50 show a very early design for the core mechanics describing how plants reproduce and the interactions between Water plants—Hydrons and Halid in the game that shipped.

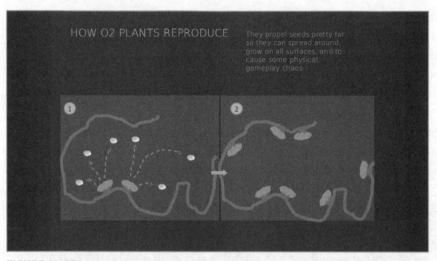

FIGURE 16-45: Initial design for Waking Mars plant reproduction

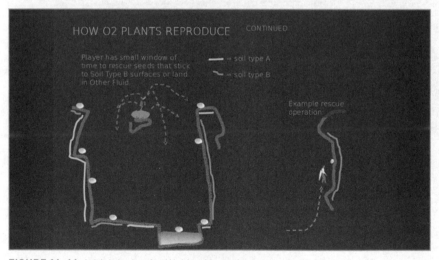

FIGURE 16-46: Initial design for Waking Mars plant reproduction, continued

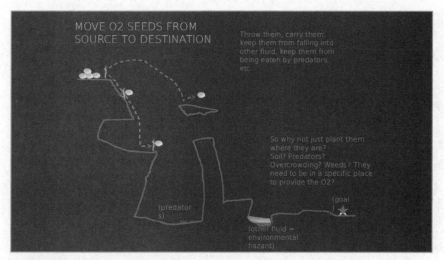

FIGURE 16-47: Oxygen plant behavior design

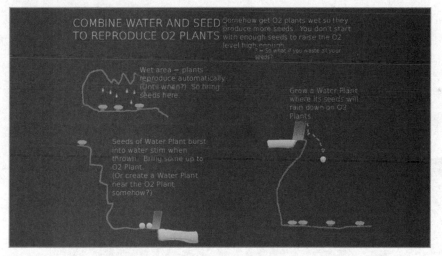

FIGURE 16-48: Design thoughts on player motivation for moving oxygen seeds

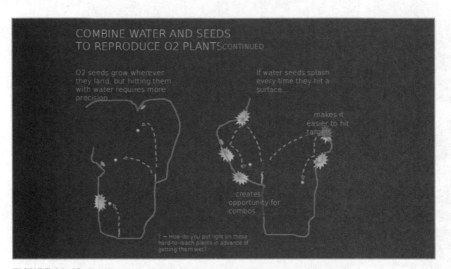

FIGURE 16-49: Design thoughts on player motivation for moving oxygen seeds, continued

"Interestingly, most of this shipped in the final game, which is rare for an early design document—specifically, the description of plants spitting seeds, which might land in good or bad locations, and the need for the player to jetpack effectively to catch seeds out of mid-air and throw seeds to target locations.

"This slide [see Figure 16-50] was written before we invented the idea of Fertile Terrain, so you can read our questions about why players don't just degenerately plant seeds wherever they happen to be standing.

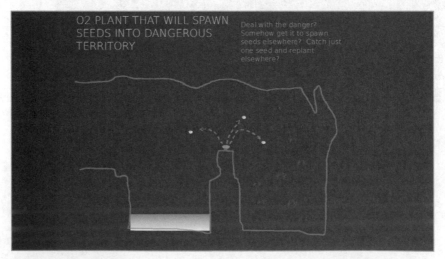

FIGURE 16-50: Planting seeds

"Each section of Waking Mars's ecosystem document kicks off with a high-level assessment of the vision and goals behind a given life form, such as the crab, known as Phyta in the game that shipped." (See Figures 16-51 and 16-52.)

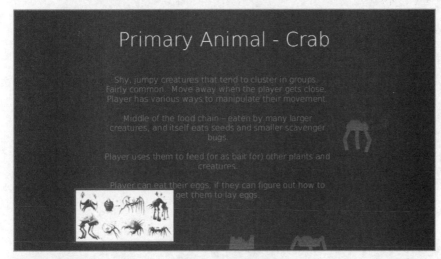

FIGURE 16-51: Design of Waking Mars's crab behavior

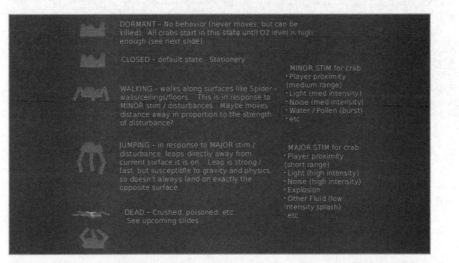

FIGURE 16-52: Crab behavior responses to stimuli

"A potential game moment we brainstormed very early on was the idea of encountering weird bumps on the cave walls, which later spring into life in a surprising way. A few incarnations of this idea were prototyped and discarded, but we kept the faith and ultimately shipped the experience in the Recovery level, where it was a big hit with our play testers." (See Figures 16-53 and 16-54.)

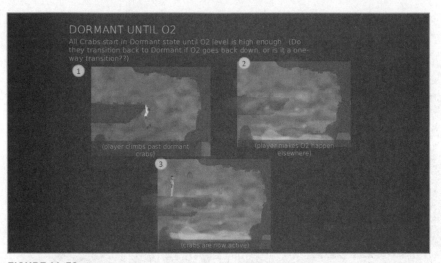

FIGURE 16-53: Crab behavior design in response to oxygen

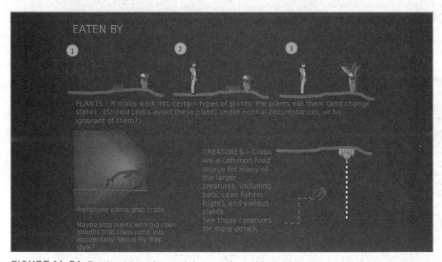

FIGURE 16-54: Design ideas for crab interaction with predators

Tone, Themes, Influences, and Inspiration

From the original design doc:

> Tiger Style's design document lays out the overall tone and theme of the game with the following descriptions, accompanied by stills from movies like Alien and Moon and photographs of the natural world.

TONE: SERIOUS, CREDIBLE, "HARD"

Fiction backed up by credible science, presented seriously enough so that players can become absorbed if they choose to.

INSPIRATION: REAL-WORLD MARS STUDY AND EXPLORATION

NASA. Human engineering versus the harsh environment of space. Speculation of the history of the planet based on observation. Childhood dream to be an astronaut.

TONE: UNEARTHLY

Rotation or distortion of concepts from Earth as though by some alien logic. Structural and logical, but the product of an unknowable mind. We want the player to feel unsettled, like this place has so many elements that are familiar, and yet nothing is ever quite as expected—e.g., music with unusual key or time signature changes, rock formations in shapes that would be impossible on Earth, creatures whose sounds are "creature-y" and yet not like anything from Earth.

INSPIRATION: THE EXOTIC, STARTLING DIVERSITY OF THE NATURAL WORLD

Every appearance, behavior, and cultural artifact in our game should be inspired by appreciation for some real-world phenomenon, not invented from scratch or contrived purely for gameplay. The crabs should move like crabs. The ecosystem has predators, prey, producers, and scavengers. The cave of giant crystals is like the one in Mexico.

THEME: ON THE BOUNDARY BETWEEN MULTIPLE INTERPRETATIONS

Players should have to look twice to figure out what they are seeing. It should be hard to categorize in Earth terms.

INFLUENCES: LEM AND HERZOG

[Author] Stanislaw Lem employs brutally hard science to speculate about the exotic natural phenomena of other planets and the unknowability of extraterrestrial life and culture. We want our life forms and sentients to be exotic, unknowable, and plausible. [Filmmaker] Werner Herzog unflinchingly observes the world with a uniquely emotional combination of disgust, love, fascination, confusion, and wonder...We don't have to shy away from the grotesque in what we portray, such as carrion bugs that eat corpses.

INFLUENCE: RED MARS

[Novelist] Kim Stanley Robinson did a ton of credible scientific research and well-informed speculation about human presence on the surface of Mars, covering the experiences of low gravity, dust storms, Martian seasons, cold temperatures, life in an outpost, underground aquifers, and more.

The first half, in particular, is a great read for anyone on the project.

THEME: FUSION OF TECHNOLOGY AND NATURE

The cave system was "engineered" by natural forces and "is powered by" the ecosystem that inhabits it. The sentients did not have technology here and nature there, instead combining them into something like future primitivism. The boundaries between technology, nature, and culture are blurred.

Waking Mars: The Higher Aspirations

The final selected slides from the Waking Mars design document lay out the developers' aspirations for the game—not only to create a commercially successful product, but also to express important ideas that elevate the game to a work of art. Maybe Tiger Style's aspirations will inspire similar aspirations in your own games. (See Figures 16-55 and 16-56.)

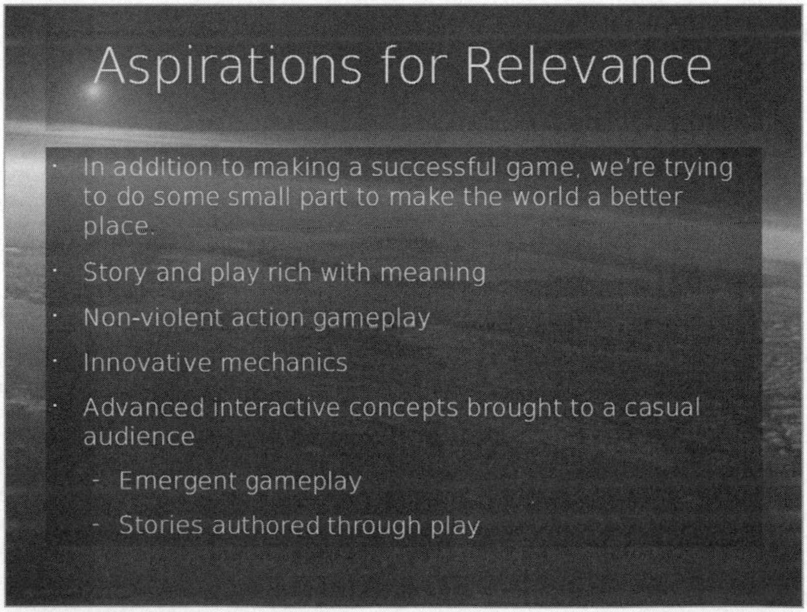

FIGURE 16-55: Waking Mars' higher aspirations

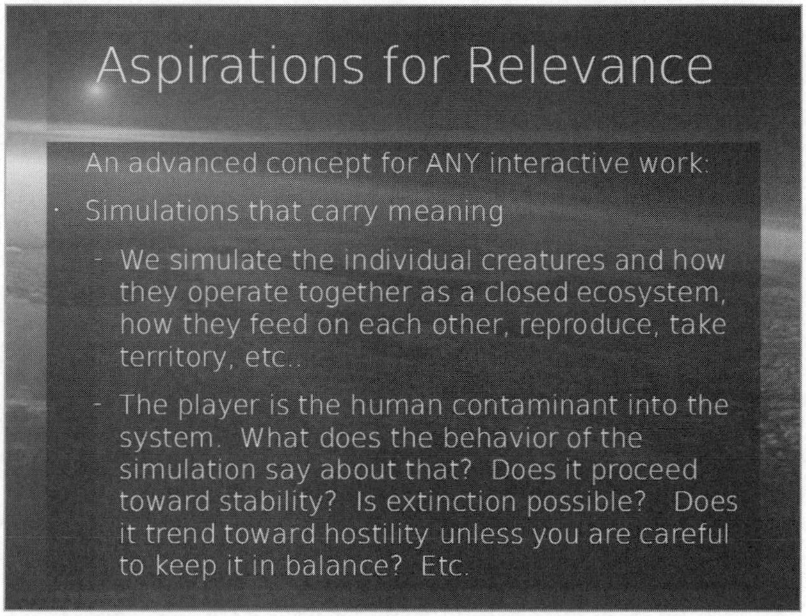

FIGURE 16-56: Waking Mars' higher aspirations, continued

SUMMARY

Here are the key points we covered in this chapter:

▸ Spider: The Secret of Bryce Manor began in its original design document with a number of features that were eventually abandoned to focus on the essence of the game—creating webs and capturing insects.

▸ The design document for Waking Mars includes everything from gameplay to story premise to artistic influences, and shows the evolution of its different gameplay features, including player interaction with the game world's complex, interconnected ecosystem and the game's signature "action gardening" mechanics.

CHAPTER 17

Concluding Thoughts Before You Start Designing

The game platforms covered in this book offer all kinds of opportunities for game designers, especially new or indie, low-budget developers. But because the market is so saturated with competition, they also give designers even more chances to fail or fall way short. However, most of the developers and experts I talked to for this book started small. Often, they had little prior experience working in the game industry or didn't even know how to write code for the games they wanted to design. But, with trial and error and persistence, they were able to turn their passion and talent into a full-fledged career of making games. In this chapter, they'll share some lessons they learned along the way—advice that'll inspire you to keep going and wisdom to help keep you focused on that ultimate goal.

LEARNING FROM LEADING DESIGNERS—LESSONS YOU'LL NEED WHEN YOU'RE READY TO DESIGN

I hope this book has answered a lot of your questions about the business side of game design on the world's three biggest platforms. But it occurs to me it hasn't answered the two most crucial questions:

> ▸ Why design games when the market is already so saturated?

> ▸ What's going to keep me going at night, when it seems like success is impossible?

These are queries worth pondering. Because as I think I've made clear, even if you were to follow all the advice in this book, the odds of succeeding are still against you. Even the few Facebook games that manage to attract millions of players can sometimes be classified as failures. Thousands of web games are played just a few hundred times, making their developers a few dollars at most. When hundreds of iOS game developers were asked how much money they made from their games, only 15 percent said they'd reached the six-figure range.

So why take the risks and keep pressing on?

Fortunately, the many developers I've talked with throughout this book have some answers, as do I. Their concluding thoughts, and mine, appear in the following sections.

Design Now Because Success Usually Comes from Unexpected Places

Nabeel Hyatt founded a social game company, sold it to Zynga, and went on to become a venture capitalist whose firm funded OMGPOP, a small New York studio that created a quirky and inventive game called Draw Something. As you might know, Draw Something unexpectedly became Facebook's most-played game in a matter of weeks.

Nabeel Hyatt says this about the observation that the market is oversaturated with games: "There have always been a lot of games." Even in the Atari and Playstation era. "It will always feel like an oversaturated, overstimulated environment. It should never stop you from action. It should raise the bar in terms of what you believe."

NOTE "The answer is not to run where nobody is; the answer is go at the place where everyone is and just raise the bar," says Nabeel Hyatt.

Instead, Nabeel Hyatt suggests that you think like this: "I'm standing on the shoulder of giants; I know what works and I want to add my voice to the industry. History bears out that breakout successes come when people start to think the market is tapped out…that's actually the right position when players are hungry for something new." When innovation is at a low point, he adds, "That's exactly the time to start building a company and go."

Design Now Because the Little Guys Still Have Special Market Advantages

Billy Pidgeon of M2 Research has built a long career analyzing the game business and keeping abreast of its many trends. "Although the free-to-play model has been around for a while and many publishers and developers have been experimenting with the business model," Pidgeon notes, "I think there is still huge potential for innovation."

> ▶ This means the little guy still has the edge in some respects.

"While it's true that some of that innovation will require big financial and technological investment beyond the reach of small developers and micro-publishers, small developers can and will try things that large publishers will not," says Pidgeon.

Small developers not only have an advantage, but also have lots of people looking to throw money their way. "Which is exactly why venture capitalists and big publishers are continuing to raise their level of investment in independent developers," says Pidgeon.

Speaking of the little guy, Pidgeon recommends leveraging platforms like Twitter, to get your game an audience: "Indies can and should market more cheaply and effectively with social media to increase word of mouth." And above all, expect to fail, and plan to come up short:

"Understand what worked in your previous games whether they failed or succeeded, and try using it in a new context next time," as Pidgeon puts it. "Also, the features and content you wanted to put into your game but didn't have the time or resources to do so can be used in your next game, or the one after.

"If you're not failing, you're probably not taking enough risks."

Design a Game You Love So Much, You Love Giving It Your All

Rob Winkler, CEO at 5th Planet, started his studio with no prior experience developing games, gave up a full scholarship at a top university to do so, devoted 60 hours a week on top of his day job to build the company's first game, and saw two founders quit along the way. Nevertheless, he persisted to release high-quality RPG games on

Facebook, like Legacy of a Thousand Suns, in the process turning 5th Planet into a profitable business boasting 32 employees. "Do something you're passionate about—it's easy to put in 100 hours a week when it's not really work," suggests Winkler.

Winkler's final piece of wisdom: "If you don't have a deep passion for what you're doing, it will probably fail."

Design with Originality in Mind, Because Imitation Is a Fool's Game

Phill Ryu's first iOS game, an innovative puzzle hybrid called Heist, earned just under $1 million in sales the first month it came out. Instead of churning out sequels or easy follow-ups, however, he spent some $250,000 and several years developing Hatch, an innovative virtual pet game he hopes will revolutionize the state of iOS gaming, and along the way, maybe teach players a little bit about themselves.

"The worst thing to do to yourself is get too cynical," says Ryu. "Don't focus too much on the crappy games that occasionally hit the lottery and have their brief day at the top of the charts. That's not a recipe for success, and if you try to emulate that as a strategy you will be throwing darts blindfolded from a mile away."

Design Even Though You Know You'll Have Setbacks as You Progress

The team at Jay Is Games turned a simple game-review blog for casual games into a go-to destination. It boasts millions of monthly visits and regularly turns obscure game developers into breakout stars. The team at Jay Is Games advises this:

"Most importantly—create, create, create! Just sit down and do it, and don't be afraid to fail. The road to success is always under construction, so expect to fall into a few potholes along the way."

Design Based on What's Worked Before, but Add Your Original Spin

Paul Preece was a Visual Basic programmer in Britain who taught himself Flash on the side. He made a web-based strategy game that was based on a popular level from World of Warcraft III, gave it some very clever twists, and wrapped it up in a style that gave it great casual appeal. After millions of people played Desktop Tower Defense, he realized the game "had changed my life." He's now co-founder of KIXEYE, a social game studio with yearly revenue approaching $100 million and a swank office in San Francisco.

Preece advises this: "Look to extend previous games. Go back to a game you enjoy playing. Not some AAA game but a nice game you liked playing, and say, 'What would I have liked to see in this game?' Start the process of re-inventing." Desktop Tower Defense, as you've learned, evolved in this way.

He continues, "Because every game is 70 percent what came before, you are going to borrow from other games. This is not a bad thing. This is something you should be doing. Then you only have to design that 30 percent, which is a good thing." Everything is a struggle in the beginning, but after the fifth game or so, he says, you'll be able to think about more innovation and risks. "You're basically going to dislike launching all of your games because you never get to that 100 percent marker, you never get to include everything you wanted. You're gonna get happier with them as you release more, and you'll get better at it."

Design Knowing that Great Games Will Find an Audience, Despite (and because of) Your Larger Competitors

Randy Smith began his career as a designer creating games for the PC, among them a groundbreaking masterpiece called Thief: The Dark Project, only to see Looking Glass, the studio of idealists who created it, abruptly closed down. He worked for a time with Steven Spielberg on a game project at Electronic Arts, only to see development on that canceled before it was released.

Now he develops his own iOS games for his own studio, Tiger Style, designing them with maximum artistic and financial control. "The distribution channels are definitely crowded with games, but even on iOS, I rarely discover something great that has gone completely overlooked," says Smith. "The overlooked games are mediocre or at best flawed. If your game is great, it will be found and people will tell each other about it. So put your emphasis into making a great game, and since it's very hard to know for sure, get outside perspectives on whether it's great yet or not."

Smith adds, "There's no substitute for play-testing. Don't be afraid to give up on ideas that aren't working. Maybe backtrack and try something else. Being invested in a bad idea won't help you, but ruthless self-editing will. Never confuse 'great' with 'huge,' either, especially when you're just starting out. We sliced Spider down to its barest essentials, the most focused version of that game possible, and threw out everything we felt was at all peripheral so we could put all our effort into nailing the core appeal. I have zero doubt this mentality was fundamental to Spider's success.

"Big, well-funded studios make polished and entertaining games, but they leave plenty of space for indies," says Smith. "My favorite games across all platforms right now are pretty evenly split between indies and mainstream. Indies are more likely to try riskier ideas and always have a sense of human personality that somehow gets scrubbed away in mainstream works. So don't be intimidated, there is room for you in this crowded market. It's been a genuine pleasure over the last several years to watch new studios spring up right out of college and elbow their way in alongside the big studios by virtue of great ideas and effective execution.

"My favorite advice to give everybody just starting out in games is to pursue the things you truly want to be doing for the rest of your career. First of all, you'll be more passionate and motivated, which means your work will be higher quality and you'll be happier every day," notes Smith. "Secondly, you'll develop your skills and over time become known as someone who does that kind of thing. The last thing you want is to pigeonhole yourself as a great Zynga cloner when you'd really rather be making innovative first-person simulations or something. So don't just take any opportunity that comes along; seek out or create the situations where you get to do what you love. I've had people thank me for this advice, and zero reports of regret so far. I feel very much like it got me where I am today."

Design because the Web, Facebook, and iOS Are Now the World's Best Platforms for Art and Creativity

I have been writing about and working on games for more than 10 years and was lucky to help develop projects that were revolutionary, if only for a while. Years before anyone was talking about alternate reality gaming, Electronic Arts' Majestic integrated voice-mail and satellite images into a multimedia experience. Years before anyone took virtual goods, avatars, and user-generated 3D content seriously, Linden Lab's Second Life stirred imaginations for several exciting years. But, for various reasons, both of these projects were ahead of their time.

It's no longer time to be ahead of your time. There is no better time to be creating games. When I started to write and develop games, tens of millions played them. Now hundreds of millions do. The platforms you've read about in this book have turned gaming into a truly mass-market medium, on a par with motion pictures. Moreover, all three platforms make it possible to build a business from your passion and develop with more freedom and opportunities to take risks than any other medium in the past. Even web games made with an intent to be serious, disturbing works of art can often find an audience in the millions—more than most works of literature or acclaimed indie movies. iOS games like Waking Mars, which gives you new ways to experience and think about the world, are finding a ready audience. Games like Hatch, which gives you new ways to think about ourselves, will likely do the same.

So the real question to ask yourself is this: Why would you want to miss the chance to develop games now, when there may never be a better time to do so?

I hope this book, dear designer, helps you answer that question for yourself. I can't wait to play your games.

SUMMARY

Here are the key points we covered in this chapter:

- ▶ Design now because success usually comes from unexpected places.

- ▶ The market has always been oversaturated with games. Big hits often come from unexpected places. Like your computer.

- ▶ Small iOS/Facebook/web developers have some special advantages over the big publishers (who often fund indie game designers for that very reason).

- ▶ It's better to design a game you love, because all the work you'll do to make it won't feel like work at all.

- ▶ It's better to design a game that's as original as possible, because imitations are risky and you probably won't love making them.

- ▶ When you do design games similar to those that have worked before, be sure to add your own spin.

- ▶ Be prepared to fail, because your first failed games are steps to ultimate success.

- ▶ Great games will eventually gain an audience, because they'll find passionate advocates.

- ▶ Games for the web, Facebook, and iOS now reach a larger audience than any before. Don't miss this chance to create for these platforms.

Part VII

APPENDIXES

Resources for Designers

This appendix contains some resources to take with you into your next stage of game design and development, starting with several resources that all developers can draw from, and then moving on to those for each particular platform.

WHERE TO GO NEXT: MY BLOG AND CONTACT INFO

nwn.blogs.com is the address of my blog, New World Notes, the first place I hope you visit after reading this book. This blog began when I was helping develop Second Life, the user-generated virtual world game platform, which I still write about (and occasionally develop in). I've since expanded the blog to cover user-generated gaming in general.

This is where you come in, game developer. Tell me about the iOS/web/Facebook games you're making, because I probably want to write about them and encourage my readers to play them. (After all, you bought my book, which pretty much proves how brilliant you are.) I also love writing about your crowd-funded game projects, because there's nothing cooler than a community of gamers coming together to help developers fund the games they're passionate about.

I'm also a part-time game developer (especially on the design, writing, and branding/marketing/business development side of things), so if you're interested in talking with me in that capacity, please contact me. In any case, I look forward to reading about your projects.

My e-mail address is wjamesau@gmail.com.

My Facebook account is Wagner James Au. (Feel free to friend!)

My Twitter account is @SLHamlet.

HOW TO CONTACT THE VENTURE CAPITALISTS INTERVIEWED IN THIS BOOK

In Chapter 15, "Is Your Game Ready to Get VC or Crowdsourced Funding?", I interviewed VCs with an impressive track record in backing iOS/web/Facebook game companies. Read what they say very carefully to decide if now is the right time to seek funding for your own studio. If you decide that's the case, you can contact them at the following addresses:

- ▶ Nabeel Hyatt, Spark Capital: nabeel@sparkcapital.com
- ▶ Jeremy Liew, Lightspeed Venture Partners: jeremy@lightspeedvp.com (Send him a two-page executive summary, ideally with user engagement and monetization data.)

GAME INDUSTRY ANALYSTS AND OTHER ONLINE RESOURCES

Billy Pidgeon of M2 Research (www.m2research.com) has been a game industry analyst for many, many years, and was also the technical editor for this book. If you gained any valuable insights from reading it, a significant part of the thanks goes to him. At M2, he tells me, "We do any-size consulting, and we can offer strategic and tactical advice based on global game industry research broken down by sector." Consider getting in touch with him: billy.pidgeon@gmail.com.

David Cole of DFC Intelligence (dcole@dfcint.com) was also a helpful resource for this book. He is another game analyst resource worth considering; see www.dfcint.com.

As the URL suggests, www.pixelprospector.com/indie-resources has a boatload of links and info for indie game developers.

Finally, I highly recommend The International Game Developers Association (www.igda.org) for its resources and community. IGDA is an organization that connects you with other developers, offers a health plan, and even curates Kickstarter funders for game developers; see www.igda.org/kickstarter.

REMOTE GAME DEVELOPER RESOURCES

Here are the resources Tiger Style founder Randy Smith recommends for developing games with a remote team:

"Tiger Style relies heavily on Google's suite of free services. We use Google Chat for video conferencing and often keep text windows open all day to stay in touch. We sometimes use Skype if we need a three-way (or more) video conference. Our company e-mail list goes through Google Groups and is an important part of our company culture, since it helps build a sense of team identity. We use Google Docs to store important files, such as task lists that need to be looked at and revised by many people frequently, and we also use Google Docs running alongside a video chat window to collaborate in real time on things like the copy for our App Description.

"For source control we use Subversion. All source control solutions have their pros and cons, but we like Subversion for its lack of overhead, minimum number of steps, and good integration into XCode. In addition to storing our buildable project files in

Subversion, we have enormous 'working' folders where source files, reference images, design documents, and so forth live and can be updated by the entire team.

"We use LeFora for an internal forum to post and discuss in-progress art, although that hasn't been adopted as readily. We've experimented a bit with fancy collaborative software like virtual whiteboards, but nothing has really caught on there. The key seems to be that effective collaboration solutions need a minimum number of steps and rapid updating. Unless we can connect right away and start seeing each other's work in real time, we probably won't give the software a second chance.

"And lastly, even though the Internet has been around for 40 years now, we still have trouble quickly shooting files much larger than 10MB to each other. [They are] too big for Gmail; none of the dropbox and mediafire-type solutions seem to work quite right, at least not without enormous hassle; and source control leaves the files around forever, which we don't want. We tend to resort to FTP, which is archaic but effective."

> **CROSSREF**   See Chapter 13, "iOS Game Developer Profile: Tiger Style and Hatch," for Smith's advice on using these tools during the design process—and read his game design document samples in Chapter 16, "Game Design Document Samples: Tiger Style's Spider and Waking Mars."

FACEBOOK GAME RESOURCES: ANALYTICS

AppData.com (www.appdata.com) is the leading analytics service for Facebook game developers. It tracks monthly and daily active users of any game on the social network and enables you to compare games by title, genre, and developer. You can access some of AppData's social game data for free, and access the full suite of utilities for a subscription fee.

> **CROSSREF**   Read Chapter 3, "Facebook Games: The Users, the Money, and the Major Players," for guidance on best using the AppData service, especially in my interview with site founder Justin Smith.

Another Facebook game analytics service, recommended by Billy Pidgeon, is Kontangent (which also does analytics for web and mobile games). "Their service has been helpful to many developers," Pidgeon tells me. For more information, visit www.kontagent.com.

FACEBOOK GAME RESOURCES: PUBLISHERS

Two of the leading Facebook game publishers covered in this book are open to the possibility of publishing indie games:

6waves
Developer's site: 6waves.com/developers.php
Contact e-mail: bd@6waves.com

EA Playfish
Developer's site: www.playfish.com/publishing

Before submitting anything, read more about both companies and general guidance for developing Facebook games in Chapter 3.

WEB GAME RESOURCES: PUBLISHERS

This section includes a survey of some leading web game publishers that accept submissions from indie developers, and includes some insights and advice from the company (when available).

Be sure to pay attention to the demographic profile of the site visitors, because that information helps you determine which publisher is ideal for your game. If your game is a bright and cheery casual game, for instance, it's probably best to go with Big Fish Games or Game House; if your game involves variations of face punching, Kongregate or Armor Games is likely the better place to look.

> **NOTE** Unless reported by the company, all demographic stats are from Google's Double Click Ad Planner, which I recommend highly as a good-if-imperfect third-party source for tracking online traffic. So make this a permanent bookmark: www.google.com/adplanner.

Also, keep in mind that web games published by these sites are often embedded on third-party sites (that's the magic of Flash!), so the monthly visitors do not necessarily reflect the publisher's entire market.

Kongregate.com

Here's how to contact the folks at Kongregate:

Developer's page: `developers.kongregate.com`

Developer's contact: Game Director Greg McClanahan at `greg@kongregate.com`

> **CROSSREF** Kongregate is covered extensively in Chapter 7, "Deep Dive into Web Gaming: Who Plays, Who Pays." I highly recommend that you read that chapter before contacting Kongregate.

Armorgames.com

Developer's page: `armorgames.com/submit` (free account for game submission required)

Estimated user base: 8.2 million (according to Google Ad Planner)

Key demographics: Aged 14–21, 75–80 percent male; 55–60 percent based in the United States; 20–30 percent in Canada/UK; and the rest from China and Europe

Site profile: Along with the preceding user demographic data, Daniel McNeely of Armor Games provides the following background on the platform.

THE MOST COMMON MISTAKES DEVELOPERS FIRST MAKE ON THE ARMOR GAMES PLATFORM

The most common mistakes include:

- **Lack of polish:** "Oftentimes, the most successful games we have seen have simple concepts that are enjoyable to play," says McNeely. "From the push of the start menu to the end screen, it's so well polished that it's an all-encompassing experience." McNeely cites something Pixar filmmaker John Lasseter and others have said about great film, and it also applies to great Flash games: "The reward is the journey, not the destination."

- **Not introducing the game's hook soon enough:** By this McNeely means the unique feature that gives the players an "aha!" moment and conveys its distinctive variety of fun or gameplay, be it a character, a story, or other element that hooks the players. If you bury that key feature too deep into the game's progression, many players may not play long enough to get hooked.

THE MOST UNIQUE FEATURES OF ARMOR GAMES VERSUS COMPETING PLATFORMS

The most unique features include content and quality. McNeely says his site's goal is not to be "the YouTube of games." Instead, "We want our portal to be the best of the best."

THE MOST IMPORTANT MONETIZATION FEATURES ON ARMOR GAMES

Armor Games has two key monetization features. First is a premium content system that developers can use to sell items in-game. Second, Armor Game licenses content from game developers on its platform.

HOW MUCH A DEVELOPER CAN EXPECT TO MAKE

From a moderately successful game, a developer can expect to make anywhere from $22,000 to $50,000, depending on how they market it and the shelf life of the game (which is usually contingent on the developer adding new content and features throughout its lifespan).

WHERE TO GET ADVICE AND GUIDANCE FROM ARMOR GAMES

Team member Justin often reviews games and gives feedback. You can contact him at this address: Justin@ArmorGames.com. McNeely also recommends visiting the user forum and seeking community feedback on your game.

mochigames.com

Developer's page: www.mochigames.com/developers/

Monthly visitors: 910,000, 230,000 from the United States

Key demographics: 57 percent of the visitors are 17 and under; 64 percent are female; 55 percent have a household income of $25,000 to $50,000.

Site snapshot: A leading ad provider for web games. Since Mochi primarily hosts games embedded across many sites, total visits to the main site are not a full reflection of total usage. In 2010, the Chinese online game publisher Shanda bought Mochi, increasing its potential to reach the Asian market.

flashgamelicense.com (or fgl.com)

Developer's page: www.fgl.com/signup.php?type=developer

Monthly visitors: N/A

Key demographics: N/A

Site snapshot: Not a game publisher in the sense of the other sites on this list, Flash Game License does exactly what its URL suggests. It licenses games submitted by developers to a portal or website. Best of all, developers and the sponsors who find each other on the service can carve out a deal as they see fit—FGL takes a commission for helping both with the matchmaking.

Miniclip.com

Developer's contact: submitgame@miniclip.com

Monthly visitors: 23 million, 6.1 million from the United States

Key demographics: 45 percent of its visitors are 17 and under; 32 percent are between 35 and 45 years old; 60 percent are female; 42 percent have a household income between $25,000 and $50,000; 38 percent have an income between $50,000 and $75,000.

Site snapshot: A huge clearing house for games of all genre types and audiences. As you'll notice, Miniclip's user base is not only significantly larger than the others, but also has the largest user base of older gamers. (Addicting Games and Game House also have a significant but slightly smaller base of older gamers; with the others, however, the age distribution starts petering out past 34.)

Addictinggames.com

Developer's page: www.addictinggames.com/game/upload.jsp

Monthly visitors: 9 million, 6.1 million from the United States

Key demographics: 46 percent of its visitors are 17 and under; 46 percent of its visitors have a household income between $25,000 and $50,000; 62 percent are female.

Site snapshot: A subsidiary of Viacom International, this site is a smorgasbord of game genres for multiple markets. (There are even "Girl Games" and "Funny Games" categories.)

bigfishgames.com

Developer's page: www.bigfishgames.com/company/game-developer.html

Monthly visitors: 8.3 million visitors, 4.2 million from the United States

Key demographics: 27 percent of its visitors are between 45 and 55; 20 percent are under 17; 79 percent are female; 53 percent have a household income between $25,000 and $50,000.

Site snapshot: Of all the publishers in this list, Big Fish's audience skews oldest and most female. It's most popular among casual game-playing moms.

WEB GAME RESOURCES: MONETIZATION

Visa's PlaySpan (www.playspan.com) is a popular payment/virtual goods solution provider that has a large number of online games, including top web-based games such as RuneScape and the web game portal Kongregate. If you're planning to monetize your web game with virtual goods (and, as discussed, you should), you'll probably also want to consider PlaySpan as a possible monetization option. Here's a summary of how the system works, via company founder Karl Mehta.

Developer Cost to Use PlaySpan

"PlaySpan's UltimatePay does not charge any upfront costs to developers for our payment services," says Mehta. "We offer a revenue share model in which we take a small percentage of game sales. The only cost to developers is the time spent to integrate the PlaySpan payment widget; these are simple REST APIs that can be implemented in days."

How Much a Developer Can Make with PlaySpan

"Revenue potential is often determined by two factors, game design and market reach," says Mehta. "Games with well-designed, engaging user experience mechanics with compelling storylines and the right balance of intrinsic and extrinsic motivators typically perform well.

"As a resource, PlaySpan is available to help game developers gain exposure for their games using our two consumer brands—PlaySpan Marketplace and the Ultimate Game Card. The PlaySpan Marketplace is an online store that merchandises and sells game publishers' virtual currency as well as PlaySpan's own virtual currency—UltimatePoints and Ultimate Game Card—that can be redeemed in games using our UltimatePay platform. The Ultimate Game Card is a pre-paid game card available at more than 75,000 retail points globally, including retailers like Walmart, Target, GameStop, 7-11, CVS, and many more. PlaySpan also actively markets the many different game titles using online, game forums, social media, and print."

PlaySpan's Value, in Comparison to Competitors

"PlaySpan has a full suite of monetization services for online games that includes over 100 payment methods from around the world, business model support for microtransactions, subscriptions, or a hybrid model," says Mehta. "Each service offers a real-time risk management application, specifically designed for the uniqueness of selling digital goods, that checks all transactions against potential fraud. All of our services are supported by a set of centralized applications that provide customer support, reporting, and detailed analytics. Our comprehensive suite of products and proven experience positions PlaySpan as a trusted partner in powering the monetization of many top game titles from leading publishers, including the top four media companies in the world."

In addition to that, the company has "game monetization metrics that provide developers with insight into their user experience flows to keep the purchase process simple and frictionless."

> **NOTE** Vindicia CashBox is another game monetization service for web developers. See Chapter 7 for more details on how they operate.

IOS GAME RESOURCES: ANALYTICS

Michael Oiknine, CEO of leading iOS analytics service Apsalar (www.apsalar.com), brought a lot of insight on gaining and monetizing mobile players to this book. Apsalar has a free analytics platform called ApScience (www.apsalar.com/apscience), which offers a customizable dashboard, cohort-based analysis, analysis by user segmentation, trending reports, and other features.

Patrick Minotti and Peter Farago of Flurry Analytics (www.flurry.com) gave great data and advice for the iOS-related portions of this book. Flurry is a free service considered powerful and easy to use, and has been used by more than 70,000 companies on over 200,000 apps. The analytics service is free and works cross-platform on iOS, Android, Windows Phone, BlackBerry, HTML5, and JavaME. The firm also offers advanced features such as Funnel Analysis, Category Benchmarks, Audience Composition, Custom Segments, and more.

IOS RESOURCES: PUBLISHERS

In Chapter 11, "Quick Survey of the iOS Game Market," I discussed a number of leading publishers who distribute indie games; read about them there before contacting/developing with them. Their info follows.

ngmoco (DeNA)

Developer's page: gamemakers@ngmoco.com

Developer's contact: developer.mobage.com

Chillingo (Electronic Arts)

Developer's pages: www.chillingo.com/developers and www.chillingo.com/about/submit-your-game/

GREE

Developer's page: developer.gree.net/en/

IOS GAME RESOURCES: CHINESE DISTRIBUTION

As I discussed with Henry Fong in Chapter 14, "Future Trends and Opportunities for iOS Gaming," China is already one of the world's largest mobile gaming markets and is on the fast track to becoming the biggest. I recommend considering Fong's company, Yodo1 (www.yodo1.com), a leading Chinese distributor of Western games, as a possible distributor. (Full disclosure: After writing this book, I became an occasional media consultant for Yodo1. I hope you take this as a double endorsement: Since I think they're a company worth working with, maybe you should too.)

Yodo1 developer's contact page: www.yodo1.com/contact.

USING PROTOTYPE SKETCHES, STORYBOARDS, AND ART AS DESIGN REFERENCES

When you are first designing your game's core gameplay elements, you'll probably want to convey a lot of these details through prototype sketches and art. As an inspirational reference guide, take a look at the following design prototype sketches and storyboards for Impending's Hatch, the virtual pet iOS game which was discussed with Phill Ryu in Chapter 13. Because they are early sketches, they represent initial evolutionary steps toward the final game and the team's beginning design process. Compare these prototypes to what was used in the ultimate game and pay close attention to the design approach Ryu and his team brought to each element.

Prototype Pet Sketches for Hatch

These are early sketches for the Fugu pet in Hatch, by artist David Lanham, and illustrate how much work it takes to create a compelling game character. (See Figure A-1.)

FIGURE A-1: Early Fugu sketches by David Lanham

"David has been dreaming up cute and fantastical creatures for most of his life," Ryu explains, "so when we started diving into Hatch, it felt like we were finally letting some of those monsters out of his head. He started by sketching a bunch of different ideas for monsters, and probably came up with enough distinct creature designs and concepts to fill a Pokemon game. We whittled those down to a few promising ones, then filtered them some more until we had the start of our current design. It's only gotten cuter since."

Designing the pet also involved choosing between two approaches for animating it: "[A] more hand-drawn look for the creature," says Ryu, "or a modular design that would be more customizable, kind of like South Park characters or a puppet." If they chose the latter option, it would be easier to create many different kinds of creatures. "But being literally a collection of parts, none of them ended up looking nearly as adorable as David's hand-animated tests." In the end, the team chose a middle ground, "going with the hand-animated style and one overall look for the creature," explains Ryu, "but with each frame done as a series of layers instead of just a flat image. That way, we can change the color and spots of your Fugu to make it unique." Doing this reflected a key design goal for the game: "It was important to make sure everyone's pet would be really cute, but just as important, they would be unique in some way to each user."

Prototype Sketch for Player Backpack UI

This sketch shows Impending's early thoughts on the user interface for the player's backpack, where pet items are stored. (See Figure A-2.) They also demonstrate the thought process needed to develop an intuitive, user-friendly UI that works well with the game's specific platform (iOS, in this case):

"We went through a lot of designs for item management in the game," says Ryu, "and, in general, it progressively became more and more focused on direct manipulation. I think it started as floating icons for food items running along the bottom of the screen to drag out, but as we removed abstract menu elements, it moved into the notebook as an inventory list. There was a disconnect, though, between managing items on a list and the items themselves, so we gravitated to the visual bag you drag items out of. People know how that works, so it's pretty self explanatory. Three-year-olds can figure it out now." This reflects Ryu's design goal to remove abstraction from the user interface, as covered in Chapter 13.

FIGURE A-2: Player backpack UI prototype for Hatch

Prototype Storyboard for Hatch Game Opening and Orientation

The storyboards shown in Figures A-3 and A-4 illustrate the design of a game's opening and on-ramping process—an extremely important aspect of a free-to-play game, since the game's beginning and orientation must be compelling and entertaining in itself, to convince first-time users to keep playing. To introduce players to Hatch, Ryu and team sketched out an appealing character named Max, who'd appear at the beginning and convey important gameplay elements in a humorous way.

KID POPS IN

USER TOUCHES EGG, IT BEGINS TO WIGGLE IN RESPONSE TO TOUCH.

APPLE STARTS GROWING IN BACKGROUND

AFTER ENOUGH PETTING THE EGG CRACKS AND HATCHES.

FIGURE A-3: Storyboard for Hatch opening

1 APPLE RIPENS ON THE
TREE READY FOR
PLUCKING.

WHEN FED THE
CREATURE LEAPS IN
THE AIR A FEW TIMES
/ WAGS ITS TAIL

3 OTHER APPLES
PROMPTLY RIPEN ON
THE TREE READY FOR
PLUCKING.

AFTER 3 MORE FRUIT
IS FED, CREATURE
BELCHES.

FIGURE A-4: Storyboard for Hatch opening, continued

"Max is our attempt to try to teach things while telling a story," says Ryu. "He's the neighborhood kid with an over-excited imagination and an imaginary pet of his own, and he thinks he knows everything about them but really is just about as clueless as the player starting out."

Creating Max made it easy to show people how to play Hatch. "We have concepts and mechanics in the game we want to teach our users early on in an efficient way," Ryu explains, "but I think as gamers we all personally hate the up-front tutorials that spell everything out. Max is great because one of his roles is asking the stupid and obvious questions and getting stumped so the user doesn't have to. That's the user's cue to figure out that mechanic or feature on their own as a simple puzzle with a clue, versus reading another line of instructions from the manual."

The game's final art, as noted, changed from this earlier version. As Ryu says, "This is an abandoned direction that was more modular and South Park style, and we ended up going with the hand-drawn frames look."

Design Principles

This appendix contains a game design "cheat sheet" that synthesizes most of the most important development, user growth, and monetization lessons covered in this book. If you're unclear on any of these principles, be sure to read the chapter in which that principle was first featured and covered in detail. At the end of each of the following lessons, I've included a cross-reference to the appropriate chapter.

BEST REASONS TO DEVELOP LOW-BUDGET/INDIE GAMES FOR IOS, FACEBOOK, AND THE WEB

There are myriad reasons to develop low-budget/indie games. The best reasons, however, include the following: largest combined market of gamers (more than 750 million), acceptance of low-budget games, shareability on social media, and portability to other platforms.

See Chapter 1, "Market Overview: iOS, Facebook, and the Web," for more information.

GAMES THAT DO BEST ON IOS

For iOS, the games that do best include 2D or 2.5D games that leverage the touch interface with short play sessions.

See Chapter 2, "iOS Versus Facebook Versus the Web: What's the Right Platform," for more information.

GAMES THAT DO BEST ON FACEBOOK

For Facebook, the games that do best include games that make use of the social network's friend-sharing features, are designed for quick gameplay sessions, and have point-and-click control.

See Chapter 2, "iOS Versus Facebook Versus the Web: What's the Right Platform," for more information.

GAMES THAT DO BEST ON THE WEB

For the Web, the games that do best include genres targeted at specific demographics. For example, match-three puzzles for women, dress-up games for younger girls, and shooter/action/strategy games for young males. Hybrid games that combine genre elements or add a twist to popular gameplay features tend to do well by attracting multiple demographics.

See Chapter 2, "iOS Versus Facebook Versus the Web: What's the Right Platform," for more information.

FACEBOOK: GAMES THAT WILL DO WELL IN THE NEAR FUTURE

In 2012-2013, puzzle/arcade games will probably be most popular, whereas casino games also have a lot of potential for indie developers.

See Chapter 3, "Facebook Games: The Users, the Money, and the Major Players," for more information.

FACEBOOK: HOW TO DETERMINE A NEW GAME IS PROBABLY SUCCESSFUL

To determine whether a Facebook game is successful, look for growth and/or strong daily user activity after three months. Also, look for a solid user base of daily users that can support the studio's development team.

See Chapter 3, "Facebook Games: The Users, the Money, and the Major Players," for more information.

FACEBOOK: HOW MANY PAYING PLAYERS CAN YOU EXPECT?

How many players will pay for your game? Between 1–3 percent is typical, whereas 5–9 percent is very good. Among your paying players, about 10 percent are generally *whales*, paying more than $20/month. A well-designed, well-monetized Facebook game will earn 50 cents to 1 dollar in ARPU per monthly player.

See Chapter 3, "Facebook Games: The Users, the Money, and the Major Players," for more information.

FACEBOOK: HOW TO FIND AN AUDIENCE AND GROW YOUR GAME

To find an audience and grow your Facebook game, find a niche genre and an under-served target group, and don't have a restrictive view of what qualifies as a game, which might exclude some potentially entertaining interactive apps. Reach players by targeting fans of similar games through Facebook's advertising platform. Design wall updates to be fun and informative, not spammy—updates with player customizations are good and user-generated content is even better. Use A/B testing, but balance it with a love of games.

See Chapters 3, "Facebook Games: The Users, the Money, and the Major Players," and 4, "Facebook Game Design: Principles for Growth and Revenue," for more information.

FACEBOOK GAME DESIGN PRINCIPLES

Generally, when designing games for Facebook, you'll want to design for long-term aspiration and communicate to players what they can do with your game months or years down the road. Also, be sure to include daily game features; they drive daily usage.

See Chapter 4, "Facebook Game Design: Principles for Growth and Revenue," for more information.

FACEBOOK MONETIZATION PRINCIPLES

Deeply integrate monetization features into your game's design, so they'll be apparent to the player from the start, alongside all the game's other main features. Make buying virtual goods part of the first-time play experience, so players know how to spend, and make the spending experience enjoyable. Price your goods (generally) high to start and offer discounts as needed. Functional enhancements tend to sell well, decorations not (usually) so much.

See Chapter 4, "Facebook Game Design: Principles for Growth and Revenue," for more information.

FACEBOOK GAME DESIGN LESSONS FROM KIXEYE'S PAUL PREECE

Paul Preece of KIXEYE offers the following game design lessons:

► Gameplay speed-ups monetize well, whereas nonfunctional virtual decor usually does not.

► Generating an emotional response in players (positive or negative) monetizes well.

► Targeted marketing through Facebook's ad platform also attracts players who monetize well.

► For strong retention, design a strong meta game that has goals above and beyond the game's specific, explicit objectives.

► Every game has about 70 percent similarity to the games that came before it—the challenge is highly evolved design.

See Chapter 5, "Facebook Design Lessons from KIXEYE and 5th Planet Games," for more information.

FACEBOOK GAME DESIGN LESSONS FROM 5TH PLANET'S ROBERT WINKLER

Robert Winkler of 5th Planet offers the following game design lessons:

► Differentiate your game with great art and music; just be economical about how you create these assets.

► A text-heavy game can work on Facebook, if you have hard-core fans who enjoy reading and sharing with other players.

► Drive viral growth with timed group experiences, such as boss battles, which encourage active players to invite their friends and fellow players to join them in the experience.

► Business advice: Get a lawyer early on, because social gaming is still the Wild West, and you'll need one.

See Chapter 5, "Facebook Design Lessons from KIXEYE and 5th Planet Games," for more information.

FEATURES YOU SHOULD CONSIDER IN FUTURE FACEBOOK GAMES

When designing or developing for Facebook games in the future, consider cross-platform games that use Facebook Connect and games that play well with mobile, especially games with shareable, user-generated content.

See Chapter 6, "Future Trends and Opportunities for Facebook Games," for more information.

WEB GAMES: WHO WILL PAY TO PLAY YOUR GAME?

Paying customers for web games are mainly between 20 and 45 years old, skewing slightly female. Big spenders tend to be in North America, Europe, and parts of Asia (particularly in South Korea).

See Chapter 7,"Deep Dive into Web Gaming: Who Plays, Who Pays," for more information.

WEB GAMES: HOW LOW-BUDGET/INDIE DEVELOPERS CAN MAKE MORE MONEY

To make the most money, you'll want to go with name brand payment options, which your players are more likely to trust. Reduce payment friction, so they don't give up in the middle of the process. Also, be sure to offer multiple payment options and revenue streams, so players have lots of ways to pay you. Finally, reward your players for paying, but also make sure you retain nonpaying customers by making sure it's fun to play the game for free. If they keep playing, they'll eventually pay.

See Chapter 7,"Deep Dive into Web Gaming: Who Plays, Who Pays," for more information.

WEB GAME DESIGN ADVICE FROM THE JAY IS GAMES EDITORIAL STAFF

Here's the top advice from the Jay Is Games staff:

- ▶ Design for overall quality, ease of use, and fun; hybrids of two or more genres are often popular.
- ▶ Obsessively remove bugs and glitches.
- ▶ If you lack passion for the game you're making, it will show.

See Chapter 7,"Deep Dive into Web Gaming: Who Plays, Who Pays," for more information.

WEB GAME DESIGN PRINCIPLES TO ATTRACT AN AUDIENCE

To attract an audience for your web game, match your game's theme to the kind of gameplay it delivers; an action game should look like one, from the advertising to the login screen. Alternatively, wrap a gameplay type into a new form that will gain a crossover audience.

See Chapter 8, "Web Game Design: Basic Principles for Growth and Revenue," for more information.

WEB GAME DEPLOYMENT PRINCIPLES TO MAINTAIN AN AUDIENCE—AND ENCOURAGE THEM TO PAY

There are many web game deployment principles to consider. To begin, distribute your games on as many sites as possible to get them in front of as many potential players as possible. To build a regular audience around all your games, create a recognizable brand they can look for. Integrate monetization features deeply into the game, so they are easy to find and use. Optimize your website so games are easy to play and advertising revenue is maximized; maintain engagement among your hard-core users with an online forum.

Also, be sure to monetize virtual goods and upgrades that give the user more convenience in their gameplay or offer exclusive access. For example, virtual goods that come in a set (like a deck of cards or figurines) can inspire a "collect them all" itch. Price your items high and adjust prices downward as needed; don't cap spending with subscriptions, because some players will prefer to pay more. Finally, if you're a new developer, consider licensing deals before advertising—you can usually make more money from the former.

See Chapter 8, "Web Game Design: Basic Principles for Growth and Revenue," for more information.

WEB GAME DESIGN LESSONS FROM DEVELOPERS WITH KIXEYE, NITROME, AND KINGDOM OF LOATHING

Players will exploit game resources in unintended, unanticipated ways, so be prepared for them to work against your own design. Power users will also play against your intentions, defeating your assumptions by putting more time and effort into your game than you probably imagined.

A good way to increase user retention is to give established players new ways to play (game modes, leveling mechanics, and so on). Revive a niche game genre you love, because there's probably a market of people who love that niche, too. Don't fall in the "it's not good enough yet" trap, and launch your game early. That way, you can improve the game after you get real user feedback.

Early on, prepare for success and ways for your game to make money. People like owning the stuff they really love, so make sure they have a means to do that with your game.

From the start, find ways to generate gameplay data, so you can figure out how players are really engaging with your game and iterate around it.

See Chapter 9, "Web Game Developer Profiles: King of Loathing, Nitrome, and Desktop Tower Defense," for more information.

FUTURE TRENDS WEB GAME DESIGNERS SHOULD WATCH FOR AND TAKE ADVANTAGE OF

Advertising-based payments and secondary markets will gain more acceptance as ways for developers to make money. HTML5 is the future of web game development, but Flash still has many years of life left in it. As 3D graphics quality for the web improves, more hard-core gamers will play there. Twitter remains a great, unexploited sharing and promotion platform for web game developers. Keep an eye on Google+ and Chrome, but keep in mind that they'll probably remain a smaller market for web and Facebook games in the short to mid term. Web games that enable asynchronous multimedia sharing will also likely become big, as will web-based app stores. Look to large publishers and investors to support and help finance your indie games, because many of them are already actively doing so.

See Chapter 10, "Future Trends and Opportunities for Web Gaming," for more information.

IOS GAMES: HOW LARGE THE MARKET IS AND HOW MUCH YOU CAN EXPECT TO MAKE FROM IT

The current market for iOS gaming is about 110 million players. Gamers aged 25–34 spend the most money on freemium mobile games. In a survey of iOS game developers, only 15 percent reported earning lifetime revenue between $100,000 and $10 million, and just 4 percent between $1 and 10 million. However, independent developers dominate the iOS game market, making 68 percent of the most successful titles.

See Chapter 11, "Quick Survey of the iOS Game Market," for more information.

IOS GAMES: HOW TO FIND PLAYERS AND GET THEM TO PAY

Unless you're going after a very specific niche market, your iOS game should be free to play and monetized with in-app payments. Although costly, targeted advertising is an important way to drive installs of your game. However, avoid offer walls, which generally don't attract paying players.

See Chapter 11, "Quick Survey of the iOS Game Market," for more information.

IOS GAMES: DESIGN PRINCIPLES FOR THE PLATFORM

Like Facebook and the Web, iOS games have their own unique design principles. To begin, design for games with short play sessions, so people can play anytime and anywhere they want to have fun. Add emerging complexity to the game, so short play sessions become longer and more frequent. And add a social sharing component, so players can tell their friends what they love about the game on Twitter and Facebook. Design iOS games to take advantage of the iOS unique strengths: the touchscreen, accelerometer, voice mic/audio, location-based detection, and so on.

See Chapter 12, "iOS Game Design: Basic Principles for Growth and Revenue," for more information.

IOS GAMES: DESIGN PRINCIPLES THROUGH ANALYTICS

Treat the user data generated by analytics as part of the design process. Analytics can't tell you when a player is having fun, but it can tell you how deeply they're engaging with the game, which is about the same thing. Release an early build of your game to a few hundred or a few thousand users, capture their gameplay information, iterate, and then release to a few hundred/thousand more. Keep gathering user data and keep improving the game based on it.

See Chapter 12, "iOS Game Design: Basic Principles for Growth and Revenue," for more information.

IOS GAMES: DESIGN PRINCIPLES FOR MONETIZING GOODS

To successfully monetize your iOS game, you'll want to frequently display the virtual goods your players can buy and give them plenty of opportunities to buy them. Offer regular, limited-time discounts or sales on special items to help get your players in the habit of checking for deals. To prevent complaints and encourage continual play, make sure that some of your free in-game items are better than the ones players can buy with in-app purchases. Consider selling virtual currency instead of virtual goods; then, you can adjust item prices as needed and avoid the app approval process that comes from adding new items.

See Chapter 12, "iOS Game Design: Basic Principles for Growth and Revenue," for more information.

IOS GAME DESIGN LESSONS FROM TIGER STYLE'S RANDY SMITH AND IMPENDING'S PHILL RYU

YouTube video footage of your game is important, especially for paid apps, because it shows potential players what they'll be paying for and why it's great. Major updates to your game will increase installs, even when it's been out for months. Creating a game with discrete levels makes it easier for players to enjoy short play sessions; leader boards increase engagement and re-playability.

Kickstarter and other crowdfunding platforms are just as important for building a fan base and marketing your game as they are for raising money. Develop a monetization plan that feels natural to the game; remove abstraction from the user interface, so that the game controls intuitively relate to what's happening onscreen.

See Chapter 13, "iOS Game Developer Profile: Tiger Style and Hatch," for more information.

FUTURE IOS TRENDS GAME DESIGNERS SHOULD WATCH FOR

Facebook will become more pervasive on mobile devices, and iOS game developers need to compete with it (or work with it) for attention. Acquisition costs will continue to rise, benefiting big publishers and making it harder for indie developers. The iPad will increasingly become a hard-core gamer platform, especially for RTS and MMO games. Location-based gaming, which uses a unique strength of the iOS, will become increasingly popular. Don't expect many future iOS games to use an old-school D-pad, which is going the way of the dinosaur.

China already has the biggest audience for iOS games, but Western designers need to know how to navigate and appeal to that market: Chinese players not only like to buy game power-ups and enhancements, they brag about them. Western social media integration doesn't work in China, since Twitter and Facebook are blocked. Be sure to avoid the "Who the hell is King Arthur?" problem by creating games with universal themes that Chinese gamers can relate to.

See Chapter 14, "Future Trends and Opportunities for iOS Gaming," for more information.

WHAT VENTURE CAPITALISTS NABEEL HYATT AND JEREMY LIEW LOOK FOR IN A GAME PROJECT

Venture capitalists Nabeel Hyatt and Jeremy Liew look for a few key items in game projects they want to fund. These include:

- ▶ Good user retention, especially day one retention toward 60 percent.
- ▶ The ability to answer two questions regarding the potential for making a game with explosive growth—"Why you?" and "Why now?" A willingness to state your weaknesses up front, while knowing your strengths.

See Chapter 15, "Is Your Game Ready to Get VC or Crowdfunding?" for more information.

HOW TO PITCH YOUR GAME PROJECT ON KICKSTARTER

To pitch your game on Kickstarter, you first need to create a video that tells the story of your project, establishes the game's premise, and clearly describes what you need to complete it. Don't be shy about promoting your Kickstarter venture, and create a viral social media campaign that targets your ideal fan base. If you're a new developer, have a playable demo to show off. Create a reward structure that makes economic sense for you and the pledgers. Be transparent with your backers; let them know how the project's going, for good and ill.

See Chapter 15, "Is Your Game Ready to Get VC or Crowdfunding?" for more information.

Glossary of Terms and Acronyms

The appendix is a glossary of acronyms and game/tech industry terms frequently mentioned throughout the book. If you're a longtime gamer or game developer reading this, a lot of them will be painfully obvious; then again, other terms will seem alien or weird. Meanwhile, readers from the business development side of things will probably know many of them quite well, while wondering what the heck terms like "physics puzzle" and "2.5D" are supposed to be. This appendix is for both kinds of readers.

2.5D game Game with graphics that appear to be 3D by using a constrained, isometric perspective. Backyard Monsters and other KIXEYE games mentioned in this book are 2.5D.

3D game Game that displays a first-person perspective or displays the game space with a camera view that rotates along the full X/Y/Z axis.

AAA game Big-budget game, generally for video-game consoles. This book is not about them, because they are a dying breed. Fewer and fewer will develop for them—especially low-budget indie folks.

accelerometer On the iOS, the feature that detects the phone's position along the X/Y/Z axis.

acquisition cost The amount you'll spend (such as on advertising) to get a new player to try your game.

A/B testing In game development, comparing user growth, engagement, and other behaviors to a feature change/addition, in relation to a control sample. Example: "We gave a few thousand players a deadly garden gnome to use in the gladiator level, and ran an A/B test to see if they played longer."

acq-hired When a corporation buys a developer's project or company for the purpose of owning its assets and turning the staff into its own employees.

advertising-based payments Form of revenue in which an advertiser offers virtual goods in a game in exchange for the user engaging with their product.

cloud deployment In gaming, broadband streaming of games directly to the end user, eliminating the need for long downloads or high-end hardware. OnLive and Gaikai are two leading cloud-deployment services.

ARPDAU Average revenue per daily active user.

ARPU Average revenue per user (as opposed to ARPDAU). Refers to the average revenue earned by a game per user on a monthly or yearly basis, or other designated timeframe.

asynchronous gaming Generally refers to multi-player games in which individual player movements are not conducted in real time, but are turn-based. Most Facebook games and many multiplayer iOS games are asynchronous. Most multi-player web games are designed for real-time simultaneous play.

boss battle Final epic confrontation at the end of a game or game segment/level.

brand-to-player payment Revenue stream in which companies run ads in one game, offering virtual currency for other games.

consumables Limited-use virtual goods, such as potions, medicine, and so on.

conversion The process of turning a free player into a monetized one.

CPI Cost-per-install—the average amount you can expect to pay for advertising and other means to get a new player.

DAU Daily active user.

DAU/MAU The percentage of a Facebook game's daily active users in relation to monthly active users. As an industry rule of thumb, a DAU/MAU rate of 20 percent or higher is extremely good.

DoD Dawn of Dragons (from 5th Planet Games).

D-pad "Direction pad," the classic compass configuration used in old-school video-game consoles.

EA Electronic Arts, one the industry's largest publishers.

Facebook Credits Formerly the social network's official currency, once mandatory for use in all Facebook games, but discontinued in June 2012.

Facebook moms Somewhat patronizing way to describe women in their 30s, 40s, and 50s who generally make up the largest audience for social games, especially casual, social, and light simulations.

forced virality (aka friend gating) In Facebook games, requiring that players invite or otherwise engage with friends in order to access selected game content. See: every single game Zynga has ever made.

freemium Game based on assets associated with and based on an existing book, movie, TV show, game, or other IP. The freemium business model is also known as F2P, or free-to-play.

hard-core gamer Audience of gamers, typically young and male, who prefer action and detail-oriented strategy/combat/building games, usually with 3D graphics, and who tend to monetize at the highest rates. Steam, Xbox 360, and PS3 are the main hard-core gamer platforms, but mid-core games are also often popular with this segment.

HTML5 Latest 3D graphics and interaction-friendly version of markup language for web pages, designed to work with powerful multimedia and interactive features (i.e., gaming).

in-app offer Advertising offer displayed within a game, usually linked to a game's virtual goods.

IAP In-app payment, generally referring to a micro-transaction conducted within an iOS game.

IP Intellectual property (such as game characters, storyline, or art assets).

launcher game Physics puzzle in which the object is to hit various objects by launching projectiles via catapult, cannon, and so on.

licensed/franchise properties Games based on assets associated with an existing book, movie, TV show, game, or other IP.

LTV Lifetime value of a given monetized player.

MAU Monthly active user. Rhymes with "cow." Usage example: "Did you know that the Facebook satire game called Cow Clicker actually attracted a lot of fans? Cow got good MAU!"

mid-core Intended for an audience at the midpoint between casual and hard-core gamers. Sometimes this relates to platform availability. KIXEYE games, for example, are often called mid-core, because they're games for hard-core players who can't bring their Xboxes to work.

MMO Massively multiplayer online game. Often used to describe iOS, web, or Facebook games that have persistent, shared gameplay elements, such as High Noon for the iOS, RuneScape for the Web, and Dragons of Atlantis on Facebook.

offer walls In these, gamers are given the opportunity to gain some kind of benefit (usually virtual goods and currency in the iOS game they play) if they install and launch a designated game at least once.

on-ramp Steps a new player must take to become a regular player, such as account creation and orientation.

physics puzzle game Game in which challenges are accomplished with the dynamic use of simulated gravity, inertia, and other Newtonian physics. Angry Birds, of course, is the killer physics puzzle game (also a launcher game).

platform agnostic A fancy way of describing a game that is playable on more than one platform (the Web, iOS, and so on).

platformer Genre of game in which a player's character must traverse a series of multilevel obstacles by running, jumping, climbing, dodging, and so on.

prepaid cards Typically sold in retail, drug, or convenience stores, cards embedded with code for redeeming virtual goods and currency in designated games.

port Conversion of a game from one platform to another, usually with most of the graphics and other key assets intact.

retention In game development, the process of turning a game's first-time players into regular players.

RPG Roleplaying game, such as Sims Social or Dawn of the Dragons.

RTS Real-time strategy game, such as Battle Pirates.

secondary market Market on which players can trade valuable items with other players, for real or virtual currency, generally on a site hosted by the company (which usually takes a commission on each sale). Diablo III now has the most well known official secondary market in western gaming.

sim Not to be confused with the EA franchise. Short for "simulation," a game in which the player must customize and control a specific, enclosed ecosystem, such as a farm or city.

SmartTV Sometimes called Hybrid TV, the next-generation line of Internet-connected, social media–integrated televisions.

SMS payment Mobile payment conducted through a short message service, generally billed through the consumer's telecom network.

Steam Valve's online game distribution service.

tower defense Genre of strategy game in which players must defend territory or resources against opponents by constructing weaponized towers and other emplacements.

UGC User-generated content. Think Draw Something.

Unity 3D graphics authoring platform compatible with Flash for the Web and iOS.

VCs Venture capitalists. The folks who can give you money.

virality Qualities and features that encourage users to share a game with friends and strangers, especially online and in social media channels. Not to be confused with forced virality.

wall updates Facebook updates posted to a user's profile where his or her friends can see them (and generally re-share with their own networks).

WebGL JavaScript-based code for rendering 2D and 3D graphics in a web browser without the need for a plug-in.

whales High-spending players in a freemium game (generally a small minority). One rule of thumb: A whale is someone who spends $20 on a single Facebook game per month.

XBLA Xbox Live Arcade.

INDEX

Index